Acc

A Family Guide to Spiritual Warfare:
Strategies for Deliverance and Healing

Our Lord taught the importance of preparing for battle, asking, "What king, going to encounter another king in war, will not sit down first and take counsel whether he is able with ten thousand to meet him who comes against him with twenty thousand?" (Luke 14:31). He also emphasized the need for good planning when He asked, "Which of you, desiring to build a tower, does not first sit down and count the cost, whether he has enough to complete it?" (Luke 14:28). No created good is under greater attack than a holy family, and yet it also remains a beacon and tower testifying to God's love in a world that hungers for it. Kathleen Beckman has drawn together in one place the resources, truths, prayers, and wisdom needed to heal, strengthen, protect, and inspire our families to mighty holiness in God's grace. May God bless her, and all who read this work.

Most Rev. Thomas J. Paprocki, J.C.D.
Bishop of Springfield, Illinois

At a time when the Catholic vision of marriage and family is under assault as never before, I pray that Kathleen Beckman's *A Family Guide to Spiritual Warfare* will serve as a beacon for the faithful and their loved ones. This book can strengthen, encourage, and equip families to defend against the evil one and strive for holiness under the protection of the Holy Family and the angels.

Most Rev. Thomas James Olmsted, J.C.D., D.D.
Bishop of Phoenix, Arizona

I am very happy to recommend Kathleen Beckman's latest book. *A Family Guide to Spiritual Warfare* is a timely work that will help to protect families in this challenging but providential age where the Lord has brought us all together.

Most Rev. Kevin W. Vann, J.C.D., D.D.
Bishop of Orange, California

The family unit, and corresponding family life, has long been understood as the core social building block to any society. But what happens when that essential structure is undermined, comes under spiritual attack, and is no longer constructed on solid ground? Kathleen Beckman's instructive work, *A Family Guide to Spiritual Warfare*, provides an eminently practical guide to the protecting, strengthening, and sanctifying of family life on a foundational level. A most timely publication.

Very Rev. Jeffrey Grob, J.C.D.
Judicial Vicar, Archdiocese of Chicago
Author, *A Major Revision on the Discipline of Exorcism*

A Family Guide to Spiritual Warfare is a great examen for any family's spiritual health and for obtaining Christ's victory over sin and evil.

Fr. Gary Thomas, M.Div.
Mandated Exorcist, Diocese of San Jose, California

Sister Lucia Dos Santos, the longest-lived visionary of the Fatima apparitions, once stated: "The final battle between good and evil will be fought over marriage and family." Without a doubt, we are in the midst of this battle today; it is raging all around us. For this reason, Kathleen Beckman's new book, *A Family Guide to Spiritual*

Warfare, could not have come at a better time. I very highly recommend this book and the wisdom it contains.

Fr. Donald Calloway, M.I.C.
Author, *Consecration to St. Joseph*

Demonic activity is on the rise, and your family is the primary target. There's no more important time to learn how to engage in spiritual warfare in order to protect your family. If you follow the advice in *A Family Guide to Spiritual Warfare*, I have no doubt that you will be victorious in the battles you face. Kathleen Beckman has done a great service to the Church in this unique treatment of how to heal and deliver your family from demonic attacks.

Dan Burke
Author, *Spiritual Warfare and the Discernment of Spirits*
Founder/President, The Avila Institute

A Family Guide to Spiritual Warfare is a must-have for every family. Kathleen Beckman offers a way to protect our families against the many extraordinary satanic snares facing us today. With the wisdom and tenderness of a mother, Kathleen shows us how to reclaim the freedom every heart desires that is found only in Christ.

Dr. Carrie Gress
Author, *The Anti-Mary Exposed, Theology of Home*

That "human nature's enemy" seeks to destroy the family, making it the principal target of his strategy to annihilate all of God's creation, should not surprise anyone. We all need to wake up to the enemy's untiringly ambitious plan, now in full view of our world. How can families defend themselves? Kathleen Beckman has written a timely guide for all families seeking to protect and defend themselves from all means of the enemy's attacks on family and family life. Buy a copy and give it to your married friends and those soon to be married. It is an essential tool for the journey ahead.

Rev. William M. Watson, S.J.
Author, *Sacred Story: An Ignatian Examen for the Third Millennium*
Founder/President, Sacred Story Institute

The devil never sleeps and wants to destroy our families, but he is powerless against Jesus. *A Family Guide to Spiritual Warfare* shows us all the ways we can tap into God's victory, providing encouragement, not fear, and inspiration to get to work. No family should be without this book and spiritual protection.

Patti Maguire Armstrong
Author, *Holy Hacks: Everyday Ways to Live Your Faith and Get to Heaven*
Correspondent, *National Catholic Register* and *Our Sunday Visitor*

A Family Guide to Spiritual Warfare is the fruit of Kathleen Beckman's many years of spiritually defending her own family as well as the expanded spiritual family that she serves in the Church. In this book, she shares strategies that are often forgotten or not realized as true weapons and protection against the enemy of our salvation, the devil. Anyone reading this book will greatly benefit in becoming a victorious prayer warrior for the family.

Fr. Miguel Maria Soeherman, M.F.V.A.
Author, *A Child Lives His Present Moment*

A FAMILY GUIDE *to* SPIRITUAL WARFARE

Also by Kathleen Beckman
from Sophia Institute Press:

When Women Pray: Eleven Catholic Women on the Power of Prayer

God's Healing Mercy: Finding Your Path to Peace, Forgiveness, and Joy

Praying for Priests: An Urgent Call for the Salvation of Souls

KATHLEEN BECKMAN

A FAMILY GUIDE *to* SPIRITUAL WARFARE

Strategies for Deliverance and Healing

SOPHIA INSTITUTE PRESS
Manchester, New Hampshire

Cover design: David Ferris Design
Cover art: Icon of the Holy family returning to Nazareth
(RYK9DX) © Godong / Alamy Stock Photo

Imprimatur: Most Rev. Kevin William Vann, J.C.D., D.D.
Bishop of Orange, July 11, 2020

Nihil Obstat: Fr. Joseph Son Nguyen, M.Div., M.A., S.T.D.
Censor Librorum, Diocese of Orange, July 6, 2020

Sophia Institute Press
Box 5284, Manchester, NH 03108
1-800-888-9344
www.SophiaInstitute.com
Sophia Institute Press® is a registered trademark of Sophia Institute.
Print edition ISBN: 978-1-64413-071-1
Electronic formats ISBN: 978-1-64413-072-8
Library of Congress Control Number: 2020941328.

5th printing

Dedication

All my love to the Holy Family and my family

Acknowledgments

To the following priests: your expertise contributed greatly to this work. I owe you a huge debt of gratitude, because you have been my teachers and have accepted me as a pupil for years. Your priesthood and friendship are great gifts to me and to the Church.

To the many prayer warriors on this list and to many others: I'm deeply grateful for your generosity in supporting me and this work spiritually. To the Censor Librorum, Fr. Joseph Son Nguyen, and Sophia Press's editor, Molly Wierman: your expertise improved my work. Thank you! To the vicar general, Msgr. Stephen Doktorczyk: thank you for not letting me give up.

Bishop Kevin W. Vann, J.C.D., D.D.

Msgr. Stephen Doktorczyk, J.C.D.

Fr. Thomas Nelson, O.Praem.

Fr. Gary Thomas, M.Div.

Fr. Dennis McManus, Ph.D.

Msgr. John Esseff

Fr. Jeffrey Grob, J.C.D.

Fr. Joseph Son Nguyen, S.T.D.

Fr. Charles Cortinovis, J.D., S.T.L.

Charlie McKinney and Sophia Press

Msgr. Stephen Rossetti, D.Min., Ph.D.

Fr. Luke Clark, O.P.

Mother Dolores Marie, P.C.P.A.

Cynthia Hunt, M.D.

Dan Burke and Apostoli Viae

Gina Witt

The Orange Diocese Team

Fr. Ambrose Criste, O.Praem.

Completed on the Solemnity of the
Most Sacred Heart of Jesus, June 19, 2020.

CONTENTS

Foreword xv
Msgr. Stephen Doktorczyk, J.C.D.

Author's Preface xix

1 **The Battle for the Soul of the Family** 1
Strategies: Fearless Faith, Vigilance, Discernment of Spirits

2 **Schooled in the Art of Spiritual Combat** 33
Strategies: Catholic Remedies, Fighting like a Knight, Healing the Heart

3 **Three Foundational Strategies for Spiritual Warfare** 57
Scripture, the State of Grace, and Authority

4 **The Language of Spiritual Combat and Six Categories of Demonic Attacks** 79

5 **Dressing Your Family in the Armor of God** 105

6 **Family Covenant of Protection** 123
Strategies: The Ten Commandments, the Beatitudes, Blessings

7 **Engaging Your Weapons: Holy Daring** 149
Strategies: Staying in Love, Building a Eucharistic Heart and Home

8 **Unmasking Dangerous Diabolical Disguises** 171

9 **Healing through Deliverance Ministry**. 203
Strategies: Renewing Baptismal Promises, the Father's Blessing, Praying for Healing, and Offering Up Suffering

10 **With the Virgin Mary and the Angels in Spiritual Combat**. 235
Strategies: Working with Mary, Devotion to Your Guardian Angel and St. Michael

Appendix A 261
Prayers for Family Healing and Deliverance

Appendix B 287
Family Deliverance Case Histories

About the Author 311

FOREWORD

As a priest living at the Casa Santa Maria in Rome, I had many opportunities to enjoy in-house meals with other student-priests residing in the house and with seminarians from the North American College, who would sometimes dine there. It was not uncommon to discuss different areas of theology, philosophy, or canon law. Doctoral students would tell others how their dissertations were coming along. It was a good sharing of information and provided opportunities for us to encourage each other in our respective studies.

Later in the fall of that same year, Fr. Gary Thomas, a priest of the Diocese of San Jose in California, took up residence there. He was only the second American priest to matriculate in the newly created exorcism ministry program at the Regina Apostolorum Pontifical University in Rome. Taking the mandate of his bishop very seriously, not only did he faithfully attend the classroom portion of the material; he also would go to a Roman parish several afternoons each week to be part of exorcisms done at various parishes in the Eternal City. What he witnessed and learned by participating in various exorcisms he shared with priests in the house during meal time. His recounting helped me to come to realize the reality of evil and the importance of taking it seriously. This was not a matter of finding the devil under every rock (on the one extreme), but rather of taking seriously the fact that evil does exist and that the Church has remedies available to those who are interested.

Since that time, while I wasn't seeking to be part of healing and deliverance ministry, I agreed to be involved with it, knowing its importance and necessity and recognizing that spiritual aid would often be received by those who presented themselves for help. While I've read various books in the past decade and a half about exorcism and healing and deliverance, to my recollection they have focused on how to deal with people who are already experiencing some form of oppression or even possession. The authors of these books have assisted many – laypeople and priests – who are in healing and deliverance ministries to help others eventually be freed from bondage, which oftentimes is not of their own making. As a complement to the many other worthy books hitherto published, the book you are now reading focuses on healing and deliverance of the family – that is, of the "domestic church."

As the reality of spiritual warfare became known and accepted and requests for help rose, some dioceses decided to make available guidelines or protocol regarding requests for healing, deliverance, and exorcism. At times, non-Catholics who have heard about the authority of the Catholic Church and her priests when it comes to authentic spiritual healing want to avail themselves of what the Church has to offer. These protocols are designed to aid clergy and laity to assist others who are suffering various levels of spiritual warfare. The protocols are not designed with prevention in mind, but simply as a response to the situation now in front of priests. In her diocese, Kathleen Beckman served as consultor as the protocol was being developed, and Fr. Gary Thomas made a presentation to the presbyterate on the day the diocesan bishop promulgated the protocol.

In her latest book *A Family Guide to Spiritual Warfare*, Kathleen Beckman takes a comprehensive approach to spiritual warfare.

If "an ounce of prevention is worth a pound of cure," families who put into practice the author's guidance might avoid walking unknowingly into potential landmines. Realizing the necessity of healthy and holy families in our Church and world, the author challenges parents (the primary educators of their children) to get back to basics – not mainly by means of avoiding certain practices, but more so by living a solid Christian life according to one's vocation. Much begins in the family. The reading of Scripture, recitation of prayers, devotion to the saints, or praying a blessing over children as they are falling asleep, while perhaps nothing new to some, cannot be assumed to be taking place in every home. A fair amount of the book is devoted to assisting people in spiritual combat, and the author offers case studies to help the reader to know that not a few people find themselves in a real battle. Thereby, the reader may perhaps avoid some of the traps others have fallen into.

We might tend to be naïve when it comes to warfare in our lives or in those of loved ones. And when one finally realizes that the Church might have the answer, some already will have tried other methods – palm-readers, fortune-tellers, or even those who claim to be in the Church but practice false mysticism. To be properly schooled in such a subject, in my opinion, is more important than ever, and the ten chapters in this book attempt to do just that.

When I think of parents who would do anything for their children, I exhort them to care first and foremost for their spiritual well-being. The world is not always in agreement with what we believe as Catholics, and parents find themselves needing to be the bearer of bad news to children, who may not always realize that what they are watching on their computers could be enough to open the door to evil.

While of course full of hope, at the same time, this book is not intended to be a "feel-good" read. Its content comes from the fruit of the author's formal and informal study and vast experience in the field of healing and deliverance. Volunteers who make up such teams have witnessed firsthand the effects of evil, not rarely upon unsuspecting families and people of good will. May you take what you learn from this book and place it into action for the good of souls. I pray that the book will inspire families to proclaim Christ's victory over sin and evil and to stand firm in the good and necessary fight.

On the memorial of St. Maria Goretti, July 6, 2020.
Rev. Msgr. Stephen S. Doktorczyk, J.C.D.
Vicar General and Moderator of the Curia
Diocese of Orange in California

PREFACE

Praised be Jesus Christ now and forever.

Pope Paul VI wrote, "Modern man listens more willingly to witnesses than to teachers, and if he does listen to teachers, it is because they are witnesses."[1] This book is a testimony that I'm compelled to offer as encouragement for families who experience spiritual warfare from the world, the flesh, and the devil. My hope is to help evangelize families about unmasking diabolical disguises. This work emphasizes how the Catholic Church provides for persons who need healing, deliverance, and exorcism. I strive to encourage families to prevent problems by practicing the proven means of protection in the Church's arsenal of spiritual weapons.

For the past twelve years, I've served in my diocese on the exorcist's team and as administrator for the healing and deliverance ministry. I field clergy calls, facilitate the exorcism protocol, accompany petitioners, and coordinate logistics for the priests and team. Often, at the request of clergy, I dialogue with the afflicted person seeking liberation from evil. I'm present at major and minor exorcism sessions as intercessor, restrainer, witness, and discerner. This is the Church's collaborative ministry of healing mercy.

Men and women seeking deliverance or exorcism frequently recount tragic experiences of emotional or physical abuse within their extended families. It's not unusual for petitioners to have

---

1 Pope Paul VI, "Address to Members of the Consilium de Laicis," October 2, 1974, quoted in Pope Paul VI, Apostolic Exhortation *Evangelii Nuntiandi* (December 8, 1975), no. 41.

sought healing from human or demonic vexation by engaging practitioners of the occult such as psychics or magicians. It's not rare to discover that within the Catholic home, religious syncretism is practiced – the combination of Catholicism with practices such as New Age or Santeria. All of this is antithetical to Catholicism. Often, people are simply unaware of the danger of such things.

I was invited into this ministry by clergy under the guidance of the bishop. My formation was initiated by two pioneers, Msgr. John Esseff and Dr. Margarett Schlientz, cofounders of the Pope Leo XIII Institute, which trains clergy and teams for deliverance and exorcism ministry. They invited me to the faculty as a case-study facilitator for priests studying at the institute. I'm grateful to Fr. Gary Thomas, exorcist for the Diocese of San Jose, California, for the experiential training he provided by welcoming my presence at several of his cases.

What is experienced during minor or major exorcism is the breathtaking power of the Chief Exorcist, Jesus Christ, working through clergy anointed for liberation from evil spirits. The Rite is a formal and solemn ritual. It is an instrument of torment to demons, and an instrument of divine mercy for souls. This book, however, is *not* about diabolical possessions or the Rite; it is about building up the domestic church.

I've attempted to avoid duplicating resources, many of which have been written already by my exorcist friends and colleagues. To my knowledge, few resources focus on the family dynamic of spiritual warfare. I believe that Catholic families should be the most well-trained spiritual warriors and that Catholic homes should be demon-free zones.

Fr. Gabriele Amorth wrote the following about exorcist assistants:

> The exorcist can be assisted by persons during the rite. As for me, I would have found it very difficult to carry out my ministry if I had had to work without my assistants. . . . The presence of qualified persons of proven faith, who are prepared to confront all that can happen during an exorcism, is important for two reasons. Above all, with their presence and their prayers of intercession, they incarnate the living presence of the Church that gathers together and loves her children, especially those who are suffering. The second is the material assistance they give to the person submitting to the exorcism, particularly if he manifests disturbances, such as the impulse to vomit or to react with movements so brusque and violent that he could harm himself and others. Helping to manage the situation physically is part of the task of the assistants. Those assisting the exorcist must be chosen with judgment: they must live an intense spiritual life, must have firm nerves, must not be easily impressionable, and must be capable of keeping secret the identity of the person possessed.[2]

The greatest witness is the transformation of these brothers and sisters in Christ and the change in their faces from tormented to peaceful following their liberation. Spiritual combat is at the heart of the gospel, not on the periphery of the Church: "The reason the Son of God appeared was to destroy the works of the devil" (1 John 3:8).

In writing this book, I give thanks to the Lord, who has given

[2] Fr. Gabriele Amorth, *An Exorcist Explains the Demonic* (Manchester, NH: Sophia Institute Press, 2016), 109–110.

me the honor of serving my brothers and sisters in Christ across thirteen countries. During international missions, I've encountered some of the most courageous, faith-filled prayer warriors who shared their need for guidance on protecting their families. Now, for the love of family, I give away the gift that I've been given in this ministry.

Our Lady of Victory, pray for us.
Kathleen Beckman
June 19, 2020
Solemnity of the Sacred Heart

1

THE BATTLE FOR THE SOUL OF THE FAMILY

Strategies: Fearless Faith, Vigilance, Discernment of Spirits

> Families are the domestic Church, where Jesus grows; he grows in the love of spouses, he grows in the lives of children. That is why the enemy so often attacks the family. The devil does not want the family; he tries to destroy it, to make sure that there is no love there. . . . May the Lord bless families and strengthen them in this time of crisis when the devil is seeking to destroy them.[3]

Tucked into the rolling hillside of the dusty Silverado Canyon is a jewel of Catholicism: St. Michael's Norbertine Abbey, home to fifty priests and twenty-five seminarians. One spring morning, after Sunday Mass, I exited the abbey's crowded church and leisurely strolled toward the parking lot, enjoying the fragrant, blooming rose garden along the way. Not far from the church

[3] Pope Francis, "Address to Participants in the 37th National Convocation of the Renewal in the Holy Spirit," June 1, 2014.

stands a large white stone statute of the great St. Michael the Archangel. Approaching it, I noticed two boys (around five and seven years old) standing in front of the impressive statue. The younger brother exclaimed to the older one: "Look! Look! He's stomping on the head of the devil! He's smashing the devil! He's squashing him! Do you see?"

The older brother bent down to examine the precise placement of the archangel's foot on top of the ugly demon's head. Then, he enthusiastically replied: "Yep, St. Michael stomped him! That devil is a goner!"

I thought to myself, "Bravo!" These young boys radiated such joy about St. Michael's victory over the devil — and so should you and I.

St. Michael is fierce in defending us from evil because that is his mission from God. Christ is gloriously victorious in the battle against sin and evil. In the words of Moses and the Israelites, "The LORD is a warrior" (Exod. 15:3) — He defends His people. And I had just received the greatest spiritual weapon, the Eucharist, of which St. John Bosco wrote, "There are two things the devil is deathly afraid of: fervent Communions and frequent visit to the Blessed Sacrament."[4] The two young St. Michael enthusiasts reminded me of my two beloved sons, whom God protected during their high school and college years when many temptations arose from the world, the flesh, and the devil. Necessarily engaging in spiritual warfare in defense of my marriage and children was agonizing but transformative for me. More memorable than any trial is God's

---

4 K.V. Turley, "Don Bosco: The Ghost, The Blessed Sacrament and The Devil," Catholic Exchange, February 2, 2015, https://catholicexchange.com/don-bosco-ghost-blessed-sacrament-devil.

amazing intervention to make all things work for good. St. Michael is one of His mighty provisions for us.

Catholic art depicts the archangel Michael's mission against the devil:

> Now war arose in heaven, Michael and his angels fighting against the dragon; and the dragon and his angels fought, but they were defeated and there was no longer any place for them in heaven. And the great dragon was thrown down, that ancient serpent, who is called the Devil and Satan, the deceiver of the whole world – he was thrown down to the earth, and his angels were thrown down with him. (Rev. 12:7–9)

The mission of St. Michael confirms that Catholics on earth are the Church Militant. What does this mean? The Church Militant is "the Church on earth, still struggling with sin and temptation, and therefore engaged in warfare (Latin *militia*) with the world, the flesh, and the devil."[5] Like it or not, we are baptized and confirmed in order to participate in spiritual warfare. What are we fighting? The enemies of our eternal salvation who would rob us of the redemption that Christ won for us.

Scripture shows us evil that comes from within the human heart: "Coveting, wickedness, deceit, licentiousness, envy, slander, pride, foolishness. All these evil things come from within, and they defile a man" (Mark 7:22–23). We also fight against enemies from without: "For we are not contending against flesh and blood, but

---

[5] John Hardon, S.J., *Modern Catholic Dictionary*, s.v. "Church Militant," Catholic Culture, accessed June 15, 2020, https://www.catholicculture.org/culture/library/dictionary/index.cfm?id=32538.

against the principalities, against the powers, against the world rulers of this present darkness, against the spiritual hosts of wickedness in the heavenly places" (Eph. 6:12). Through sacramental communion with Christ, we are anointed to imitate Him in destroying the works of the devil (see Rom. 12:21).

The language of spiritual warfare is not always appreciated outside or even inside the Church, and it is often misinterpreted or corrupted. Internal and external spiritual struggles are challenging. We err to ignore them or to become excessively preoccupied with them. By grace, we learn to respond peacefully to the challenge of spiritual warfare. In his Post-Synodal Apostolic Exhortation *Vita Consecrata*, Pope St. John Paul II teaches: "The path to holiness thus involves *the acceptance of spiritual combat*. This is a demanding reality which is not always given due attention today."[6] The truth is that spiritual combat is at the heart of the gospel. The life of Christ Crucified and Risen is an icon for "fighting the good fight" (see 1 Tim. 6:12). The whole Church is actively involved in Christ's mission of healing and deliverance.

"The Devil Does Not Want the Family"

These words of Pope Francis strike at our hearts, since we intimately identify with our families. So vital is the family that Pope St. John Paul II said, "The future of humanity passes by way of the family."[7] Family life is to be *prioritized*, *protected*, and *promoted*. To quote that

---

[6] Pope John Paul II, Post-Synodal Apostolic Exhortation *Vita Consecrata* (March 25, 1996), no. 38, emphasis original.

[7] Pope John Paul II, Apostolic Exhortation *Familiaris Consortio* (November 22, 1981), no. 86.

beautiful summary of St. Teresa of Calcutta's teaching, "If you want to change the world, go home and love your family." The saint reminds us to focus on the soul of the family. We'll find our Calcutta within the home, in service to the souls entrusted to us.

Today, there is profound spiritual need in the domestic church. St. Teresa of Calcutta asked: "Do we know the poor in our house, in our family? Perhaps they are not hungry for a piece of bread. Perhaps our children, husband, wife, are not hungry, or naked, or dispossessed, but are you sure there is no one there who feels unwanted, deprived of affection?"[8] Evil spirits often aim for the family member who perceives himself to be unlovable. Many of us have some area of insecurity. A fundamental task of marriage and family is to radiate God's affection and affirmation of the dignity of the human person. Pope St. John Paul II taught, furthermore, that no person can thrive without affection: "Man cannot live without love. He remains a being that is incomprehensible for himself, his life is senseless, if love is not revealed to him, if he does not encounter love, if he does not experience it and make it his own, if he does not participate intimately in it."[9]

Families are a diverse unity of persons — a man, woman, and children — with different temperaments, strengths, and weaknesses. The kind of love that wills the good of the other is the equalizing unifier. We must not lose our focus and become distracted by the world, the flesh, and the devil. Yet we must fight courageously against these three enemies if we're to remain free and available to love and serve our families.

---

[8] Mother Teresa, *No Greater Love* (San Francisco: New World Library, 1997), 101.

[9] Pope John Paul II, Encyclical Letter *Redemptor Hominis* (March 4, 1979), no. 10.

In his *Letter to Families*, Pope St. John Paul II reflects on Christ at the wedding feast at Cana — specifically, how the Lord responded to the couple's need. When the Blessed Mother said, "They have no wine" (John 2:3), Christ's response was extravagantly generous. Equally generous is His response to the needs of today's families as they strive to live their mission and defend the domestic church from its enemies. The Polish pope encourages: "*Do not be afraid* of the risks! God's strength is always far more powerful than your difficulties! . . . *Spouses and families, remember at what price you have been 'bought'* (cf. 1 Cor 6:20)!"[10] If we truly perceived our dignity before God, we'd be less inclined toward sin and evil, and more protected from them.

The papal *Letter to Families* also speaks of two opposing civilizations: the civilization of love and the civilization of death. Pope St. John Paul II emphasizes the joy of the civilization of love within the family *and* warns of opposition to it: "*Opposed to the civilization of love* is certainly the phenomenon of so-called 'free love' . . . a love 'liberated' from all conditionings, [which] means nothing more than to make the individual a slave to those human instincts which Saint Thomas calls 'passions of the soul.' 'Free love' exploits human weaknesses; it gives them a certain 'veneer' of respectability with the help of seduction and the blessing of public opinion."[11] This is a clarion call to vigilance, virtue, and valor.

In our culture of death and unbelief, with its hyper-sexualization and hyper-egocentricity, the great need arises for families to

---

10 Pope John Paul II, *Letter to Families* (Manchester, NH: Sophia Institute Press, 2015), 95, 92, emphasis original.

11 Ibid., 60, 61, emphasis original.

cultivate the civilization of love from within. Even in 1981, Pope St. John Paul II recognized this, writing in *Familiaris Consortio*: "At a moment of history in which the family is the object of numerous forces that seek to destroy it or in some way to deform it, and aware that the well-being of society and her own good are intimately tied to the good of the family, the Church perceives in a more urgent and compelling way her mission of proclaiming to all people the plan of God for marriage and the family."[12] Since God calls us to be defenders, life-givers, and lifesavers of the family, He equips us for the mission. It's awe-inspiring to consider what a precious treasure God has entrusted to us.

Demons know that Christ has sealed us in the sign of the cross through Baptism; that the Lord has claimed us; and that the Holy Spirit has come to dwell in us. No evil spirit may claim us unless we intentionally invite it. Unfortunately, some people are unwittingly opening doorways for demons to enter the domestic church. Whether languishing, surviving, or thriving, every family is called to be vigilant against a real foe who "prowls around like a roaring lion, seeking some one to devour" (1 Pet. 5:8). Love requires protecting the beloved. Demons attack the family because of its enormous significance in God's plan of salvation. "The devil does not need to possess us. He poisons us with the venom of hatred, desolation, envy and vice. When we let our guard down, he takes advantage of it to destroy our lives, our families, and our communities," writes Pope Francis.[13]

---

12 Pope John Paul II, *Familiaris Consortio*, no. 3.

13 Pope Francis, *Rebuking the Devil* (Washington, DC: United States Conference of Catholic Bishops, 2019), 9.

St. Paul's exhortation to the Corinthians reminds us to be brave: "Be watchful, stand firm in your faith, be courageous, be strong. Let all that you do be done in love" (1 Cor. 16:13–14). It takes brave men and women to enter a sacramental marriage, to have children according to God's plan, and to raise them in the Faith. This struck me recently when I watched our eager youngest son and his lovely bride exchange marriage vows at the altar of our parish church. I prayed for them to be brave in their witness to Christ, brave in the face of enemies of the family. I prayed that they would keep God at the center of their married life and attain the goal of marriage, which is the eternal salvation of both souls.

After more than forty years of marriage and motherhood, I understand the reality of spiritual attacks aimed at destroying the inestimable beauty of familial love, and I know how necessary it is to stand firm in Christ against the fiery darts of the devil. Pope Francis calls the devil a "loser" and tells us, "Don't forget it!" I call demons bullies, and I kick bullies out of my house by calling upon the name of Jesus Christ and invoking the Precious Blood over the family.

The art of loving and serving the family demands bravery because true love compels you to sacrifice everything for the sake of the beloved. Family life demands total self-giving that is rewarded by the discovery of a joy not to be found elsewhere. Your yes to family is an echo of the yes of the Holy Family. Their yes to the Father reveals complete surrender to the adventure of love, even when this love pierced their hearts. The depth and intensity of your yes, too, show the measure of your surrender to God.

Consider how few families take the Holy Family as their model today. The standard of the Holy Family is not impossible since God called your family into existence and equips you with grace.

He will form your family incrementally according to His will for your eternal salvation. Scripture reveals how the devil pursued the Holy Family from the start: Joseph was tempted to divorce Mary until God intervened through a dream (see Matt. 1:19–22); and Herod gave an edict to slaughter all male infants in an attempt to kill the Infant Jesus (see Matt. 2:16–18).

At the opening Mass for the 2015 Ordinary Synod of Bishops on the Family, Pope Francis preached:

> Our experience today is, in some way, like that of Adam: so much power and at the same time so much loneliness and vulnerability. The image of this is the family. People are less and less serious about building a solid and fruitful relationship of love: in sickness and in health, for better and for worse, in good times and in bad. Love which is lasting, faithful, conscientious, stable and fruitful is increasingly looked down upon, viewed as a quaint relic of the past. It would seem that the most advanced societies are the very ones which have the lowest birth-rates and the highest percentage of abortion, divorce, suicide, and social and environmental pollution.[14]

In this painful picture, we are faced with the reality of sin and evil. The Church was so concerned with the way of the family that a synod of bishops was called to consider ways to aid the family's mission in the world. So strong is our drive for family that "people today — who often ridicule this plan — continue to be attracted

---

14 "Homily of His Holiness Pope Francis," Holy Mass for the Opening of the XIV Ordinary General Assembly of the Synod of Bishops, October 4, 2015.

and fascinated by every authentic love, by every steadfast love, by every fruitful love, by every faithful and enduring love. We see people chase after fleeting loves while dreaming of true love; they chase after carnal pleasures but desire total self-giving."[15] The family will persist according to God's will, but He enlists us to prioritize, protect, and promote it.

Christ's Victory

A victorious spiritual warrior has internalized his identity with Christ Crucified and Victorious (Risen). The spirituality of a Catholic warrior is transformation in Christ. The life of Christ within us allows us not only to withstand spiritual combat but also to obtain victory over our sinful nature and demonic attacks. Faith teaches that the devil is defeated by Jesus Christ, but still makes war on earth. When we resist sin and evil by cooperating with divine providence, we participate in Christ's victory.

St. John Chrysostom penned a beautiful reflection on Christ's victory:

> "The power is Yours," Christ says. For this reason, no matter how many forms your weakness may take, you may still rightly be confident in the battle. You have the kind of Sovereign who's able to accomplish everything necessary that concerns you, and to do it with ease. Not only can God free you from the dangers you face; His power is great and His glory is beyond telling — they are both limitless

[15] Ibid.

> and never come to an end. See how He has in every way anointed you, His champion, and surrounded you with confidence?[16]

Scripture is a weapon; it forms the sword of the Spirit (see Eph. 6:17). Let's internalize Scriptures about God's victory over sin and evil. Prayerfully take time to engrave Scripture on your heart so that if the devil tries to terrify you, you will be secure in these truths. When the devil attacks, pray these Scriptures (even aloud) as a litany of victory over the fallen angels:

> God crushes Satan under our feet: Rom. 16:19–20. God delivers the one who fears Him: Sir. 33:1. Enemies of God will perish: Ps. 92:9. God fights for us: Deut. 3:22. God gives us the victory: Deut. 20:3–4. God guards us from evil: 2 Thess. 5:3. God is our hiding place and shield: Ps. 119:114. God keeps us from all evil: Ps. 121:7. God laughs at the wicked: Ps. 37:13. God leads us in the triumph of Jesus Christ: 2 Cor. 2:14. God is like a man of war: Isa. 42:13. God never sleeps: Ps. 121:4. God prepares a table for us in the presence of His enemies: Ps. 23:5. God is a refuge and fortress: Ps. 91:2; 94:22. God reigns forever: Rev. 11:15. God rescues us from every evil: 2 Tim. 4:18. God is a strong tower: Prov. 18:10. God scatters His enemies: Rev. 11:17; 19:6–7. God is a warrior who gives victory: Zeph. 3:17.[17]

---

16 Quoted in Paul Thigpen, "Know Your Commander" insert, in *Spiritual Warfare Bible* (Charlotte, NC: Saint Benedict Press, 2017).

17 "Topical Index," in *Spiritual Warfare Bible.*

God never asks you to "go it alone," or to bear the heavy weight of human or diabolical trials without leaning on Him. Exorcists teach that even demonic possession can be a school of holiness. How? The process of liberation from evil spirits requires conversion of heart, which in turn requires a radical acceptance of God and the gospel. God may allow spiritual warfare to help reorder your hierarchy of values in order to set you (or loved ones) free.

Throughout the New Testament, the Christian life is defined as *warfare*:

> The Christian life is . . . warfare (2 Cor. 10:4), struggle (Phil. 1:30; Col. 1:29; Heb. 10:32; 12:4), a fight (1 Tim. 1:18), an athletic contest or *agonia* (1 Cor. 9:24), a boxing-match with oneself (1 Cor. 9:27), a readiness to kill things in ourselves and in our relationships (Rom. 8:13), a conflict between good and evil (John 5:29; Rom. 7:21), light and darkness (Luke 11:34–36; John 3:19), truth and falsehood (John 8:44), life and death (Rom. 6:13, 23). In this conflict we are participants and not just spectators, agents but also victims dependent on the power of Christ if we are to survive it.[18]

Strategy: Fearless Faith: Avoiding Sin and Evil

"Faith is a way of knowing. The more we know who Christ is — his absolute lordship over the whole universe, his victory over sin and death won on the cross, his unconditional love for every human

[18] Fr. Vivian Boland, O.P., *Spiritual Warfare: Fighting the Good Fight*, Deeper Christianity (London: Catholic Truth Society, 2007), 5.

being, the more faith we have. That faith is what enables us to pray against sickness and infirmity with confident authority."[19] With faith, we do not succumb to the enemy; we are not victims, but victors.

It's time to be braver in driving out sin and evil in our families, so that our homes can be demon-free zones. St. Catherine of Siena teaches: "Start being brave about everything. Drive out the darkness and spread light. Don't look at your weaknesses. Realize instead that in Christ crucified you can do everything."[20] St. Catherine was born in Italy during the outbreak of the Black Death in 1347. She was the twenty-fifth child of her mother, who was forty years old when Catherine was born. Imagine growing up with twenty-four siblings!

What we needn't stretch our imagination about is St. Catherine's experience of the Black Death, since we are currently experiencing the horror of the COVID-19 pandemic. Like ours, St. Catherine's culture was immersed in turmoil, fear, and death. St. Catherine brilliantly demonstrated bravery in her life by her battles with and victories over demons. Providence graciously raises up saints to bless the world by their brave witness in times of cultural chaos, confusion, and suffering. This present moment begs for the holy daring of saintly family witness.

In 2015, the canonization of Louis and Zélie Martin, the parents of St. Therese of Lisieux, shed light on the profound influence of family life. "When they were beatified in Lisieux in 2008,

---

19 Mary Healy, *Healing: Bringing the Gift of God's Mercy to the World* (Huntington, IN: Our Sunday Visitor, 2015), 89.

20 St. Catherine of Siena, *Letters*, quoted in Carmen Acevedo Butcher, *A Little Daily Wisdom* (Brewster, MA: Paraclete Press, 2008), 1014, Kindle.

Cardinal Jose Saraiva Martins of the Vatican's Congregation for the Causes of Saints emphasized in his homily, 'Louis and Zélie understood that they could sanctify themselves not *despite* marriage but *through*, *in* and *by* marriage, and that their nuptials would be considered as the starting point for a mutual rise.'"[21] Zélie Martin gave birth to nine children, five of whom entered religious life. This is the transformative power of family life lived according to God's design. Family life is a tremendous force for good.

Pope St. John Paul II's parents, Karol and Emilia Wojtyla, offer another example of domestic sanctity. On May 7, 2020, the causes for their canonization opened in Wadowice, the pope's birthplace. A Catholic News Agency article describes the Wojtyla family as follows:

> Karol Wojtyla, an army officer, and Emilia, a school teacher, were married in Kraków in 1906. They had three children. The first, Edmund, was born that year. He became a doctor but caught scarlet fever from a patient and died in 1932. Their second child, Olga, died shortly after birth in 1916. Their youngest, Karol junior, was born in 1920, after Emilia refused a doctor's advice to have an abortion because of her frail health.[22]

To think that Emilia was advised by her doctor to abort Karol Jr. speaks volumes. It's hard to imagine the world without the

---

[21] Fr. Roger Landry, "Louis and Zélie – St. Thérèse's Incomparable Parents and Church Builders," *National Catholic Register*, July 9, 2019, www.ncregister.com/blog/fatherlandry/incomparable-parents-and-church-builders.

[22] "St. John Paul II's parents' sainthood cause has officially opened," Catholic News Agency, May 7, 2020, https://www.catholicnewsagency.com/news/st-john-paul-iis-parents-sainthood-cause-has-officially-opened-69386.

influence of Pope St. John Paul II, who was a treasure of the twentieth century.

The compelling heroism of saintly families isn't relegated to the past. Today, there are many heroic Catholic families standing against sin and evil. But each family will endure attacks from evil ones who "do not want the family" to exist in the form ordained by Christ. No matter how difficult a family trial may be, hope arises from faith in God. We learn through the lives of the saints how even the greatest sinners can be transformed into saints. So it is with family members. Even if you are the only person in your family who is practicing the Faith right now, God can work wonders through you, prayer warrior! When we are in the thick of spiritual combat, it's hard to perceive God's presence, but we hold fast to the truth. The same Lord Jesus who healed and delivered people in the gospel continues to do so today. It cannot be otherwise.

Resistance to sin is the heroism of saintly families. Fighting against personal and communal sin prevents diabolical development. Fr. Dennis McManus, an exorcist, teaches that sin is one of the most common entryways for evil spirits: "Sin is a soul-stealer; a serious matter." In breaking from sin, you must invite the Divine Physician to enter all the imperfect areas of your human story to heal it. The *Catechism of the Catholic Church* teaches: "Sin damages or even breaks fraternal communion. The sacrament of Penance repairs or restores it.... The forgiven penitent is reconciled with himself in his inmost being, where he regains his innermost truth. He is also reconciled with his brethren whom he has in some way offended and wounded. He is reconciled with the Church. He is reconciled with all creation" (CCC 1469). Catholic healing is about reconciliation with God, self, and others.

Referring to Pope St. John Paul II's Encyclical *Veritatis Splendor*, Fr. John Hardon, S.J., explains a fundamental premise of demonic activity:

> Millions of people in the modern world have been deceived into disclaiming that there is such a thing as an inherently or intrinsically evil action. Nothing that a man does is ever evil by itself. It is only circumstances, or the motives, or the situation in which people act, that determine the morality of their conduct. Once people accept this principle, there is nothing that two thousand years of Christianity has taught that are still called sins.[23]

Redemption is about the forgiveness of our sins. To live in His truth, we must call a sin a sin. Otherwise, the domestic church, mired in sin, opens doors for evil spirits.

The devil tempts those who are seriously trying to remain faithful to God to worry, to be anxious and discouraged, and to believe that the Christian life is burdensome, boring, or oppressive. He encourages people caught in habitual sin to give in to their worldly desires without worry because, after all, there is no sin. Besides, the devil tells us, God will be merciful, and so we can do whatever we like. Beware of these demonic lies. Rely on daily examination of conscience and frequent Confession, which make all the difference in combatting sin and evil.

Family life is a rewarding mission of love. God wants to be involved in the details of domestic life because He is the source of

[23] Fr. John A. Hardon, *Meditations on the Angels* (Bardstown, KY: Eternal Life, 2006), 73.

the love that ties families together. All vocations are the purifying means of sanctification by which we journey toward God, who alone is the fulfillment of all desire. What happens in family life influences all vocations: single life, married life, religious life, and the ordained priesthood. Family love is tender and fierce – qualities of a spiritual warrior's heart.

Merciful Healing

The following case of a young person's deliverance illustrates God's infinitely creative providence for persons seeking liberation from evil spirits. The person's mother, who practiced Satanism and was married to a Satanist high priest, consecrated her unborn child to Satan. The person's life was terribly tragic, and his soul was tormented until, as a young adult, the person encountered a Catholic prayer group, the members of which led the person to a priest exorcist. As part of the team, I saw that after the Rite was prayed, while the person was resting from the physical and spiritual battle, the person spontaneously went into the fetal position and began crying copious tears. After several minutes, the person ceased crying and calmly said: "My mom [who was deceased] came to me somehow. I saw her weeping, begging for me to please forgive her. She was so sorry for what she did to me. So very sorry! She didn't mean to hurt me; she didn't know. I told mom that I will forgive her. Then, suddenly, my mother faded away, and the Virgin Mary seemed to hold me like a baby in her arms, rocking me." Healing tears glistened on the person's face. This was another layer of deep healing for the poor soul. Prior to this vision, at the end of the Rite, the priest had invoked Our Lady to step on the head of the serpent that tormented this person. God answered the prayer of the exorcist in a glorious way: He sent His Mother to do battle and to heal.

Heaven hears the cry of a tormented soul. Here is a beautiful example of how God reconciles families. He heals our "mother wounds" and our "father wounds." In the thick of spiritual warfare, remember that God is omnipotent, omniscient, and omnipresent — all powerful, all knowing, and everywhere. Christ doesn't give up on a person, so we are called to hope for God's intervention for the family.

Strategy: Vigilance

Ignorance about diabolical attacks from without and within the family increases the likeliness of casualties among loved ones. The spiritual barrier protecting the domestic church can be compromised if we reject certain teachings of the Faith, such as contraception, cohabitation, adultery, and abortion. Not a few of us prefer the path of self-gratification and comfort, instead of the arduous way of sacrificial service to the family. A soldier for Christ battles against selfishness and demonic temptations of worldly comfort.

Fr. Dwight Longenecker challenges our tendency to go with the flow:

> The story of Satan's fall is the legacy of the war which has, for four thousand years, been the foundation of the Faith—the lens through which we have understood God's great gamble. But we, in our lily-livered age, apathetic in our affluence and cowardly in our comfortable lives, have studiously avoided the language of war. We are frightened

> of offending others. . . . We are embarrassed by the whole idea of the "Church Militant" and wish The Salvation Army would change its name.[24]

This book is for the unashamed Church Militant who desire to be braver in casting out sin and evil from within the family. To live according to God's hierarchy of values is countercultural and necessarily requires resistance to the world, the flesh, and the devil. Cunning evil spirits tempt us to choose to be served, not to serve. Lucifer himself told God, "Non serviam"—Latin for "I will not serve." An effective diabolical tactic against the family is to perpetuate demonic rebellion against God's plan. Then, spouses, parents, and children will no longer desire to serve one another. Demons don't want us to focus on the family: they'd prefer we let them destroy it.

In an interview with the Italian magazine *Tempi*, exorcist Fr. César Truqui warned that "everything that is harming the family, including divorce, pleases the devil." Fr. Truqui also explained that there is "a demon who specializes in the attack on the family, also cited in the story of Tobias [the Old Testament book of Tobit], called 'Asmodeus.'"[25] We mustn't blame the devil for all the troubles in marriage and the family, but diabolical influences do contribute to their breakdown. To better protect loved ones, we should intentionally strategize about how to defend the family against sin and evil. Demons, cunning as they are, can be unmasked and

---

24 Fr. Dwight Longenecker, *Immortal Combat* (Manchester, NH: Sophia Institute Press, 2020), 13, 14.

25 Fr. Romeo Hontiveros, "Exorcist Fr. Cesar Truqui Says There's a Demon That Targets the Family," Pagadian Diocese, May 27, 2016, www.pagadiandiocese.org/2016/05/27/exorcist-fr-cesar-truqui-says-theres-a-demon-that-targets-the-family/.

crushed under the weight of divine and human love interwoven in the family. You are called to "fight the good fight of faith; take hold of the eternal life to which you were called" (1 Tim. 6:12). To take hold of eternal life, we must let go of that which is not of God; we must renounce even the slightest association with sin and evil. We can do this only by God's grace.

This book aims to affirm the resiliency of the family in times of spiritual combat. The world has great need of the divine light that shines forth from faithful Catholic families. We do not only *fight* evil spirits: we *conquer* them, as St. Paul taught the Romans: "We are not overcome by evil, but overcome evil with good" (Rom. 12:21). Families *overcome* evil in God's name!

Strategy: Discernment of Spirits

A primary strategy for wisdom in spiritual combat is called *discernment of spirits*, by which we live and move *with* the Holy Spirit *against* the world, the flesh, and the devil.

The word *discern* comes from the Latin *discernere*, which means "to separate" or "to distinguish." The *Catechism* explains discernment as follows: "The Holy Spirit makes us discern between trials, which are necessary for the growth of the inner man, and temptation, which leads to sin and death. We must also discern between being tempted and consenting to temptation. Finally, discernment unmasks the lie of temptation, whose object appears to be good, a 'delight to the eyes' and desirable, when in reality its fruit is death" (CCC 2847). St. Paul uses the term this way: "Solid food is for the mature, for those who have their faculties trained by practice to distinguish good from evil" (Heb. 5:14). St. John tells us, "Do not believe every spirit, but test the spirits to see whether they are of God" (1 John 4:1). The fundamental discernment to be made is among the human spirit, the Holy Spirit, and an evil or false spirit, which is not from God. Spiritual warriors rely on the gifts of the Spirit (1 Cor. 12): fear of the Lord, piety, counsel, fortitude, knowledge, understanding, and wisdom to help us discern.

Discernment is the ability to understand the spirits working against or for us so that we know to respond according to divine wisdom. In family interactions, we can train ourselves to discern which spirit is operative among us. By discerning the spirits, we are able to join God in fighting demons that attack us and our loved ones.

Be encouraged that God wants us to know His will, and He aids us in discerning it. Fr. Jean-Pierre de Caussade, S.J., teaches, "If we could lift the veil and if we watched with vigilant attention, God would endlessly reveal himself to us and we should see and rejoice in his active presence in all that befalls us."[26]

The Spiritual Exercises of St. Ignatius of Loyola are a proven method of discernment of spirits. I recommend Dan Burke's book *Spiritual Warfare and Discernment of Spirits* for learning the Ignatian way of discernment related to spiritual combat.[27] Ignatian spirituality concerns the movement of spirits with many variables: consolation and desolation, good and evil spirits, movements toward and away from God. Fr. Timothy Gallagher, O.M.V., an expert on the Spiritual Exercises, writes about St. Ignatius's Threefold

---

26 Quoted in Timothy M. Gallagher, OMV, *The Discernment of Spirits: An Ignatian Guide for Everyday Living* (New York: Crossroad Publishing, 2005), 11.

27 Dan Burke, *Spiritual Warfare and the Discernment of Spirits* (Manchester, NH: Sophia Institute Press, 2020).

Paradigm. This paradigm reflects the heart of St. Ignatius's Spiritual Exercises.

1. *Be aware* of what is stirring in you—in your thoughts and in your heart.
2. *Understand* what in these stirrings comes from God and what does not.
3. *Take action* to accept and live by what is of God and to reject what is not.[28]

Prayerfully wait for peace of soul, or *consolation*, before making vital marriage and family decisions. If your soul is in turmoil, or *desolation,* you will be much less inclined to follow God's will, because in desolation, we tend to move away from God.

The ardent invocation of the Holy Spirit is key to discernment because the Holy Spirit helps us to judge correctly. "Discernment of the Holy Spirit is listening and responding to the voice of the Holy Spirit arising in the midst of daily activities. It is being aware of the internal fluctuations of our hearts and learning to discern those movements that flow from the Holy Spirit from those that do not. The Epistles and the Gospels invite us to be disciples 'in the Holy Spirit,' the third person of the Blessed Trinity."[29]

As soldiers for Christ, through prayer and spiritual exercises, we grow in knowledge of His Heart and ours. The goal is that our hearts remain closely united to the Lord's:

---

[28] Gallagher, *Discernment of Spirits*, 17.

[29] Fr. Dick Hauser, S.J., "Following Christ in the Holy Spirit: Discernment of the Holy Spirit," United States Conference of Catholic Bishops, September 15, 2019, http://www.usccb.org/beliefs-and-teachings/how-we-teach/catechesis/catechetical-sunday/prayer/adult-faith-formation-hauser.cfm.

> The key discipline for a Christian following Christ in the Holy Spirit is consciousness of his or her quality of heart. We all experience fluctuations of heart daily. Some of them arise from our propensity to sin. Initial and ongoing conversion in the life of the disciple is critical. In this pursuit, the basic question for conscientious Christians becomes, "In what situations in my day is my heart not moving with the desire to love, and therefore not experiencing the peace of the Holy Spirit?" Just as the experience of peace normally accompanies responding to the Holy Spirit, absence of this peace—anxiety and restlessness—normally accompanies our lack of response.[30]

To protect marriage and family, pray for keen awareness of the dynamic Holy Spirit, our divine counselor dwelling in us. As soon as we sense a spiritual battle within our family, we can pray: *Come Holy Spirit. Please reveal the truth of this situation and lead me to respond according to your will and timing.* Sometimes, I shorten the prayer: *Holy Spirit, what's going on? Help us!*

Family Empathy, Encouragement, and Empowerment

I believe that family life calls for the most well-trained spiritual warriors. The following three experiences have made me keenly aware of the many demonic attacks on the family:

---

[30] Ibid.

1. Personal experience of defending my family through years of spiritual combat, especially following the murder of a loved one
2. International travels to give conferences or lead retreats where I spoke and prayed with Catholics who shared stories of family warfare
3. My work as diocesan administrator of deliverance ministry and as a member of the exorcist's team

I've traveled to thirteen countries to speak and pray with people who shared their personal stories—stories of teenagers addicted to porn, alcohol, or drugs; stories of parental abuse, spousal abuse, hateful divorces, devilish child-custody battles, serial marital infidelity, serial abortions, and infested homes; stories of family members who practice witchcraft and other occult practices and who curse one another. Many people are battle-worn and need encouragement. I want to offer *empathy*, *encouragement*, and *empowerment* to families.

If I could accompany you on the journey, I'd whisper: "Do not give up! Stand firm. Christ never abandons your family. Your marriage and family are worth it. You are braver than you imagine when you abide in Christ. Lean on the Blessed Mother, who is fierce in battle. Tap into the Church's spiritual arsenal. Be a brave soldier, because God is with you." I want to support your family, as others have supported mine. When you are in need, find a good priest or trusted faith community to accompany your family. Draw on the Church's resources. I pray this book will be of some help.

For increasing numbers of people, their family experience is one of loneliness, fear, shame, abandonment, and violence. The inhumane, violent, and abusive behavior of a person within his family is more surprising, and perhaps more painful, than demonic activity. For a person to act inhumanely toward relatives is heartsickening. Sadly, statistics show that this reality is on the rise.

Above all, we must emphasize God's unfailing miraculous intervention for the family. God knows the burdens we carry for our loved ones. Christ does not want us to be crushed in spirit—that's the devil's tactic. Jesus helps us up, breathes new life into our soul, and empowers us with torrents of grace.

The Lord Jesus is a warrior because He is the divine lover of souls. As His disciples, we are called to be warriors because we are first called to be lovers. If you desire more prayer power for spiritual combat, pray first that you love the Lord more. Fall in love with Christ, because love alone compels a warrior to fight against sin and evil and to attain victory over himself and demons.

Evil spirits are keenly aware of God's omnipotence. They know they are limited according to the divine will, but they do not want you to realize this. If you know the truth about spiritual combat, then, when a demon bullies you, you'll discern who truly loves you and who does not. Demons have nothing but disdain and jealousy for humans, while God cares for you and your family. Sometimes, you will be the object of demonic attack—but you will also be the recipient of unending divine assistance.

My Story of Family Spiritual Combat

To show you how deeply I can relate to family spiritual warfare, I'll share my family's experience of spiritual attack and of the Church's lifesaving help for my wounded family through the clergy, my Rosary prayer group, eucharistic life, Church teaching, and the example of the saints.

My family was nearly destroyed by the trauma of seeing my beloved father-in-law bludgeoned to death. Dad was beaten until he was unrecognizable and then was left in a pool of blood on the street in front of his business. That trauma, combined with our laxity in family prayer, our worldliness, and our waning faith, created a perfect storm. In the aftermath of Dad's murder, division undermined my family immediately. Communication ceased; greed, rage, resentment, rivalry, and revenge were rampant. Each of us retreated to our own safe corners.

Coping with this trauma was hellish. I liken it to a bomb of evil that detonated in our homes. Unrelenting temptations assailed me: run from this chaotic family; wall up my heart; throw my energy and time into worldly things; anesthetize the pain. Demons attacked me, saying: "You were not called to this marriage and motherhood after all; it's all a big mistake. It hurts too much. Suffering is useless—run away."

My saving grace was running to Christ at daily Mass and Adoration. I wrestled with the Lord and poured out my tormented emotions to Him. I was deeply traumatized and crushed in spirit because, for the first time, I no longer intuitively perceived good in people. Now I was suspicious of others and even of God's goodness. I raged at what a human being could do to another person.

In Adoration, Jesus graciously led me to understand that only forgiveness could save me. I knew that few family members would embrace the path of forgiveness. I had no control over anyone but myself. After a few weeks, during Adoration, Jesus animated His words from the Gospel: "Father, forgive them; for they know not what they do" (Luke 23:34). That scriptural scene became exceedingly dynamic, profoundly personal. With His agonizing last breath, Christ prayed *for me*, "Father, forgive them; for they know not what they do" (Luke 23:34). I deeply internalized the undeserved gift of divine forgiveness. Receiving the abundance of divine mercy, could I become a vessel of mercy—even for a murderer? I was jarred. With the Holy Spirit's help, I realized that I would never desire a soul's eternal damnation. I couldn't know the disposition of the murderer the day Dad died. I understood that divine justice is intertwined with divine mercy. I decided to forgive and to pray for the murderer for love of Jesus. As evidence of the power of forgiveness, I regained faith, peace, joy, patience, love, and hope. Family restoration was realized over a twenty-year period of suffering and spiritual warfare. Forgiveness was the necessary medicine. Reconciliation was the fruit of "washing the feet" of my family (see John 13:3–17).

I became the family intercessor. Poor in spirit, I offered a sacrifice of praise through daily Mass, Adoration (often multiple holy hours), meditation on Scripture, spiritual reading, daily Rosaries, and Chaplets of Divine Mercy. I grew to love prayer because I deepened my love for the Lord; communing with Him drew me out of myself.

To aid my healing, a priest of the Oblates of Mary led me through the Spiritual Exercises of St. Ignatius. For one year, in weekly sessions, Father augmented the Exercises with Pope St. John Paul II's teaching on marriage and family. In the 1970s, when we were married, my husband and I were twenty-year-old college students. Our preparation for marriage consisted of three meetings with a priest over dinner. Thankfully, we also had the shining example of our faith-filled Catholic parents and their sacrificial commitment to family to prepare us for our life together.

As I learned the Church's teaching on the dignity of marriage and family, I valued it more. The harder the devil tempted me to quit, the more determined I was to be all in. A scholarly priest director formed me to internalize Christ's victory and to identify as a soldier for Christ. This priest championed our family against demonic attacks and taught us God's wisdom. The vital lesson is that God entered the depths of our very imperfect family and defended us against enemies, both human and diabolical. Thanks be to God!

Caution: Abandoning God

In part, the proliferation of diabolical attacks is related to the rejection of God, faith, and the gospel, and the embrace of relativism, moral compromise, and love of the world. Our times are troubled, but long ago, Venerable Fulton Sheen reminded us of God's plan:

> God will not allow unrighteousness to become eternal. Revolution, disintegration, chaos, must be reminders that our thinking has been wrong, our dreams have been unholy. Moral truth is vindicated by the ruin that follows when it has been repudiated. The chaos of our times is the strongest negative argument that could ever be advanced for Christianity.... The disintegration following an abandonment of God thus becomes a triumph of meaning, a reaffirmation of purpose.... Adversity is the expression of God's condem-

> nation of evil, the registering of Divine Judgement. . . . Catastrophe reveals that evil is self-defeating; we cannot turn from God without hurting ourselves.[31]

When I (or a family member) choose something other than God, a door for evil opens. God won't allow us to be comfortable in situations contrary to our salvation; He is compelled to unsettle us for our good. Sometimes, He allows evil spirits to purify the domestic church.

A practical example of how demons drive loved ones apart to the point of contempt is found in C. S. Lewis's classic *The Screwtape Letters*. In the book, Screwtape, a fictional devil, teaches another devil, Wormwood, how to execute the mission of driving loved ones apart:

> When two humans have lived together for many years it usually happens that each has tones of voice and expressions of face which are almost unendurably irritating to the other. Work on that. Bring fully into the consciousness of your patient that particular lift of his mother's eyebrows which he learned to dislike in the nursery, and let him think how much he dislikes it. Let him assume that she knows how annoying it is and does it to annoy—if you do your job he will not notice the immense improbability of the assumption. And, of course, never let him suspect that he has tones and

---

[31] Fulton Sheen, "Signs of Our Times" (radio address, Light Your Lamps series, January 26, 1947), quoted in Fr. Richard Heilman, "Why I'm Passionate about Spiritual Warfare – This Happened in the Span of My Lifetime," Roman Catholic Man, July 9, 2019, https://www.romancatholicman.com/why-im-passionate-about-spiritual-warfare-this-happened-in-the-span-of-my-lifetime/.

> looks which similarly annoy her. As he cannot see or hear himself, this is easily managed.
>
> In civilised life domestic hatred usually expresses itself by saying things which would appear quite harmless on paper (the *words* are not offensive) but in such a voice, or at such a moment, that they are not far short of a blow in the face.[32]

Screwtape's insight is relatable and beckons us to vigilance about how typical family annoyances may be diabolically exaggerated. It is incumbent upon us to protect the fragility of family relationships. There may be family members who do very evil, cruel things to loved ones. But if there are family members who do very good things to save the family, the good overcomes the evil. "For though we live in the world we are not carrying on a worldly war, for the weapons of our warfare are not worldly but have divine power to destroy strongholds" (2 Cor. 10:3–4). Families can destroy demonic strongholds!

Spiritual Warriors for the Family

I met a priest while I was speaking at a prayer breakfast on a Caribbean island. He was exhausted when he arrived. He kindly greeted me and then privately whispered:

> I can't keep up with the demand. At 3:00 a.m., a family knocked on my rectory door. I answered the door and saw a family trying to restrain their teenager who was manifesting

---

32 C. S. Lewis, *The Screwtape Letters*, rev. ed. (New York: Macmillan, 1982), 17.

> evil spirits with superhuman strength, inhuman body contortions, yelling blasphemies. It was the middle of the night; the family was panicked. I did the best I could for them. For a long time, I prayed until the unusual manifestations ceased. My heart breaks for their troubled teen, for what the family endures. Kathleen, please pray for us, and pass the coffee pot; I need coffee.

This Caribbean island is located on the drug-trafficking route to the United States, so drug lords are situated throughout the city. Islanders shared how the drug cartels effectively curse the drugs they peddle to make them more addictive. No wonder the priest was exhausted: he accompanies many families whose children are addicted to drugs. One mother shared that she had three sons who were addicted to opioids or methamphetamines—gateways for evil spirits. But she would not give up on them. She claims Christ's victory and praises Him in the midst of battle. That's dynamic faith!

A group of mothers invited me to attend Mass on the day after the prayer breakfast. Afterward, the women prayed the Rosary together. Before beginning, each voiced her prayer intentions: "For my sons, who are addicted to opioids"; "For my husband, who is having an affair"; "For my daughter, who won't baptize her newborn." What touched me most about these brave women was their genuine joy and untiring hope. They are fierce in battling against evils that threaten their family. Their secret? They offered God a sacrifice of praise ahead of the victory to come.

St. Michael the Archangel,
pray for and protect us, please.

2

SCHOOLED IN THE ART OF SPIRITUAL COMBAT

Strategies: Catholic Remedies, Fighting like a Knight, Healing the Heart

For a monumental struggle against the power of darkness pervades the whole history of man. The battle was joined from the very origins of the world and will continue until the last day, as the Lord has attested. Caught in this conflict, man is obliged to wrestle constantly if he is to cling to what is good, nor can he achieve his own integrity without great efforts and the help of God's grace.[33]

Rome Course: Lessons on Spiritual Warfare

I was a student at the International Association of Exorcists course "Exorcism and Prayers for Liberation," held in Rome in May 2017. The class is offered for clergy, especially those serving as mandated exorcists. A limited number of seats are given to lay persons who serve on the exorcist's team if their bishop writes a letter of request.

[33] Vatican Council II, Pastoral Constitution on the Church *Gaudium et Spes* (December 7, 1965), no. 37.

Since I serve in such capacity, my good bishop advocated for me and our team psychiatrist to attend the course.

One of the professors, Cardinal Angelo Amato, then prefect of the Congregation for the Causes of Saints, gave a stirring conference featuring three points:

- the diabolical component of the July 26, 2016 murder of French priest Fr. Jacques Hamel at his parish, Saint-Étienne-du-Rouvray (a sign of the devil's attack on priests and the Church)[34]
- the devil's assault on new life (abortion), children, and family (the confirmation of Sr. Lucia's prophecy about the family)
- the urgent relevance of the Virgin Mary's message at Fatima, and the role of the three seers

Cardinal Amato shared how he was preparing for the upcoming canonization of the Fatima seers, which, at the time of the course, was only a few days away. He commented:

> Fatima helps us to understand the signs of the times. Children see hell. They are exposed to this terror [and] enlisted to help save souls by prayer and penance. The children respond in faith with obedience to the revelation. They understand the key word: penance!

---

[34] French priest Fr. Jacques Hamel (November 30, 1930 – July 26, 2016) was murdered at the altar in the middle of a Mass. Eyewitness Sr. Danielle confirmed that, before dying, Fr. Hamel called out twice, "Begone, Satan!" She added that "this does not mean that [the assailant] Adel Kermiche was possessed, but that Satan was at work in a powerful way. Father Jacques wanted to exorcise this evil. Those were his last words. Satan does not like the Eucharist." The cause for the beatification of Fr. Jacques Hamel has begun. Elizabeth Scalia, "Eyewitness report: Father Jacques Hamel's last moments," Aleteia, October 4, 2016, https://aleteia.org/2016/10/04/witnesses-to-martyrdom-father-hamels-last-moments/.

> The event of Fatima underscores the victory of Mary over Satan. Mary is the protagonist. She comes to us in a time of war, anti-Catholic persecution, communism, fascism, Christian terrorism, and oppression of any religious values.
>
> The free will of man is to choose between good and evil. Sometimes the future is presented in an irrevocable way: the vision of a city in ruin; a bishop in white is killed; martyrdom (the future of the Church in the twentieth century). Pope John Paul II acknowledged his own fate. The maternal hand of Mary says, "There is no unchangeable fate." Prayer is stronger than a gun! Mary shows us this.[35]

Do you believe that *your* prayer power is heavy artillery, stronger than any other weaponry against the enemy of your soul and salvation? Do you instead assign more attention and power to Satan and his minions than to Jesus Christ, King and Savior? When our family is the target of diabolical vexations, the paralysis of fear and doubt often leads us down a dark and disordered path. Fear is useless—immediately pray an act of faith in Christ.

The Cardinal contrasted the Fatima seers with the *youth of today*, noting that "too many young people falsely believe that Satan is good—a positive being, and the real father of humanity. The God of Christianity is seen as negative." He emphasized the need to teach young people the truth of good and evil and to combat the lie that Satan is a good, harmless character. Television shows portray Lucifer, vampires, and dark and evil beings as

---

35 My personal unpublished notes taken at the twelfth annual International Association of Exorcists course "Exorcism and Prayers of Liberation," Pontifical Athenaeum Regina Apostolorum, Rome, May 2017.

"humane" and Our God and Creator as punitive and judgmental. The family, especially children, must be catechized in the truth and protected against the allurement of the world. Children, too, are invited through prayerful intercession and witness to be active participants in the battle for the family.

Defending children from evil is the responsibility and privilege of parents. In her *Diary*, St. Faustina writes:

> I suddenly saw a crowd of children who seemed to be no older than five to eleven years of age. When they saw me, they surrounded me and began to cry out, "Defend us from evil," and they led me into the chapel which was in this convent. When I entered the chapel, I saw the distressful Lord Jesus. He looked at me graciously and said that He was gravely offended by children: You are to defend them from evil. From that moment, I have been praying for children, but I feel that prayer alone is not enough.[36]

Aware of Jesus' message to St. Faustina, we must redouble our efforts to protect children by unmasking demonic disguises to protect their innocence and beauty.

Sr. Lucia was a little child when the Mother of God entrusted to her a message for the world, with prophetic insights into spiritual warfare. In October 1917, Sr. Lucia received an apparition of Mary and St. Joseph, who held the Child Jesus in his arms. Imagine the inexpressible beauty!

---

[36] *Diary of St. Maria Faustina Kowalska: Divine Mercy in My Soul* (Stockbridge, MA: Marian Press, 1987), no. 765.

Sr. Lucia writes: "In times such as the present, when the family often seems misunderstood in the form in which it was established by God, and is assailed by doctrines that are erroneous and contrary to the purposes for which the Divine Creator instituted it, surely God wished to address to us a reminder of the purpose for which He established the family in the world."[37] This is an elegant statement confirming that family life is assailed by false teachings. The first step in being spiritual warriors for the family is grasping the weight of its purpose in the world. We must know the precious thing we defend in combat. I'm not going to fight hard if I'm really not invested in the thing I'm protecting.

If we stray from our vocation to the family, we often unknowingly end up in the grip of the enemy of our soul. The evil spirits do not play fair and are happy to kick us when we are down or distracted. We can easily fall into escapism, which is imbued with diabolical snares. Our spiritual armor must remain well oiled with the balm of faith-filled prayer.

In 1981, Sr. Lucia wrote in a letter to Cardinal Carlo Caffarra: "The final battle between the Lord and the kingdom of Satan will be about marriage and the family. Don't be afraid . . .because whoever works for the sanctity of marriage and the family will always be fought against and opposed in every way, because this is the decisive issue. . . . Nevertheless, Our Lady has already crushed his head."[38]

---

37 Sister Lucia, *Calls From the Message of Fatima* (Still River, MA: Ravengate Press, 2005), 162.

38 Joseph Pronechen, "Fatima's Sr. Lucia and John Paul II: Why Every Family Should Be a Holy Family," *National Catholic Register*, December 29, 2019, https://www.ncregister.com/blog/joseph-pronechen/sister-lucia-and-st-john-paul-ii-explain-holy-families-for-holy-family-sund.

This is our invitation from Our Heavenly Mother to join in the battle for the preservation of the family. Our battle cry in the name of Jesus Christ is "Get behind me, Satan!" Pray for the Holy Spirit to increase faith in Christ's victory, and for Our Lady's miraculous intervention for the family.

Cardinal Amato continued his discussion of Fatima and spiritual warfare as follows:

> We have tools to dominate evil. Christianity is not a religion of discouragement. When we face evil that God permits, He helps us. We place our hope in Him, entrusting ourselves more to God in our weakness. And we entrust ourselves to Mary, sharing in her work of extending God's victory. The key is to enrich and share with neighbors in the Church, to form Christian people in the biblical theological view of angels and demons.
>
> Fatima introduces the symbol of the Blood [of the Lamb]; it reveals the battle between Satan and the Virgin Mary. The message throws light on the world today. Fatima opens a new vision of our future: a dark future enlightened by hope because of the maternal Heart of Mary. Fatima is a prophetic vision of the war waged against the Church and of immense suffering. We cope with the battles of this life with Mary and the Eucharist.[39]

We may call upon the power of the Precious Blood for our loved ones by praying: *Lord Jesus, I implore you to cover my loved one*

[39] My personal unpublished notes.

in your saving Blood. For the family, we pray: *May the Precious Blood of the Victorious Lamb flow within us, bring us to conversion, and anoint us for spiritual combat.*

"In the power of belonging to Christ we become participants in the battle and not just beneficiaries of its outcome."[40] No servant is greater than the Master. The life of Christ is the proclamation of victory. The Virgin Mary continues to be the exemplar for proclaiming God's victory over evil. Mary's complete yes to God echoes throughout the spiritual realm. For devils, her yes is crushing.

Cardinal Amato articulated five vital points about spiritual combat:

- Formation in spiritual warfare empowers authentic, victorious discipleship.
- Discernment of spirits is key for evangelization.
- Fatima informs and confirms the Virgin Mary's role in the salvation of souls.
- Children are capable of fulfilling their call to learn and live the art of spiritual combat as part of their mission in the family and world.
- Mary and the Eucharist are pillars of protection in the battles of this life.

According to Cardinal Amato, after the attempt on his life on May 13, 1981, Pope St. John Paul II asked for the Fatima file to be delivered from the Vatican to the Agostino Gemelli hospital in Rome, where he was recovering. There, he *again* reviewed the file in light of the attempted assassination.

---

40 Boland, *Spiritual Warfare*, 56.

The Congregation for the Doctrine of the Faith records that "on 25 May 1984 in Saint Peter's Square, while recalling the *fiat* uttered by Mary at the Annunciation, the Holy Father, in spiritual union with the Bishops of the world, who had been 'convoked' beforehand, entrusted all men and women and all peoples to the Immaculate Heart of Mary."[41] This time, as part of the complete Marian consecration of the world, the Holy Father wrote a *deliverance prayer*. The prayer is included in appendix A of this book.

Mary's Deliverance Team

Msgr. John Esseff, an exorcist and spiritual son of St. Padre Pio, cofounded the Pope Leo XIII Institute (www.popeleo13institute.org) with Dr. Margarett Schlientz in 2010. The institute provides a two-year postgraduate course to train clergy for the office of exorcist. At the institute, I served as an exorcism case-study facilitator for clergy students. For five years, I attended lectures given by the exorcist professors: Fr. Francesco Bamonte, Fr. Gary Thomas, Fr. Dennis McManus, Fr. Jeffrey Grob, Fr. Chad Ripperger, Fr. Cliff Ermatinger, and others. In 2016, I was asked to coordinate the annual summer conference for clergy and laity who serve in exorcism ministry. The theme that year was "The Virgin Mary's Role in Spiritual Warfare."

At the conference, Msgr. Esseff presented a slide labeled "Mary's deliverance team" featuring a picture of the children of Fatima. These three children were chosen to assist the Mother of

---

41 Congregation for the Doctrine of the Faith, "The Message of Fatima," Vatican, June 26, 2000, https://www.vatican.va/roman_curia/congregations/cfaith/documents/rc_con_cfaith_doc_20000626_message-fatima_en.html.

God in the salvation of souls. What do they teach us about spiritual combat?

- The Eucharist is vital, as the angel expressed in the prayer he taught the children. (*My God, I believe, I adore, I hope, and I love you. I ask pardon for those who do not believe, do not adore, do not hope, and do not love you.*)
- We must remain in the state of grace.
- The Rosary is a powerful weapon against evil.
- Marian intervention saves souls.
- Marian consecration is efficacious.
- Fasting is a powerful way to overcome evil.
- Reparation for sins saves souls from falling into hell.
- Unconfessed sin puts a person in spiritual danger.
- Hell exists, and too many souls are going there.
- God works miracles to advance our salvation.
- Daily conversion of heart is the way of discipleship.
- Penance is necessary, and even children can do penance.[42]

Mary's deliverance team also teaches us not to worry about what others think of us and not to fear reproach or rejection. The children suffered greatly because their own parents doubted them and didn't visit them when they were imprisoned. These children teach us to be faithful to our mission without compromise. How often do we bow down, back off, compromise, or water down the

42 "Jesus' call to conversion and penance, like that of the prophets before him, does not aim first at outward works, 'sackcloth and ashes,' fasting and mortification, but at the *conversion of the heart, interior conversion*. Without this, such penances remain sterile and false; however, interior conversion urges expression in visible signs, gestures and works of penance" (CCC 1430).

truth because we care so much what others think? Even when it comes to our loved ones, we are often tempted to tune out disordered behavior or patterns of sin occurring under our roof. We are at a loss to address some of the most vital life-and-death issues for those entrusted to us. Even an act as simple as praying grace before meals with extended family can cause fear, embarrassment, or conflict.

To battle the pride of being politically correct, the vanity of people-pleasing, and the fear of presenting the truth in love, we need lively faith, fortitude, and fearless charity. The world has redefined marriage and hijacked the word *love*. Not a few Catholics have succumbed to disordered tolerance and have relinquished discipline. In reality, love cohabitates with truth and justice. We must be brave to descend beneath the surface of the family, beyond the vanities of daily life. It takes courage, not cowardice, to live out God's call for the family and to learn the art of being graciously authentic and charitable in the face of nonbelieving family members. There's profound beauty in what Catholics bring to the table. We should radiate to others the joy of knowing and loving Christ; we should attract them by the beauty of our Faith.

A perennial call to arms, the events and witnesses of Fatima offer confirmation that divine providence chooses the family to thwart the devil's plans. Here's some evidence for the importance of Fatima: when news broke about the fall of the Berlin Wall in 1991, my father-in-law commented, "This is the result of a generation of Catholic families praying the Rosary as Mother Mary requested at Fatima." Dad then gleefully dangled his rosary in front of me. As the *New York Times* reported, "The Communist regime was prepared for everything 'except candles and prayers.'"[43] I will elaborate on the weapon of the Rosary in another chapter.

Caution: Diabolical Influence through Sin

Fallen man is self-centered. We orbit ourselves instead of God. In this state, we enter enemy territory. Satan is a tempter, and as with the Fall, he still directly influences us to reject divine grace and to choose sin. Though he doesn't force us, he can seduce us into sin if we don't resist temptations. Scripture teaches that temptation is the devil's ordinary mode of action (see 1 John 3:8–10). By deception and psychic violence, the devil tempts us to sin, seduces us to participate in evil. The diabolic aim is to separate us from God: the devil knows that if we reject God, the darkness gains some power over us. The enemy has no access to your will unless you hand over the key (though he doesn't want you to know this). As a result, it is the flesh, not the soul, that may become diabolically infested through the doorway of sinful cooperation with evil. If we yield to an evil spirit's temptation to sin, how can we not be united with that evil spirit at some level?

Perhaps we can think of a sinful lifestyle as a kissing affair with the devil, who won't let the relationship cease at a kiss. He'll seduce us until the ungodly relationship develops further, and he may ultimately gain access to our bodies in an effort to mock the very Incarnation of Christ. Demons can never be life-giving; therefore, they must take by force and manipulation what they both

[43] Katrin Bennhold, "The Fall of the Berlin Wall in Photos: An Accident of History That Changed The World," *New York Times*, November 9, 2019, https://www.nytimes.com/2019/11/09/world/berlin-wall-photos-30-year-anniversary.html.

despise and desire—us! God took possession of you and me at Baptism. We are possessed by the Holy Spirit, and our foreheads are engraved with the sign of the cross. Do not let demons be more aware of this than you are—know to whom you belong.

All sin, including the sin of Adam and Eve, is based in distrust of God. The devil still whispers in our ears: "God isn't trustworthy," and "You can be like God." Cultivate a vigilant heart, aware that "out of the heart come evil thoughts, murder, adultery, fornication, theft, false witness, slander" (Matt. 15:19). The book of Deuteronomy speaks of the paths to sin as a straying heart, surrender to idolatry, and a refusal to listen (30:15–20). The book of Sirach warns us against setting "your heart on your wealth," "walking according to the desires of your heart," and saying, "Who will have power over me?" (5:1–3).

Sometimes, we pour all our energy into our family's outward appearance, without much concern for the interior life of the souls within our homes. Our actions make evident our attitude about families. What does it say about us when, at Mass, we sneer at the mothers of crying children or at couples with many children? The devil is a patient predator who studies his prey and knows well our weaknesses. Cultivate a *vigilant, virtuous, valiant* heart.

Strategy: Genuine Catholic Remedies

If you or your family need liberation from evil spirits, please do not be tempted to seek remedies outside of the Catholic Church. In appendix B, you will read the stories of families who, knowingly or not, became diabolically afflicted by enlisting the help of occult practitioners posing as healers. Often, people seeking liberation from diabolical vexation expect to see the exorcist immediately. They hope Father will quickly pray away any demonic suffering so they can resume normal life. Sometimes, their lifestyle includes habitual sin and a long break from friendship with God. Issues such as cohabitation and nonsacramental unions need to be regularized for lasting liberation from evil because deliverance occurs through reconciliation with God.

When demonic affliction occurs, seeing an exorcist is not the first step. It may be helpful to consider that when we are physically sick, we do not immediately see a surgeon. At first, we may try to treat mild symptoms at home. If the physical sickness persists, we call our doctor for an appointment. The doctor will then examine us and perhaps order tests to determine a diagnosis and treatment. Many diocesan protocols for deliverance and exorcism are similar to the medical model.

The afflicted person (and his family) should begin praying deliverance prayers, renouncing evil, repenting of sin, repairing damage done to others, and solidifying his relationship with God and the Church. Often, genuine relief from diabolical attacks can be attained by making a good sacramental Confession, praying daily deliverance prayers, fasting, and leading a sacramental life. These are effective, proven remedies. All levels of demonic affliction require such remedies.

If a person, together with a parish priest, has discerned that he is experiencing diabolical vexation beyond ordinary temptation, an appointment is made for a prayer session. Sometimes, when I call a person to schedule his appointment for minor or major exorcism, he reports that, by going to Confession regularly, attending Mass as often as possible, receiving spiritual direction from a priest, saying deliverance prayers, and renouncing sin and evil, he no longer needs to see the exorcist. The person is already experiencing liberation from demonic affliction by cooperating with the Chief Exorcist and by exercising his baptismal authority to cast out any evil spirits in protection of his soul.

Sometimes, healing the whole person requires a team of people. Often, a medical or mental-health professional's consultation is helpful. Why? It's not that the Church disbelieves the afflicted person's story; rather, the Church must discern how to heal the whole person. We can't compartmentalize the soul and the body; they are incorporated. Also—and this is important—we live in a very medicated society, and the side effects of prescription drugs can mirror diabolical problems. Our priests are the shepherds and anointed physicians of souls, but they are not medical doctors or mental-health professionals. A medical or psychiatric evaluation is performed only to help *you and the priest* discern the true origin of your suffering. Some dioceses work in collaboration with the excellent apostolate of the Catholic Medical Association (www.cathmed.org). Our team enlists medical professionals; one of our members is a psychiatrist. I'm aware that not a few people have had negative experiences with mental-health professionals. Discernment is vital. Each spiritual-combat situation is unique and requires a tailored course of action. I implore parents to make deliverance prayers part of daily life to protect their families. It's helpful if your family establishes a good rapport with your parish priest, who can pray periodic blessings upon you and your home.

For cases of *extraordinary* spiritual warfare, make an appointment with your parish priest. A word about the importance of *jurisdiction*: demons are extremely legalistic and know who has authentic spiritual authority over them. The diocesan bishop has jurisdiction in his diocese, as do the mandated exorcist and his team. Your parish is considered your spiritual home; your parish priest, your spiritual father. For your spiritual protection, be aware of authority and jurisdiction.

Thankfully, many bishops are establishing diocesan protocols for deliverance and exorcisms. If your family is experiencing spiritual combat and needs more help after you have made a good Confession and exercised your baptismal authority through deliverance prayers and fasts, make your needs known to your parish priest. *Every* priest can offer healing and deliverance prayers, spiritual counseling, and sacraments to relieve demonic vexation.

Even in the midst of dire spiritual combat, by God's grace, you can be lifted above the battle to grasp the greater purpose of God's providence, which is aimed at the salvation of souls. Remember that you are anointed to be a soldier for Christ. Renounce evil and cling to God, and He will not forsake you. Then, you will be prepared to "fight like a knight" for the Lord you love and the family you cherish.

Strategy: Fight like a Knight

The phrase "fight like a knight" refers to a message that Christ dictated to St. Faustina.[44]

In Krakow-Pradnik, Poland, on June 2, 1938, Christ directed the young Polish Sister of Mercy on a private three-day retreat. Jesus began, "My daughter, I want to teach you about spiritual

---

[44] St. Faustina, *Diary*, no. 1760.

warfare." Here, I'll highlight a few parts of Jesus' message to St. Faustina. The entire retreat can be found in appendix A.

In the text below, the words of Jesus taken from St. Faustina's *Diary* are printed in bold. The commentary is mine.

- **Bear with yourself with great patience.** The virtue of patience disarms the tactics of the devil, who loves drama. Demons tempt us to treat ourselves and family members impatiently. These temptations turn us against ourselves and loved ones, making us angry and resentful. Bearing with yourself requires patience. Bearing with your loved ones calls for greater patience.
- **Do not neglect interior mortifications.** Scripture teaches that some demons can be evicted only by prayer and fasting. Interior mortification is a powerful weapon. Small sacrifices offered with love strengthen our armor. Promote a form of fasting in your family.
- **If someone causes you trouble, think what good you can do for the person who caused you to suffer.** Mercy is a weapon for the good. When others hurt us, we can train ourselves to respond with goodness. This takes practice! Remember that we can break a curse by returning it with a blessing: "Bless those who curse you, pray for those who abuse you" (Luke 6:28). Pray only for blessings for your family, even for your extended family, whose members may aggravate you.
- **Do not be guided by feeling, because it is not always under your control; but all merit lies in the will.** All merit lies in the will because love is an act of the will. Even a daily communicant may exit the Church, enter the work-

place or the home, and become an agent of darkness by the duplicity of his heart. Your will is always free—the devil can't touch it. He can only seduce you with temptations. Your free will can assent to God's will, or the devil's, or your own.

- **I will not delude you with prospects of peace and consolations; on the contrary, prepare for great battles.** St. Faustina was prepared for great battles by daily carrying her cross. Families are prepared for battles by daily resistance to countless temptations from the flesh, the world, and the devil. When we take up the daily crosses that God allows into our lives, we are being faithful soldiers in Christ's army that is engaged in great battles against sin and evil.
- **Know that you are on a great stage where all heaven and earth are watching you. Fight like a knight, so I can reward you. Do not be unduly fearful, because you are not alone.** You and I are on a great stage where heaven and earth are watching. What message is your family life radiating? Do you live in the light, the darkness, or shades of gray? The way you live attracts more light or more darkness. If the devil does not succeed in pulling you into darkness, he'll attempt to keep you in a lukewarm state. "So, because you are lukewarm, and neither cold nor hot, I will spew you out of my mouth," God tells us (Rev. 3:16). Lukewarmness is a spiritual danger zone. A lukewarm heart becomes self-absorbed in lazy living that stifles sacrificial love. Lukewarm people live to satisfy their own comfort. Gradually, such Christians end up being content with a mediocre life, while Christ calls us to the abundant life (see John 10:10).

Christ's words to St. Faustina can become a motto for the family: "Fight like knights." A knight knows the nobility of his mission. With assuredness of victory, the knight fights to the end, even at the cost of his life, for he defends a cause greater than himself.

St. Faustina and Jesus Christ converse heart to heart in the language of holy love. You, too, are called to divine intimacy. It's only for love's sake that a soldier fights like a knight. We fight the foe in front of us for the loved one standing behind us. "Resist the devil and he will flee from you" (James 4:7). In the same verse, St. James tells us, "Submit yourselves therefore to God." To submit yourself to the Lord means to receive His love humbly and to be formed by Him and His Church. Fidelity to your family vocation is the fruit of submitting to Christ.

Family is where love should flourish. Some people are reluctant to acknowledge spiritual combat in the home. Others may have family members who are absorbed in doing their own thing, unaware of the pain their loved ones may be experiencing. We may be tempted to look the other way to keep peace in the home. But nothing is gained unless we face the truth of our family situations.

If you believe that your spouse or child is addicted to pornography, alcohol, or drugs, or is practicing witchcraft or playing an occult game, you may struggle to address the problem. Love compels you to do the hard thing. Realize that God will offer a lifeline through you. You may be ridiculed or rejected. Call your family to order anyway, and allow them to call you to order. Each member of the family is called to holiness and healing. The ideal family is a team of spiritual warriors who strengthen one another in virtuous love.

St. Faustina battled the devil on several occasions. In this example, we learn how the devil tempted her to abandon intercessory prayer and divine mercy:

> The tempter went on: "Why should you bother about other souls? You ought to be praying only for yourself. As for sinners, they will be converted without your prayers. I see that you are suffering very much at this moment. I'm going to give you a piece of advice on which your happiness will depend: never speak about God's mercy and, in particular, do not encourage sinners to trust in God's mercy, because they deserve a just punishment.... You see, to live as a good nun, it is sufficient to live like all the others. Why expose yourself to so many difficulties?"[45]

Demons attacked St. Faustina's vocation and her mission. Our vocation and mission in the domestic church are subject to the devil's parade of temptations and clever assaults by way of doubt, mediocrity, secrecy, and disobedience. These are the hallmarks of devilish temptations, and their intensity causes grief if we don't resist and rebuke the devil.

STRATEGY: HEALING THE HEART OF THE FAMILY

The *Catechism* defines the heart beautifully:

> The heart is the dwelling-place where I am, where I live... the place "to which I withdraw."... The heart is the place of

---

45 St. Faustina, *Diary*, no. 1497.

> decision, deeper than our psychic drives. It is the place of truth, where we choose life or death. It is the place of encounter, because as image of God we live in relation: it is the place of covenant. (CCC 2563)

The family has a vulnerable heart. The devil aims to crush a person's spirit, to break his heart, to cut off his friendship with Christ, and to alienate him from his family so that the devil can replace these supports. While the battlefield is our mind, it is our heart that demons aim to wound. When we lose heart, hopelessness settles in, despair weighs down, depression engulfs, and demons gain some ground in us.

There is one Heart that rescues, one Heart that suffices for healing and liberation from evil. It is the human and divine Heart of the Incarnate Word, the victorious Heart of the Chief Exorcist who rescues us from the devil's grip. It is the Heart that was knit together in the womb of the holiest Virgin Mother; the Heart made flesh for the revelation of divine love; the obedient Heart of the son of Joseph the carpenter; the broken Heart of the rejected Savior; the Holy Thursday Heart of the Priest in agony; the pierced and bleeding Good Friday Heart of the Redeemer who paid our ransom; the victorious Easter Heart of the Risen King; the Heart consoled by saints and wounded by sinners; the Heart that absorbs your pain and brokenness so that you receive a new heart: His Heart.

Christ's Heart is the home where human vulnerability is safe. It is from God's Heart that family love arises. Within the family, you are called to radiate fully the *One Heart* that heals. Pray ardently for one another's healing and deliverance; tend to one another's wounds; seek liberty for anyone bound by the diabolical chains of sin. Pope St. John Paul II often repeated, "Man cannot fully find himself except through a sincere gift of himself." We can pray the prayer that Pope Francis learned from his grandmother: "Jesus, make my heart more like yours."[46]

We expect to be safe with and cherished by our parents and siblings. For our safety and happiness, our family should intentionally welcome Jesus, Mary, and St. Joseph into their hearts. Pope Francis teaches:

> Each Christian family can first of all—as Mary and Joseph did—welcome Jesus, listen to Him, speak with Him, guard Him, protect Him, grow with Him; and in this way improve the world. Let us make room in our heart and in our day for the Lord. As Mary and Joseph also did, and it was not easy: how many difficulties they had to overcome! They were not a superficial family, they were not an unreal family. The family of Nazareth urges us to rediscover the vocation and mission of the family, of every family. And, what happened in those 30 years in Nazareth, can thus happen to us too: in seeking to make love and not hate normal, making mutual help commonplace, not indifference or enmity. It is no coincidence, then, that "Nazareth" means "She who keeps", as Mary, who—as the Gospel states—"kept all these things in her heart" (cf. Lk 2:19, 51). Since then, each time there is a family that keeps this mystery, even if it were on the periphery

---

[46] Kathleen N. Hattrup, "The 7-word prayer Pope Francis learned from his grandmother," Aleteia, June 8, 2020, www.aleteia.org/2020/06/08/francis-shares-7-word-prayer-he-learned-from-his-grandmother/.

> of the world, the mystery of the Son of God, the mystery of Jesus who comes to save us, the mystery is at work. He comes to save the world.[47]

In considering the beauty of the Holy Family, we shouldn't believe that our family can't measure up. One of the devil's means of attack is *unbelief*. Even if most of our loved ones are prodigal now, we keep our post as watchmen, wisely waiting with hope that won't disappoint. I know of many dire family situations that have been turned into victories through the persistent intercession of one family prayer warrior—often a grandmother or grandfather with a rosary in hand.

Five Common Entryways for Demons

At the Avila Institute's 2019 summit, Fr. Dennis McManus gave a conference that provided pertinent information about doorways through which demons enter a person:

1. *Sin*. Sin is a serious matter; it's soul-taking. Demons watch us sin and accuse us afterward. When we sin, we choose something other than God.
2. *Wounds*. Demons want us to believe that we equal our wounds. If we are our wounds, we live in them, and so can demons.
3. *Inheritance*. Parents can consecrate a child to Satan. We can also inherit curses from our ancestors, especially if they practiced Freemasonry.

---

47 Pope Francis, General Audience (December 17, 2014).

4. *Contracts.* Many make contracts with the dark world through the sex trade or the drug trade, for instance. When you profit from secret knowledge, you enter a contract with demons and give them rights over you.
5. *Demons who choose us.* Demons are extremely lonely. They have lost all possibility of love. Human beings are very consoling to them. Some pick us out, saying, "I want you." You can't destroy them, but you can chase them away. An exorcism severs the relationship.

In summary, demons are not contagious. They can enter when a person willfully assents to demonic temptations, usually to gain power, money, or control over others. Our choices have consequences, so prudence dictates that we discern our choices well. We should not be afraid, but should rely on the Holy Spirit's guidance. Pray about everything! God is in the details of our lives. Faith in God prevents us from being nervous about spiritual warfare, which all of Christ's disciples experience. When we are cognizant of our identity in Christ, we have nothing to fear. We should be ready for spiritual combat, not preoccupied by it. Our preoccupation must always be the glorious truth of God's protective and providential love for us.

Lord Jesus, unite my heart to yours, please.
Our Lady of Fatima, pray for us, and protect our children.

3

THREE FOUNDATIONAL STRATEGIES FOR SPIRITUAL WARFARE

Scripture, the State of Grace, and Authority

The devil . . . plants evil where there is good, trying to divide people, families and nations. But God . . . looks into the "field" of each person with patience and mercy: he sees the dirt and the evil much better than we do, but he also sees the seeds of good and patiently awaits their germination.[48]

In spiritual warfare, the fundamental tripod is (1) Scripture, (2) spiritual authority, and (3) the state of grace. These are a spiritual warrior's basic weapons. Our Captain, Jesus Christ, used these against demons.

If you're seeking for a way to protect yourself and your family, look no further than the *Person of Jesus Christ*. He is *the* way! Think, act, pray like Jesus Christ. In spiritual warfare, it is your

[48] "Pope Francis Prays for Peace in the Middle East," Vatican Radio, July 20, 2014, http://www.archivioradiovaticana.va/storico/2014/07/20/pope_francis_prays_for_peace_in_the_middle_east/en-1103115.

incorporation into Christ that ensures victory over sin and evil. In the Acts of the Apostles, this principle is exemplified by the sons of Sceva, who were itinerant Jewish exorcists:

> And God did extraordinary miracles by the hands of Paul, so that handkerchiefs or aprons were carried away from his body to the sick, and diseases left them and the evil spirits came out of them. Then some of the itinerant Jewish exorcists undertook to pronounce the name of the Lord Jesus over those who had evil spirits, saying, "I adjure you by the Jesus whom Paul preaches." Seven sons of a Jewish high priest named Sceva were doing this. But the evil spirit answered them, "Jesus I know, and Paul I know; but who are you?" (19:11–15)

The demons recognized the Lord and His disciple St. Paul, but they wouldn't obey the commands of the Jewish exorcists because, while they used the name of Jesus, they weren't authentic disciples: they invoked Him for their own gain. So the demons attacked the inauthentic exorcists. Let's not forget this story.

Note also how God used this situation to bring forth good:

> And the man in whom the evil spirit was leaped on them, mastered all of them, and overpowered them, so that they fled out of that house naked and wounded. And this became known to all residents of Ephesus, both Jews and Greeks; and fear fell upon them all; and the name of the Lord Jesus was extolled. Many also of those who were now believers came, confessing and divulging their practices. And a number of those who practiced magic arts brought

> their books together and burned them in the sight of all; and they counted the value of them and found it came to fifty thousand pieces of silver. So the word of the Lord grew and prevailed mightily. (Acts 19:16–20)

It was Christ through St. Paul who worked miracles of healing and deliverance. Christ's disciples are still called to manifest the Lord's power to the amazement of the world. Be brave and pray for miracles in your family. We insult the Lord God when we fail to ask for big miracles with expectant faith. If your spouse or child needs radical conversion to Christ, anticipate the miracle.

When the Eternal Father looks at you, He sees the image of His Son Jesus Christ woven into the fabric of your baptized being. When you pray against evil spirits, demons recognize Christ in you. The devil recognizes that you belong to Jesus. Demons know *if you know* your identity and with what authority you act. If you are exercising your *rightful authority* in Jesus' name, demons will obey your command: "Begone, Satan!" (Matt. 4:10).

Exorcists emphasize that God can use spiritual combat to our great benefit for the salvation of our soul. Through trials, we strengthen our faith and bear witness to how Christ defended us from attackers. Christ carries us along surprising paths to new depths and heights, revealing His power and beauty so that we know our life is truly in His almighty hands.

Caution: Perfectionism

All families have difficulties; there are no perfect ones. In my retreat work, I've met and prayed with many people who seem disappointed about the way their families are functioning. Spouses and parents feel that they have personally failed because family life is not as they expected. Sometimes, the problem lies in our unrealistic expectations. Perhaps the secular world's portrait of the ideal family has influenced us more than we realize.

I was once yoked by a spirit of perfectionism that led to my need to control everything—especially my family and my home. I rarely recall dreaming, but there is one dream I won't forget. In the dream, I was a young wife and mom sitting on the floor with building blocks. I was trying to build the perfect house for the perfect family. Just when I was close to finishing, the whole structure would fall apart. I had to start over, rebuilding, trying to pull it all together. But it always fell apart. I became very frustrated. I wanted perfection, but couldn't make it happen.

Then, in the dream, Christ came and sat down on the floor across from the pile of wooden blocks. Looking into my pouting eyes, the majestic Lord gently, patiently said, "Are you ready to let me build it now?" Intuitively, I understood that my loved ones and my home *were not mine* to perfect. I understood that each family member belongs to God, and it is for Him to design each person's adventure according to what he needs for eternal salvation. I started to turn over control of my children to the Lord and Mary. This was very healthy for my family. Many years later, I had a second dream in which I was invited to entrust my husband to St. Joseph. I began to do this and saw good fruit. Divine providence knows how to provide for each precious soul.

We worry about our loved ones, especially the prodigals. Christ is even more preoccupied than we are with their eternal salvation. But God does not violently invade a soul or take it by force. As much as Christ desires it, He won't insist that a person love Him. However, He does insist on pursuing the person, waiting for the slightest opening in his heart, that He may be welcomed there. God also arranges circumstances to guide the prodigals home. His love is extremely creative; His timing is perfect.

Discernment of spirits helps us to know when to be silent and when to speak according to God's will. Timing is important in the family and in combat. Sometimes, Christ says, "Stand back, and watch what I do for your family!" Other times, He urges, "Pick up your sword and fight!"

In this chapter, we'll learn more about the *three foundational* Catholic strategies for defending the domestic church in times of spiritual combat. The first of these strategies is *Scripture*. God's Word is a resounding, powerful weapon. When Jesus was tempted, for instance, He quoted Scripture to rebuke the devil. In my experience, when Scripture is read aloud during the Rite, the reactions of demons reveal their torment. In particular, they react strongly to the prologue to John's Gospel.

In the Old Testament, we find many examples of spiritual warfare, and in the Gospels, we learn from the exorcisms performed by Jesus, our model for spiritual combat.

Mark 1:21–28 (an Exorcism)

> And they went into Capernaum; and immediately on the sabbath he entered the synagogue and taught. And they were astonished at his teaching, for he taught them as one who had authority, and not as the scribes. And immediately there was in their synagogue a man with an unclean spirit; and he cried out, "What have you to do with us,

> Jesus of Nazareth? Have you come to destroy us? I know who you are, the Holy One of God." But Jesus rebuked him, saying, "Be silent, and come out of him!" And the unclean spirit, convulsing him and crying with a loud voice, came out of him. And they were all amazed, so that they questioned among themselves, saying, "What is this? A new teaching! With authority he commands even the unclean spirits, and they obey him." And at once his fame spread everywhere throughout all the surrounding region of Galilee.

With *seven words from the mouth of Christ*—"Be silent, and come out of him!"—the evil spirit leaves. The man is made clean; he is set free. The Word effects radical change. In this Scripture passage, we learn three fundamental strategies for spiritual combat: *Scripture*, *authority*, and *sanctity*.

Mark 5:1–20 (the Gerasene Demoniac)

> And when [the demoniac] saw Jesus from afar, he ran and worshiped him; and crying out with a loud voice, he said, "What have you to do with me, Jesus, Son of the Most High God? I adjure you by God, do not torment me." For he had said to him, "Come out of the man, you unclean spirit!" And Jesus asked him, "What is your name?" He replied, "My name is Legion; for we are many." And he begged him eagerly not to send them out of the country. Now a great herd of swine was feeding there on the hillside; and they begged him, "Send us to the swine, let us enter them." (5:6–12)

Jesus sent them into the swine, and the herd of about two thousand rushed down a steep bank into the sea, where they drowned. Mission accomplished! As Jesus was getting into the boat to leave, the man who had been healed pleaded to go with Him. Jesus wouldn't permit him, saying, "Go home to your family and announce to them all that the Lord in his pity has done for you" (Mark 5:19, NABRE).

One exorcist professor used this Scripture to highlight the importance of family. Rather than allowing the healed man to accompany Him, Jesus sent him home to his family not only to tell them the good news of his liberation but to receive inner healing. Jesus had expelled his demons, but the man's inner healing would occur within his family.

Then, the exorcist told a story about a college student who saw herself as an outcast. Estranged from her family, she was extremely lonely at school. Alone in her dormitory one night, she sank to the floor of her bathroom and frantically cried out: "Is there anyone out there who will become my friend? Please!" Her desperate summons was heard and answered by a demon, who then entered her. Quickly, her life got worse, and the befriending demon tormented her for some time. She was liberated after a series of deliverance prayer sessions. The exorcist told this story to emphasize how family can provide a spiritual hedge of protection. Obviously, if a person's family is the source of his abuse or woundedness, that's a different story altogether.

Exorcists teach that college students are targeted strategically by satanic cults. I believe in God's unfailing protection of our children, but we can't look away from the raw truth of dangers, spiritual or otherwise. There are human predators, and then there are demonic ones. There are age-appropriate ways to instruct youth about the reality of angels, good and bad.

Tobit 3:7–10 (a Cursed Bride and the Breaking of a Curse)

> Sarah, the daughter of Raguel, was reproached by her father's maids, because she had been given to seven husbands, and the evil demon Asmodeus had slain each of them before he had been with her as his wife. So the maids said to her, "You are the one who kills your husbands! See, you already have had seven and have had no benefit from them. Why do you beat us? Because your husbands are dead? Go with them! May we never see a son or daughter of yours!"
>
> On that day she was deeply grieved in spirit and wept. When she had gone up to her father's upper room, she intended to hang herself.

As if the devil Asmodeus isn't enough for Sarah to deal with, her maids also curse her, adding insult to injury. Then, she faces the temptation to hang herself. Demons torment us today in similar ways.

The next chapter of Tobit reveals how to break a curse: humbly prostrate yourself in prayer, believe in God's covenant, and invoke His blessing. Sarah's new husband, Tobias, breaks the curse by praying:

> Blessed are you, O God of our fathers. . . . You made Adam and gave him Eve his wife as a helper and support. From them the race of mankind has sprung. You said, "It is not good that the man should be alone; let us make a helper

> for him like himself." And now, O Lord, I am not taking this sister of mine because of lust, but with sincerity. Grant that I may find mercy and may grow old together with her." And they both said, "Amen, amen." Then they both went to sleep for the night. (8:5, 6–9)

We need modern-day Tobiases who pray fervently for God's blessing to cancel the curses on our loved ones.

Similarly, the apostle St. Peter speaks of returning a curse with a blessing: "Do not return evil for evil or reviling for reviling; but on the contrary bless, for to this you have been called, that you may obtain a blessing" (1 Pet. 3:9).

Matthew 2:16–18 (Infant Sacrifice)

King Herod, fearing the birth of the long-awaited Messiah, decreed the slaughter of the innocents. This is similar to modern-day abortion, is it not? The devil aggressively seeks child sacrifice. A friend who owns multiple pro-life clinics confided that intense spiritual warfare perennially plagues pro-life workers. The point is that modern-day Herods exist. The devil is the most anti-life creature of all.

1 Samuel 4:1–11 (Using God as a Good Luck Charm)

In the first book of Samuel, we read how the Israelites were defeated by the Philistines. The Israelites ask, "Why has the Lord put us to rout today by the Philistines?" (4:3). They decided to get the Ark of the Covenant from Shiloh and bring it into battle with them. Then, the Israelites were defeated again, and the Ark of the Covenant was captured. Why?

The lesson in spiritual warfare here is important. The Israelites used the Ark as a kind of *talisman* (a good luck charm). But the Lord doesn't honor those who use Him or articles of faith as a talisman. God desires true interior conversion, not exterior acts of superficial faith performed for a person's own ends. We can't make God do our bidding or use Him to get our way. He is the Lord God whom we humbly serve and reverently honor for His glory, not ours.

Strategy: The State of Grace

The state of grace gives us strong protection. Being in the state of *mortal sin* robs us of the protection of divine authority. Demons perceive whether we are in right communion with God. Exorcists teach that being in the state of grace makes your prayers for the family *more* efficacious.

The state of grace doesn't ensure that demons won't attack you—when demons are threatened by a person's sanctity and influence for good, they will attack. But there's nothing to fear if you're living in the state of grace.

In Mark's Gospel, an evil spirit cries out: "What have you to do with us, Jesus of Nazareth? Have you come to destroy us? I know who you are, the Holy One of God!" (1:24). The evil one knows who Jesus is. He recognizes His identity—the Holy One of God! *The evil spirits fear holiness*! The armor of God can be summed up in three words—*state of grace*.

What is the state of grace? The *Catechism* explains:

> The grace of Christ is the gratuitous gift that God makes to us of his own life, infused by the Holy Spirit into our soul to heal it of sin and to sanctify it. It is the *sanctifying* or

> *deifying grace* received in Baptism. It is in us the source of the work of sanctification.... Sanctifying grace is an habitual gift, a stable and supernatural disposition that perfects the soul itself to enable it to live with God, to act by his love. *Habitual grace*, the permanent disposition to live and act in keeping with God's call, is distinguished from actual graces which refer to God's interventions, whether at the beginning of conversion or in the course of the work of sanctification. (CCC 1999, 2000)

The *Catechism* then offers a beautiful insight on the universal call to the life of grace:

> All Christians in any state or walk of life are called to the fullness of Christian life and to the perfection of charity. All are called to holiness. (CCC 2013)

God's grace is active unless, and until, you cut off the flow of grace via mortal sin. That's the horror of sin: it cuts us off from the life of grace. Without grace, we're doomed. God's provision for you to remain in the state of grace is Confession. The sacrament of Reconciliation is so powerful that, according to exorcists, "one Confession is more effective than one hundred exorcisms." Confession is a sacrament, while the Rite is a sacramental.

Remember that each family has direct recourse to the Chief Exorcist. Living in right relationship with Jesus Christ protects us. The challenge is that, sometimes, family members serve the sinful world, the darkness that disguises itself to seduce a person away from God. Habitual small sins still open doors for demons. "Sin renders the soul miserable, weak and torpid, fickle in good, cowardly in resisting temptation, slothful in the observance of God's commandments. It deprives her of true liberty.... It makes her a slave to the world, the flesh and the Devil."[49]

Strategy: Authority

> And the unclean spirit, convulsing him and crying with a loud voice, came out of him. And they were all amazed, so that they questioned among themselves, saying, "What is this? A new teaching! With authority he commands even the unclean spirits, and they obey him." (Mark 1:26–27)

Because evil spirits are extremely legalistic, they fixate on the issue of authority. It's to our benefit to live within the divine construct of authority.

The *Catechism* teaches, "We are obligated to honor and respect all those whom God, for our good, has vested with his authority" (CCC 2197). In protecting families, we must exercise *baptismal, spousal,* and *parental authority*. Spiritual authority is conferred upon us sacramentally, and it reinforces the power of our prayer.

The Divine Economy of Authority

Demons know and must obey the *divine structure*. Mortal sin robs you of the good effects of the divine economy of authority. Your

[49] Venerable Louis of Grenada, *Manual for Spiritual Warfare* (Charlotte, NC: TAN Books, 2014), 173.

prayers for the family are more efficacious when you are in the state of grace *and* operating within the divine economy of authority. When a person attempts to practice Catholicism combined with another spirituality, such as Santeria or New Age, his religious syncretism causes him to step outside the divine economy of authority.

Authority differs from power in that the term *authority* suggests a right to, or fittingness for, the power that goes with it. Fr. Chad Ripperger writes about spiritual authority in his widely acclaimed book *Deliverance Prayers for Use by the Laity*:

> It is when we remain under the authority structure that God has established by the divine positive law (i.e. the authority of the Church) and the natural law, that we remain protected. For this reason, if the laity always remain within the confines of the authority that God has given to them by the natural law, such as commanding the demons to leave their own bodies or those over whom they have authority by the natural law (such as their children or wife, etc.), then they will experience little to no retaliation, as a general rule.
>
> This is also true in relation to rights which grant authority in relation to the object of the right. By this we mean that spouses . . . by virtue of the marital contract (a covenant is just another name for a solemn contract according to the traditional authors) have rights over each other's bodies by virtue of the conceding of those rights to each other on the day of their marriage. For this reason, wives may command the demons to leave their husbands' bodies and the husbands, their wives' bodies. For the husband it is a two-fold

authority; the one as head of the household and the other by virtue of the rights over his wife's body.

From experience, most exorcists concede that there is an ability to command the demons to depart (observing the prescription given above by the Congregation for the Doctrine of the Faith regarding not doing it publicly and in not trying to get the name of the demon, etc.) in relation to those of one's *immediate* family. It appears due to the nature of the obligations of the Fourth Commandment, that children, when saying binding prayers and other prayers of this sort for the parents, do not seem to be affected. This may flow from the fact that they have the obligation to take care of them in their need as a result of the natural law. For this same reason, exorcists have noted a lack of retaliation when the prayers are said for one's siblings. This does not appear to be the case for godparents or grandparents since they do not have the same obligations under the Fourth Commandment.

Nevertheless, despite the fact that one may not have the requisite authority to command the demons, one can always modify the prayer to petition Christ or Our Lady to drive the demon out. For example, one of the standard forms of the binding prayer begins with the words: In the Name of Jesus, I command the spirit of N. These words may be only used as we have delineated above. However, when one does not have authority, rights or duties in relation to another, one could change the words to the following: Jesus, *I ask Thee* to bind the spirit of N.[50]

---

[50] Fr. Chad A. Ripperger, *Deliverance Prayers for Use by the Laity* (self-pub., Sensus Traditionis Press, 2018), 8–9.

Baptismal Authority

Each of the baptized is commissioned as priest, prophet, and king. You serve as priest by your sacrificial efforts to bring people to God; as prophet by your witness to truth in word and deed; and as king when you lead others to engage their talents to advance the kingdom of God (see CCC 1241).

Rediscovering the gift of Baptism strengthens you for spiritual warfare. At Baptism, you are granted the authority of a Christian; at Confirmation, you are sent as a "soldier for Christ." Praying deliverance prayers for yourself is a holy duty for which you have baptismal authority.

During the celebration of Baptism for children, the following exorcism prayer, or a variant of it, is said:

> *Lord God Almighty, who sent your Only Begotten Son to endow humankind, imprisoned in slavery to sin, with the freedom of your sons and daughters, we pray most humbly for these children, whom you know will experience the allurements of this world, and will fight against the snares of the devil: by the power of the Passion and Resurrection of your Son deliver them now from the stain of Original Sin, strengthen them with the grace of Christ, and guard them always on their journey through life. Through Christ our Lord. Amen.*[51]

[51] *The Order of Baptism of Children: English Translation According to the Second Typical Edition* (Chicago: Liturgy Training Publications, 2020), quoted in Archdiocese of Milwaukee Office for Worship, "The Order of Baptism of Children, Second Typical Edition," Office for Worship Newsletter, February 2020, https://www.archmil.org/ArchMil/Resources/OFW/OFW-Resources/February2020Newsletter.pdf.

Your sacramental Baptism confers inestimable spiritual protection against sin and evil and provides a reservoir of grace to which you always have recourse.

We ardently pray for Catholic parents who decide not to baptize their children out of resistance to the Faith. Baptism is a sacrament of faith, which is a free gift from God. Accordingly, the Church requires ongoing conversion and provisions for raising children in the Catholic Faith. Thus, on the part of families, the critical choice is to convert or not to convert.

A priest friend active in deliverance ministry noted that, in his experience, unbaptized children suffer more and are more vulnerable to diabolical attacks. He urges his parishioners to bring their unbaptized children to him for the sacrament. We are blessed to have many influential adult converts in the Church today—so there's always hope for adult Baptism.

Spousal Authority

"I want you to understand that the head of every man is Christ, the head of a woman is her husband, and the head of Christ is God" (1 Cor. 11:3). For spouses, the conjugal act is a spiritual event, a sacred act ordained by God. The blessing will be realized in its fullness if the conjugal act is performed with purity and in right relationship with God. Anything less *may* invite demons actively to attack the soul.

Authority is given to the spiritual head of the family, the father. The father should lovingly pray deliverance prayers for his wife and children. Since husband and wife minister the sacrament of Matrimony to one another, the wife has a *sacramental* mantle of authority for her husband, for whom she should lovingly pray deliverance prayers. Exercising spousal authority in praying for healing and deliverance protects and blesses the couple. Ideally, it also deepens their intimacy. Strive not to break the "couple bond" because you are much stronger together in defense of your family.

On maintaining marital unity, Pope Francis writes:

> I offer this advice to spouses: argue as much as you want, but don't let the day end without making peace. Do you know why? Because "the cold war" of the day after is extremely dangerous. How many marriages are saved when they have the courage at the end of the day to not make speeches but rather offer a caress, and peace is made! It is true, there are more complex situations, when the devil gets involved and entices the man with another woman who seems more beautiful than his wife, or when the devil entices the woman with another man who seems better than her husband. Ask for help straightaway. When this temptation comes, ask for help immediately.[52]

Parental Authority

A parent has both power and authority over his children in the order of nature. A parent's relationship to his child intrinsically

52 Pope Francis, "Address of the Holy Father," Meeting with Priests, Religious, Seminarians, and Pastoral Workers, October 1, 2016.

engenders a web of responsibilities, rights, and powers. Parents have spiritual authority and a holy duty to pray for their children. This includes deliverance prayers because children can be targeted by evil spirits. Have confidence in God; be diligent in prayer; stay engaged in all areas of your children's lives. This goes especially for parents of teenagers, who are vulnerable to spiritual attack. Parental presence offers enormous protection for the domestic church.

Whenever I completely missed a sign of trouble in one of my children, the Lord covered my blindness with grace. Sometimes, God resolved an issue before I was aware of it. God calls us to exercise diligence to the best of our ability, but we know that He has our back!

Clerical Authority

Clergy have spiritual authority by virtue of the sacrament of Holy Orders. All priests have authority to pray imprecatory prayers commanding a demon to leave. Demons know the powerful authority of the ordained priesthood and obey the commands of its members.

Our priests are spiritual doctors, ordained and anointed to be Christ's ministers. As previously stated, if your loved one experiences ordinary (temptation) or extraordinary (oppression, obsession, possession) demonic attacks, discern the spirits prayerfully and exercise your baptismal and spousal or parental authority, as appropriate, to pray deliverance prayers for him. If needed, ask for an appointment with your parish priest.

Knowing the three foundations of spiritual combat (Scripture, authority, and the state of grace) is part of knowing Christ—heart to heart, in reciprocal love:

> Do you really know the living Jesus—not from books but from being with Him in your heart? Have you heard the loving words that He speaks to you? . . . The devil may try to use the hurts of life, and sometimes our own mistakes—to make you feel it is impossible that Jesus really loves you, is really cleaving to you. This is a danger for all of us. And so sad, because it is completely opposite of what Jesus is really wanting, waiting to tell you. Not only that He loves you, but even more—He longs for you.[53]

Exorcist Teaches How to "Talk Back"

At the 2019 Avila Institute summit, exorcist Fr. Dennis McManus presented a conference entitled "Talk Back." Tailored to lay persons, Father's teaching was a call to imitate Christ's response to the devil, who tempted Him in the desert (Matt. 4:1–11). Father reminded us that we are not called simply to "endure" the fiery darts of the devil all day long. We are called to defend ourselves with Scripture.

When you're harassed by many temptations that bombard you, stop and pray with a Scripture such as "He who is in you is greater than he who is in the world" (1 John 4:4). Below are some examples. First, call to mind your baptismal authority, and then pray these passages with conviction.

---

53 Letter of Mother Teresa to her spiritual family, quoted in "In Mother Teresa's Own Words: 'I Thirst, I Quench,'" *Franciscan Spirit* (blog), July 11, 2016, https://blog.franciscanmedia.org/franciscan-spirit/in-mother-teresa-own-words-i-thirst-i-quench.

1. **Matthew 4:10: "Begone, Satan!"** Christ spoke these words to Satan when He was tempted in the desert. When you, your spouse, or your children are attacked by evil spirits, authoritatively repeat Christ's words.
2. **Matthew 16:23: "Get behind me, Satan!"** "But he turned and said to Peter, 'Get behind me, Satan! You are a hindrance to me; for you are not on the side of God, but of men.'" This powerful, brief Scripture is very effective! Of course, if, like St. Peter, a family member offers you an opinion that's not in accord with God's will, I don't recommend calling your loved one Satan! But we should keep this passage in mind and be aware of similar scenarios in our families. A loved one may offer an opinion contrary to God's commandments, such as "I recommend an abortion," or "You should get a divorce," and the like.
3. **Romans 8:37: "In all these things we are more than conquerors through him who loved us."** Personalize this Scripture: *In all these things* I am *more than a conqueror through Christ who loves* me. When the evil one pushes you, push back with God's Word. When the devil notes your determination and sees that you have faith in Christ, he'll leave.
4. **Romans 14:11: "As I live, says the Lord, every knee shall bow to me, and every tongue shall give praise to God."** Personalize: *Thank you, Lord, that every knee shall bow to you, and every tongue shall give praise to you, for you are the Lord of all! You are my Lord and Savior. I trust in you.* Exalting the Lord Jesus pierces the devil's pride and helps us to focus on Christ, not Satan.

St. Therese, the Model of a Fearless Warrior

St. Therese was docile to God's grace, which gently formed her into a fearless little warrior. Fr. Dwight Longenecker writes:

> Thérèse [of Lisieux] says on her cruel deathbed, "When I think I'm dying in bed, I would want to die in an arena!" She wrote that she wanted to "die in a battlefield, arms in hand.... I would not fear going to war. With what joy, for example, at the time of the Crusades, I would have gone to combat heretics. Yes! I would not have been afraid to be shot; I would not have feared the fire!"
>
> She was so brave and resolute that those who knew her said, "Under a suave and gracious aspect, [she] revealed at every instant, in her actions, a strong character and a manly soul." Pope Pius XI said she was "a manly soul." Her battle was for holiness and against Satan. With great vigor she cried out, "Sanctity! It must be won at the point of a sword!"

Fr. Longenecker continues:

> The First World War broke out just 17 years after her death. There were some 40 recorded apparitions of Thérèse to soldiers on the battlefield. She appeared holding a cross or sometimes a sword. The soldiers reported that they saw her, spoke to her—and she to them. She helped them with temptations, calmed their fears and protected and converted them.

> The stories were recorded and published in 1920, just before her canonization. The *Laudem Gloriae* blog records how the French soldiers called her "my little sister of the trenches," "my war patroness," "the shield of soldiers," "the angel of battles" and "my dear little Captain."...
>
> More astoundingly, the men of the French military named artillery pieces and planes after Sister Thérèse. Whole regiments were consecrated to her, and witnesses said relics of the saint miraculously stopped rifle bullets like real shields, saving the lives of the soldiers who carried them.
>
> In our modern world, where warfare is total and Christians seem wary of war, Thérèse reminds us that we are all engaged in a fight to the death.[54]

What an astounding soldier for Christ! God chooses little souls to procure big victories over sin and evil. Little souls are weapons in God's hand.

St. Therese, please pray that we may be faithful,
fearless, and fruitful spiritual warriors. Amen.

[54] Fr. Dwight Longenecker, "St. Thérèse: Little Flower, Little Warrior," *National Catholic Register*, October 1, 2014, https://www.ncregister.com/daily-news/st.-therese-little-flower-little-warrior1.

4

THE LANGUAGE OF SPIRITUAL COMBAT AND SIX CATEGORIES OF DEMONIC ATTACKS

> These cruel spirits torment me quite frequently, but they do not frighten me in the least. For I am convinced that they cannot move except by God's permission. . . . They have no power except against cowardly souls who surrender their weapons.[55]

Often, family relationships rupture due to misunderstanding of words, actions, or omissions. In order to cause confusion, resentment, and division, the evil spirits may influence our understanding of what we communicate to one another. This isn't limited to families, but it is within the family that miscommunication can cause the most serious damage to vital relationships. In spiritual combat, words and context matter. Understanding the language of deliverance and exorcism equips us to make necessary distinctions in spiritual warfare.

55 St. Teresa of Avila, *Autobiography*, chap. 31, quoted in *Spiritual Warfare Bible*, 1150.

The art of spiritual warfare requires that we "consider the source." As Pope Francis states: "A Christian cannot be calm, assuming that everything is fine. He must discern things and really look at where they come from, what their root is.... Where does this come from? What is the origin of this opinion, these phenomena...?"[56] In families, these are vital questions for what is taught to our children in schools or through the media.

The Language of Spiritual Combat

In many of the definitions below, I will quote the *Catechism* because it provides authoritative teaching and demonstrates that the Church is quite aware that evil exists in our world.

Binding prayer. A prayer to Jesus to bind evil spirits that are tempting or oppressing you or someone in your family for whom you have spiritual authority (spouse, children). Below is an example:

> *Spirit of N., I bind you in the Name of Jesus, by the power of the most Precious Blood of Our Lord Jesus Christ and by the intercession of the Blessed Virgin Mary, St. Michael the Archangel, the blessed apostles, Peter and Paul and all of the saints, and I command you to leave N. (Name of person or object) and go to the foot of the Holy Cross to receive your sentence, in the Name of the Father, the Son and the Holy Spirit.*[57]

---

[56] Pope Francis, "The well-mannered evil one," Morning Meditation in the Chapel of Santa Marta, October 9, 2015.

[57] "Binding Prayer," Sensus Traditionis, accessed May 10, 2020, http://www.sensustraditionis.org/Binding.pdf.

Blessings. The United States Conference of Catholic Bishops (USCCB) teaches:

> Blessings consist of prayer, scripture, and sometimes a special ritual sign (see *Catechism of the Catholic Church*, no. 1668).
>
> People are accustomed to seeing bishops, priests, and deacons blessing objects or persons in the name of the Church. Indeed, "the more a blessing concerns ecclesial and sacramental life, the more is its administration reserved to the ordained ministry" (*Catechism of the Catholic Church*, no. 1669).... However, there are other blessings...that can be prayed by anyone who has been baptized, "in virtue of the universal priesthood, a dignity they possess because of their baptism and confirmation" (*Book of Blessings*, no. 18). The blessings given by laypersons are exercised because of their special office, such as parents on behalf of their children.[58]

Blessings make God manifest, or present, in one's life, in one's body, in one's home, in one's institution. To the degree that God is present is the efficacy of the blessing. The reciprocal, yet unequal in strength, is the curse. Blessings and curses present two sides of creation, and echo these two aspects. The blessing received through one's relationship with God overshadows all else, namely the curse.

---

58 "Sacramentals (Blessings)," United States Conference of Catholic Bishops, accessed April 10, 2020, http://www.usccb.org/prayer-and-worship/sacraments-and-sacramentals/sacramentals-blessings/index.cfm.

Sample blessings:

1. Numbers 6:24–26: "*The LORD bless you and keep you: the LORD make his face to shine upon you, and be gracious to you; the LORD lift up his countenance upon you, and give you peace.*" This can be prayed in return for a curse.
2. In your own words: *Eternal Father, I confide to your goodness those people who have cursed me or my loved ones. I implore you to cover them in the Precious Blood of your Son, Jesus. Graciously bless them with the light of truth and conversion of heart. Thank you for the infinite protection of divine love that surrounds me and my family. Amen.*
3. St. Edmund: "*O, Lord, into Your hands and into the hands of Your holy angels, this day I entrust my soul, my relatives, my benefactors, my friends and enemies, and all Your Catholic people. O Lord, by the merits and prayers of the Blessed Virgin Mary and of all Your saints, keep us today from all evil and unruly desires, from all sins and temptations of the devil, from a sudden and unprovided death, and from the pains of hell. Grant that I may ever be obedient to Your commandments. Let me never be separated from You, O God, who live and reign with God the Father and the same Holy Spirit forever. Amen.*"[59]

Curses. A curse is the inverse of a blessing. Fr. Jose Fortea writes: "A curse is an action that is done to harm another with the help of demons. There are specific curses to cause one to be possessed, to make things go bad in business, and to make someone sick, etc. Curses are effective only if God allows them to have

[59] "Prayers for God's Blessing upon the Day," Our Catholic Prayers, accessed July 15, 2020, https://www.ourcatholicprayers.com/prayers-for-Gods-blessing.html.

effect. The more one prays the more one will be protected against these things."[60]

Are curses really effective? Fr. Fortea explains:

> The first thing that has to be said is that whoever *does* the curse—as well as the person who may have asked for the curse to be done—will be the first ones affected by the demonic. Without a doubt, they suffer some type of demonic influence, possession, or sickness. The evil they wish on another will come back to them. A demon is never invoked in vain. But is a curse effective against the person to whom it is directed? This depends on the will of God. That is to say, it is the same as with accidents, illnesses, or misfortunes. During our time on earth, God allows us to experience both good and evil because this life is a period of trial, of purification. Of course, the person who prays and lives in God's grace is protected. The more one prays and lives a spiritual life, the more one is protected.[61]

What can be done to counteract a curse? Fr. Fortea teaches: "If [a person] is truly under a curse, the only way to remove it is to do just the opposite. That is to say, if a person has invoked a demon to do evil, then one has to invoke God to protect, help and bless him. Good is always stronger than evil."[62] This echoes Scripture: "I say to you that hear, Love your enemies, do good to those who hate

---

60 Fr. Jose Antonio Fortea, *Interview with an Exorcist* (West Chester, PA: Ascension Press, 2006), 110, Kindle.

61 Ibid., 111, Kindle.

62 Ibid., 112, Kindle.

you, bless those who curse you, pray for those who abuse you" (Luke 6:27–28). The origin of curses can be in the past or the present. Depending on the severity of the curse, a priest (not necessarily an exorcist) may be needed to break it. To break Freemasonic curses, for example, a priest leads the afflicted person in a series of long renunciations.

Fr. Fortea continues: "In cases where a person's medical problems are the result of a curse but the exorcist sees that there is no demonic influence remaining, the person's illness, then, it is like any other sickness and needs to be cured by medical treatment. There is no further need for supernatural remedies."[63]

A curse can be effective when family members are involved in grievous groups and activities such as gangs, the mafia, drug traffickers, child abuse, and prostitution. A curse that is generated in the present may result from cult or coven members' placing a curse, hex, or spell to thwart the work of God by cursing priests, churches, families, and officials. Playing video games or reading books that promote the practice of spells or curses fosters a climate of ill-wishing.

Cursed objects. Exorcists teach that objects can be cursed by some work of magic, voodoo, satanic rituals, or witchcraft. Cursed objects are sometimes unknowingly ingested, or they may cause harm by being touched or by being kept in a person's home. Cursed objects should be blessed, broken, and buried, which breaks the curse. Priests caution us about purchasing artifacts from foreign countries, since they may be cursed. Not infrequently, when a home is infested, we find a cursed object that has been placed there, knowingly or not.

---

[63] Ibid., 113, Kindle.

Deliverance. Msgr. Charles Pope of the Archdiocese of Washington explains:

> Deliverance is prayer and ongoing ministry that uses numerous approaches to bring healing and wholeness to those who, after baptism, have come to struggle significantly with bondage to sin and sinful drives, the influence of demons, or the effects of psychological and/or spiritual trauma....
>
> Even after baptism, it is possible that we open doors to Satan enabling him some degree of access to our heart and mind. When this is the case, a Christian, working with clergy and fellow believers alike, must take a stand against the schemes of the devil by repenting of sin and renouncing any form of agreement with the deceptions of the enemy. Deliverance involves coming to an understanding of the tactics of the evil one and recognizing the flawed thinking that often infects our minds. It involves coming to know and name these tactics and the deep drives of sin within us. It involves repenting of them and steadily renouncing their influence so that we come to greater serenity, peace, and healing—to deliverance.[64]

Demon. "Demon is the name applied to all varieties of evil spirits, including the devil or Satan. Demons, like angels, are pure spirits, which means they do not have bodies and are invisible;

64 Msgr. Charles Pope, "Getting Unbound: A Reflection on Deliverance Ministry," *Community in Mission* (blog), August 6, 2017, http://blog.adw.org/2017/08/getting-unbound-reflection-deliverance-ministry/.

nevertheless, they sometimes manipulate or possess the human or animal body (cf. Gen 3:13; Isa 34:14)."[65]

Deprecatory prayer. This prayer invokes God's power to protect from evil spirits. As with imprecatory prayers, lay persons can and should pray deprecatory prayers for themselves and for those for whom they have spiritual authority.

Deprecatory prayers are a helpful means of general intercession for extended family for whom lay persons *do not have authority*. For example, when you are interceding for a nephew for whom you *do not have spiritual authority*, it would be appropriate to pray: *Lord Jesus Christ, by the infinite merits of your life, death, and resurrection, mercifully liberate my nephew Ryan from any and all evil spirits that are attacking him. Graciously fill him with your Holy Spirit. Thank you, Lord.*

Devil. This word literally means "one who hurls"[66] himself against God and His faithful. "The devil and the other demons are fallen angels who have freely refused to serve God and his plan. Their choice against God is definitive. They try to associate man in their revolt against God" (CCC 414).

Evil. St. Thomas Aquinas defines *evil* as "the absence of the good, which is natural and due to a thing."[67] The *Catechism* explains:

> God is infinitely good and all his works are good. Yet no one can escape the experience of suffering or the evils of nature which seem to be linked to the limitations proper to creatures: and above all to the question of moral evil. . . . The revelation

---

[65] Scott Hahn, *Catholic Bible Dictionary* (New York: Doubleday, 2009), 210.

[66] Brian Kelly, "The Temptations of Christ in the Desert," Catholicism.org, June 14, 2016, https://catholicism.org/the-temptations-of-christ-in-the-desert.html.

[67] St. Thomas Aquinas, *Summa Theologica* I, q. 49, art. 1.

> of divine love in Christ manifested at the same time the extent of evil and the superabundance of grace. We must therefore approach the question of the origin of evil by fixing the eyes of our faith on him who alone is its conqueror. (CCC 385)

Exorcism. "Exorcism is a specific form of prayer that the Church uses against the power of the devil. . . . There are instances when a person needs to be protected against the power of the devil or to be withdrawn from his spiritual dominion. At such times, the Church asks publicly and authoritatively in the name of Jesus Christ for this protection or liberation through the use of exorcism."[68]

Fall of the angels. "Behind the disobedient choice of our first parents lurks a seductive voice, opposed to God, which makes them fall into death out of envy. Scripture and the Church's Tradition see in this being a fallen angel, called 'Satan' or the 'devil.' The Church teaches that Satan was at first a good angel, made by God: 'The devil and the other demons were indeed created naturally good by God, but they became evil by their own doing'" (CCC 391).

Imprecatory prayer. This prayer spoken to demons issues a direct summons, adjuration, or command for them to leave. Lay persons can and should pray imprecatory prayers for themselves or for those for whom they have spiritual authority. For example: *In the name of Jesus Christ, by the infinite power of your holy Cross, I cast out from me (or my spouse or child) the demon of lust (name the spirit/temptation). Evil spirit, be gone from me. Holy Spirit, grant an infusion of divine love to strengthen me. Amen.*

---

68 "Exorcism," United States Conference of Catholic Bishops, accessed March 20, 2020, http://www.usccb.org/prayer-and-worship/sacraments-and-sacramentals/sacramentals-blessings/exorcism.cfm.

Magic. "In popular language, white magic is said to be magic that is used for good, whereas black magic is used for evil. But both types of 'magic' are useless. Strictly speaking, any paranormal effect achieved through magic is accomplished through the intervention of demons, not the result of a particular person's magical powers. The very magic they practice opens them up to demonic influence and even possession."[69]

Minor or major exorcism. The USCCB explains the difference between these two forms of exorcisms:

> Simple or minor forms of exorcism are found in two places: first, for those preparing for Baptism, the *Rite of Christian Initiation of Adults* (RCIA) and the *Rite of Baptism for Children* both call for minor exorcisms; secondly, the appendix of *Exorcisms and Related Supplications* includes a series of prayers which may be used by the faithful.
>
> The second kind is the solemn or "major exorcism," which is a rite that can only be performed by a bishop or a by priest, with the special and express permission of the local ordinary (cf. Code of Canon Law, can. 1172). This form is directed "at the expulsion of demons or to the liberation [of a person] from demonic possession" (*Catechism of the Catholic Church*, no. 1673).[70]

Nature. "The essence of a being considered as the principle of activity.... In contrast with God, it is the created universe. In

---

69 Fortea, *Interview with an Exorcist*, 114, Kindle.

70 "Exorcism."

contrast to the life and operations of divine grace, it is that to which a human person has claim, as creature, as distinct from a share in God's own life, which is the supernatural."[71]

Occultism. Fr. Gabriele Amorth defines *occultism* as follows:

> Occultism is, in other words, the great umbrella under which all the practices and forms of satanic adoration are gathered in order to be drawn upon by those who wish to profit from its gains. The most significant forms of occultism are magic, astrology, fortune-telling, and/or spiritism. At its base is the belief in the existence of spiritual forces that cannot be experienced through one's external senses (i.e. touch, sight, and so forth); therefore, they are esoteric or hidden. By controlling these forces through techniques into which one is initiated and after practicing them appropriately, one can dominate the reality. These entities as we shall see, are the unclean spirits commonly called devils.[72]

Preternatural. "That which is beyond the natural but is not strictly supernatural. It is preternatural either because natural forces are used by God to produce effects beyond their native capacity, or because above-human forces, angelic or demonic, are active in the world of space and time."[73]

Rebuke. A prayer to Jesus in which you express sharp disapproval

---

71 Hardon, *Modern Catholic Dictionary*, s.v. "nature," Catholic Culture, accessed March 27, 2020, https://www.catholicculture.org/culture/library/dictionary/index.cfm?id=35071.

72 Amorth, *Exorcist Explains*, 30.

73 Hardon, *Modern Catholic Dictionary*, s.v. "preternatural," Catholic Culture, accessed March 27, 2020, https://www.catholicculture.org/culture/library/dictionary/index.cfm?id=35762.

of demons because of their evil actions. For example: *In the name of Jesus, I rebuke you, evil spirit of impurity. Be gone from me, in Jesus' name.*

Renunciation. A prayer to Jesus in which you say in a formal way that you will give up evil, such as the occult or pornography, and not have anything more to do with it. For example: *In the name of Jesus, I renounce the way that I have used my sexuality for sin against myself and others. With your grace, Lord Jesus, I will cease to misuse my sexuality.*

Sin. "As a result of original sin, human nature is weakened in its powers, subject to ignorance, suffering and the domination of death, and inclined to sin (this inclination is called 'concupiscence')" (CCC 418).

Spiritual warfare. Regarding spiritual warfare, the *Catechism* teaches:

> The consequences of original sin and of all men's personal sins put the world as a whole in the sinful condition aptly described in St. John's expression, "the sin of the world." This expression can also refer to the negative influence exerted on people by communal situations and social structures that are the fruit of men's sins. This dramatic situation of "the whole world [which] is in the power of the evil one" makes man's life a battle: "The whole of man's history has been the story of dour combat with the powers of evil, stretching, so our Lord tells us, from the very dawn of history until the last day. Finding himself in the midst of the battlefield man has to struggle to do what is right, and it is at great cost to himself, and aided by God's grace, that he succeeds in achieving his own inner integrity." (CCC 408–409)

Supernatural. "The ensemble of effects exceeding the powers of the created universe and gratuitously produced by God for the purpose of raising the rational creature above its native sphere to a God-like life and destiny. The meaning of the phrase fluctuates with that of its antithesis, the natural order."[74]

The Six Categories of Demonic Activity

Ordinary Activity: Temptation

Temptation is the devil's ordinary mode of action (see 1 John 3:8–10). Satan is the tempter (1 Thess. 3:5), and just as he incited the Fall, he still directly influences us to reject grace and commit sin. Temptation is common to all.

Not all temptations arise from diabolical influence. From *original sin* arises the weakness of our faculties. We can develop sinful habits without the devil's influence. The flesh and the world provide an abundance of temptations. Evil spirits take advantage of our fallen nature. Indirectly, through our five senses, they suggest evil ideas. These can be subtle or strong. When we misuse our five senses, evil spirits may enter (and exit during deliverance ministry). Exorcists teach that evil spirits cannot read our thoughts, but, by observing our behavior, they can read our weaknesses.

The devil tempts us to sin by several means: deception, accusation, doubt, seduction, and provocation. These are ways of disquieting us and of arranging circumstances that will likely stir us to commit deadly sins of pride, greed, anger, envy, lust, gluttony, and sloth.

---

[74] Joseph Sollier, "Supernatural Order," in the *Catholic Encyclopedia*, vol. 14 (New York: Robert Appleton Company, 1912), https://www.newadvent.org/cathen/14336b.htm.

In his excellent book *The Devil You Don't Know*,[75] Fr. Louis Cameli articulates four ordinary, common means of diabolical temptation: deception, division, diversion, and discouragement. In my experience, we could add distance, destruction, disobedience, and duplicity. Below, I'll demonstrate these and other ordinary demonic temptations common to all.

The goal of temptation is to entice us to commit sin. If we sin, *the responsibility is ours*, not the devil's, because grace is always sufficient to avoid sin. By resisting and rebuking the following tactics of temptation, we will avoid sin.

Accusation. The devil is the accuser of Christians (see Rev. 12:10). He bullies us, saying: "You're a loser, no good, and will amount to nothing. Look what you have done—you ruined your marriage (or your family or career). You're a failure." In marriages where one of the spouses had an extramarital affair, the devil may accuse the faithful spouse—"You drove your spouse to have the affair." Or, if one's child turns out to be a criminal, the temptation may be "You failed as a parent." Sometimes, the devil tempts one family member to believe that another has abused him. This is why St. Ignatius instructs us to bring temptations to the light of prayer, Confession, or spiritual direction.

Provocation. In the book of Job, we have an example of how, through adversity, the devil tempted Job to give up—to despair completely. In this case, *Job's wife* is the mouthpiece of the evil one: "Curse God and die" (2:9). In the family, we can provoke one another subtly or blatantly. A child can undermine parental trust by trying to provoke his siblings to go against parental rules. One

---

75 Louis J. Cameli, *The Devil You Don't Know* (Notre Dame, IN: Ave Maria Press, 2011).

family member may entice another to use an illicit drug, or to view pornography, or to steal or lie. Television is often used to provoke rebellion against family and God.

Deception. "'A murderer from the beginning, ... a liar and the father of lies,' Satan is 'the deceiver of the whole world.' Through him sin and death entered the world and by his definitive defeat all creation will be 'freed from the corruption of sin and death'" (CCC 2852). Demons deceive people with false promises: "You will be like God" (see Gen. 3:5). A diabolical tactic is the distortion of reality: good is made to look bad, and bad is made to look good. True and false are inverted. In Scripture, St. Peter differentiates not so much between good and evil, as between truth and falsehood. Peter emphasizes that Christ's disciples need to be "established" in truth (see 2 Pet. 1:12) to be protected from the devil, father of all lies.

Doubt. Temptations to unbelief can include subtle-to-intense doubts about oneself, God, the Church, and so forth. Faith, as we learn in Scripture, moves God's Heart and provides a hedge of protection.

Unbelief is a dangerous spiritual state that should be taken to prayer for healing. Sometimes, the root of unbelief is a demonic lie. "Take care, brethren, lest there be in any of you an evil, unbelieving heart, leading you to fall away from the living God" (Heb. 3:12).

Division. "Every kingdom divided against itself is laid waste, and no city or house divided against itself will stand" (Matt. 12:25). Demons persistently try to divide spouses, children, extended families, colleagues, and the Church. Seeds of discord are sown across our lives. Discern the *source* of the division. In the family, reward unity, not division.

Beware of preferring relationships with people who move you *away* from your family or away from God and the Church. I remain close to family members who are opposite thinkers on politics, business, and religion. They understand that I love Christ and the Church. We are connected through desire for one another's good, by family ties, and in times of joys and sorrows that knit us together. Love unifies. Demons initiate or exacerbate divisions in families. Clear the air. Demons are spirits of the air: they hear what we speak. Custody of the tongue pays big dividends in families. Purity of heart protects us from rash, harsh judgments.

Diversion. "But take heed to yourselves lest your hearts be weighed down with dissipation and drunkenness and cares of this life" (Luke 21:34). In some cases, we've noted how evil spirits have undermined the good of marriage and family by seduction into worldly pursuits (workaholism), or addictions (pornography, alcohol, and so on) that interrupt a person's duty to the family. The evil ones try to thwart God's call, timing, or plan for families. Knowing that good people won't be tempted to obvious evil, evil spirits often tempt us to choose a lesser good or immediate gratification. Diabolical diversions may prevent us from fulfilling our mission, to the detriment of loved ones.

Distance. Temptations arise to distance you from God, family, friends, and communities. This includes temptations to the orphan-spirit (which says, "I'm unlovable, rejected, alone"). The difference between the temptations to distance and division is that you may be well disposed toward a person (not divided), but you are nonetheless tempted to isolate yourself, disengage, put on a mask, hide your real state of being, and shun community and relationships. By distancing yourself from loving relationships, you may create a void that demons try to fill.

Destruction. "The thief comes only to steal and kill and destroy; I have come that they may have life, and have it abundantly" (John 10:10). Demonic seduction aims to destroy families, marriages, godly friendships, good works, and holy intentions. In some cases, religious men and women who lived their vocations for a while were demonically attacked to destroy their vocations to the point of leaving.

Disobedience. "You were dead through the trespasses and sins in which you once walked, following the course of this world, following the prince of the power of the air, the spirit that is now at work in the sons of disobedience" (Eph. 2:1–2). That demons tempt us to disobedience is an understatement. Disobedience and pride are like two sides of the same coin. Beware when you are tempted to disobey lawful, authentic authority such as God's commandments and the Church's moral teaching. Disobedience has led many souls away from the Church into the occult or the demonic.

Duplicity. "Let what you say be simply 'Yes' or 'No'; anything more than this comes from the Evil One" (Matt. 5:37). To be duplicitous is to be double-minded, two-faced, irresolute. We all know of popular politicians who boldly claim to be Catholic while vehemently legislating for anti-Catholic causes such as abortion, contraception, and same-sex marriage. In some family cases, the demonic hook originates from the duplicity of one spouse who leads a double life (by having an extramarital relationship, for example).

The devil observes Christians who pray piously in church in the morning and then go home or to work, where they act the complete opposite of a Christian. Think of those who loudly claim to be Catholic despite working in the abortion industry, corrupt political groups, or drug cartels.

Discouragement. Our word *acedia* comes from a Greek word meaning, essentially, "I don't care." Lethargy about God and the spiritual life due to weariness, overwhelm, or disappointment is a common temptation. The Desert Fathers referred to it as the "noonday devil." Discouragement dampens faith, hope, love, joy, generosity, and judgment. The Fathers taught that discouragement is the most dangerous of all temptations because it thwarts progress toward the goal of being with God and attaining eternal life. Many deliverance cases begin with deep-seated, paralyzing discouragement.

Discouragement has no place in the home. Each loved one benefits from encouragement. The devil delivers enough discouragement to lead people to a place of darkness. Let's resist discouraging words and actions in the domestic church.

The above is a partial list of some *ordinary action of demons* experienced in families. Now we will move on to the *extraordinary ways* in which the devil attacks us.

The Extraordinary Actions of the Devil

According to Fr. Francesco Bamonte[76], "the extraordinary actions of the devil refer to his particular actions on matter. Important: it

[76] Fr. Francesco Bamonte is president of the International Association of Exorcists, a member of the Servants of the Immaculate Heart of Mary, and an exorcist of Rome.

is far more interesting to demons to keep people enslaved to sin and to bring them ultimately to the greatest misfortune—eternal damnation—than it is to provoke a series of misfortunes."[77]

Infestation. Signs of diabolical infestation of a place, such as a home, include:

> Sounds or blows to a house's roof or inside of it on the floor, doors, windows, or furniture; sounds of someone or something stepping around the place but nothing is seen; loud sounds of chains or irons; voices, screams, laughter, yelling, shouting; the disappearance of objects which are either not found or are found in improbable areas of the house; sudden gusts of wind in environments that are completely without any other airflow; wind that snuffs out candles; sudden and intense odors of something burning, excrement, sulfur, rotten meat, or incense; doors and windows thrusting open and shut rapidly; windows break; plates, glasses, bottles shatter; pictures or paintings detach from the wall and fall down for no reason; clothes, sheets, blankets that levitate for no reason; spontaneous fog, smoke, fires; sudden increase or decrease of the temperature in a room; invasions of small animals or insects which the person is not able to rid the house or place of (bats, reptiles, owls, toads, cats—that quickly disappear into nothing); apparitions of various shadows, persons

[77] My personal unpublished notes taken during Fr. Francesco Bamonte's presentations at the twelfth annual International Association of Exorcists course "Exorcism and Prayers of Liberation," Pontifical Athenaeum Regina Apostolorum, Rome, May 2017; and Fr. Bamonte's lectures at the Pope Leo XIII Institute clergy class, May 2012.

> or monstrous beings; pets are suddenly terrified and run away without explanation.
>
> In discerning the above manifestations of infestation of a place, the criterion is this: Everything that is outside of the laws of nature which does not come from God comes from Satan. There are no intermediate conditions. A rigorous investigation should be done to determine the cause of a manifestation upon a place. A natural causation should be ruled out.[78]

Possible origins of diabolical infestation may include "curses against the place; séances were held in the dwelling; rituals or rites were performed by practitioners of magic who lived in the house; heinous crimes, suicides, abortions occurred there (intercessory prayer is required to heal this); rites of evocation or devotion to the devil have been performed there; or holy things or objects have been profaned there (in all these cases, reparation is also needed)."[79]

Extraordinary Demonic Activity Exercised on a Person: Oppression, Obsession, Possession

According to Fr. Bamonte, "whenever the diabolical action is exercised on or inside of a person's body, one speaks of 'vexation' (sometimes referred to as oppression), 'obsession,' or 'diabolical possession.' Sometimes the boundaries between these forms of diabolical action are not clearly defined."[80]

---

78 Ibid.

79 Ibid.

80 Ibid.

Fr. Bamonte taught about the following causes for some extraordinary actions of the devil upon persons:

- Through our own fault: the sins of superstition and of the occult. Wide openings for demons are created by participation in these activities.
- Participating or being present at séances.
- Consulting mediums or talismans, especially those given by a practitioner of magic who has performed rites of evocation on them.
- Practice of certain techniques of Transcendental Meditation; Reiki; opening chakras (yoga); and association with the New Age movement.
- Use of divination—for example, with a pendulum.
- Undergoing sessions to receive potions or skin preparations to prevent bad luck or the evil eye.
- Possessing objects, such as souvenirs, that have been used in local magic rituals.
- Practicing or being present at voodoo or macumba rituals.
- Having participated in sects or associations in which esoteric rites or occult practices were performed.
- Having participated in satanic sects or even sporadically in Satanism (for example, making blood pacts with the devil, attending or participating in black masses, participating in ritual homicides, or profaning the Holy Eucharist).
- Having listened for a long time to music that incites people to worship Satan or to commit acts of violence, blasphemy, homicide, or suicide. Individuals are even

more susceptible to the influence of such music when the superstitious practices and forms of occultism described above are combined with addictive vices, such as drinking heavily, using drugs, performing sexually depraved acts, and blaspheming. Blasphemy in particular puts a person in harmony with the devil, who, by his nature, curses God with absolute hatred.

- Being the recipient, even unknowingly, of a rite of malefice. For instance, a parent may consecrate a child to Satan. A person may have been cursed while in the womb, as well as later in life. In such cases, the subsequent malefice often reinforces the preceding one.[81]

Demonic oppression. Sometimes called diabolical vexation, oppression refers to "physical aggressions of demons against a person which may manifest in burns, scratches, bites, beatings, and blows that leave bruises, swelling, bloody sores, or bone fractures. Some have experienced letters, words, or symbols appearing as incisions on their skin. These persist for a time and then disappear."[82]

Demonic obsession. Fr. Bamonte explains demonic obsession in this way:

> Demonic obsessions are cases of the devil's aggression in which, although he does not block the intellectual faculty and the free will of the person during a crisis, he is able to communicate obsessive thoughts or images that are at times rationally absurd to the victim's mind (i.e. the imagination

---

[81] Ibid.

[82] Ibid.

and the memory) but which they are not able to ward off. In these cases the person feels tormented by a fixed idea or an image that seems to really be his own. The obsessions can be of different forms and of different graces and intensities and reach a point at which they completely dominate a person's mind.

They may take up all of the attention of the person and are insistent, despite determined and well-imposed resistance, which may be necessarily heroic. Only abandoning oneself to God helps the afflicted to not succumb to this submersion, and exorcism is sometimes necessary to liberate a person from the exterior or interior violence.

Diabolical obsession is different than personal obsessions such as excess handwashing, or obsessive thoughts such as "Did I leave the stove on?" These are related to anxiety, not the diabolical. Exorcists rely on the medical advice of mental-health professionals to help them distinguish between human anxiety and diabolical attacks.

Discerning obsessions can be difficult because of the absence of physical signs or manifestations that usually accompany oppression and possession.... Like physicians who study the efficacy or inefficacy of a medical treatment to arrive at a correct diagnosis, priests may apply the same idea in evaluating diabolical obsessions.[83]

Fr. Bamonte also offered the following example of a case of diabolical obsession:

---

83 Ibid.

> A girl who had one exam left to complete to graduate was no longer able to study; as soon as she opened her books, her mind immediately became filled with images from a romance novel that she had read a few years before, which were incredibly vivid, colorful, and intense. Nothing like this had ever happened to her before. Despite great effort, she could not block these images from coming into her mind. Her parents, who were oblivious to everything, were not able to understand what was happening to their daughter. Immediately after the exorcist prayed mentally, saying, "*In the name of Jesus, I break every malefic tie with the romance novel that is present in you . . . and with the two protagonists of the romance novel, N. and N.*," the girl felt relieved of a weight, and when she returned home, she was finally able to take up her studies again, and she happily graduated.[84]

Demonic possession. Diabolical possession is relatively rare, although exorcists have been reporting an increase in cases. A brief overview will suffice for a general idea of this most severe diabolical condition. Possession markers include the following:

- superhuman strength and unnatural physical contortions; whites of eyes showing
- knowledge of languages the person has never studied
- knowledge of secrets the person could not have obtained by normal human means (for example, in one case, a demon revealed, "If you are not directly under my power,

---

[84] Ibid.

it is because your mother has been praying for you, and she has put up a wall of prayer!")

- strong aversion to the sacred, such as churches, Holy Communion, prayer, holy water, rosaries, relics of saints, or the Bible

Demonic Subjugation

When an individual or group of people voluntarily submit themselves to Satan, this is called demonic subjugation. People fall into this form of relationship with Satan by volunteering to make a blood pact with the devil or to consecrate themselves to Satan.

Fr. Gabriele Amorth: "Who Must Be Afraid, Us or the Devil?"[85]

In his book *An Exorcist Explains the Demonic*, Fr. Amorth offers us the following assurance:

> The letter of James says textually: "Submit yourselves therefore before God. Resist the devil and he will flee from you" (Jam 4:7). The demon keeps his distance from the one who nurtures his faith, who frequents the sacraments, and who wishes to live devoutly. Why? Simply put, the devil hates God and is in terror of Him and anything that even has the odor of sanctity.... The devil can greatly disturb a person who nurtures faith, but he does so unwillingly because he is "forced" to by the power of a spell. He prefers far and away

---

[85] Amorth, *Exorcist Explains*, 21.

> to be involved with those who have distanced themselves from God. In these circumstances he is freer to act. Satan fears the sons of God, those seeking to conform their lives to Jesus: "I have been crucified with Christ; it is no longer I who live, but Christ who lives in me" (Gal 2:20).[86]

Diabolical attacks can go only as far as the Lord allows for our good—for purification, tests of faith, and growth in holiness. Providence allows what is necessary for the salvation of a soul and always gives us necessary graces in our trials.

Eternal Father, graciously commission an army of Catholic soldiers to help set the captives free and to proclaim the victory of the Cross.

[86] Ibid., 21–22.

5

DRESSING YOUR FAMILY IN THE ARMOR OF GOD

Therefore take the whole armor of God, that you may be able to withstand in the evil day, and having done all, to stand. Stand therefore, having fastened the belt of truth around your waist, and having put on the breastplate of righteousness, and having shod your feet with the equipment of the gospel of peace; besides all these, taking the shield of faith, with which you can quench all the flaming darts of the Evil One. And take the helmet of salvation, and the sword of the Spirit, which is the word of God. (Eph. 6:13–17)

Recently, when I was flying back to the West Coast after speaking at a conference on the East Coast, a large group of U.S. Army soldiers boarded the plane. Men and women with the same brown-and-green camouflage uniform, big boots, and bursting backpacks took their seats as a chorus of passengers expressed joyful gratitude for their service. Buckling my seatbelt, I realized that their presence comforted me. After reflecting on the bravery of these young people, I considered their diverse ethnicities, blurred by their identical uniforms. Now, they represented the country's army and had an esprit de corps: a common loyalty and fellowship. I wondered if, in the same way, heaven sees one united troop of Catholic soldiers wearing the same armor of God.

In the domestic church, the family who dresses in the armor of God is ready to "overcome evil with good" (Rom. 12:21). Conversely, the family who is not dressed in God's spiritual armor is vulnerable to attacks from the evil one. Your family may have only one practicing Catholic to wear the armor of God, but one uniformed soldier standing guard is far better than none. God will uphold and use you, lone soldier. Don't abandon your post; wear the uniform. You're part of the domestic church's universal army. Heaven outfits you, good soldier.

Jesus Christ Is a Warrior

Many Catholics are familiar with St. Paul's Letter to the Ephesians, in which he urges believers to put on God's armor. Before St. Paul, the Old Testament prophet Isaiah wrote about God's armor:

> Righteousness shall be the belt of his waist, and faithfulness the belt of his loins. (11:5)

> He saw that there was no man, and wondered that there was no one to intervene; then his own arm brought him victory, and his righteousness upheld him. He put on righteousness as a breastplate, and a helmet of salvation upon his head. (59:16–17)

The book of Wisdom also describes God's armor:

> The Lord will take his zeal as his whole armor, and will arm all creation to repel his enemies; he will put on righteousness as a breastplate, and wear impartial justice as a helmet; he will take holiness as an invincible shield, and sharpen stern wrath for a sword, and creation will join with him to fight against the madmen. (5:17–20)

The New Testament reveals that the warrior God of the Old Testament has called those who belong to Christ to stand beside Him in battle. The mighty sword of the Spirit is placed in the humble hands of the Christian (Eph. 6:17). But if the sword is purely spiritual, where is its power? "The weapons of truth, integrity, eagerness of the gospel, faith, salvation and the Word of God build a spiritual kingdom not an earthly one."[87] These spiritual truths become weapons for the Christian, who is baptized in Christ to build His heavenly kingdom and smite the head of the serpent.

Fr. Dennis McManus teaches, "If you are not a warrior, you'll be a victim." I used to resist the whole idea of a "warrior identity" until twenty-five years ago, when I saw how the evil spirits were attacking me and my family. I chose to wear God's armor to defend myself, my marriage, and my children. During exorcisms, we see a fierce battle for a person's immortal soul. My faith in the need to wear the full armor of God has greatly increased.

Describing the enemy we face in Christ's name, Fr. Amorth said: "The original sins of the angels are the same as those who

---

[87] Amorth, *Exorcist Explains*, 57.

implicitly or explicitly adhere to Satanism. Angels and men who follow Satan base their existence on three principles and practical rules of life: you can do what you wish, that is, without subjugation to God's laws; you obey no one; and you are the god of yourself."[88] He then added: "One day during an exorcism, Father Candido Amantini—a Passionist priest and my great teacher—asked a demon: 'How many are you?' The demon responded: 'We are so many that if we were visible we would obscure the sun.' The demon on that occasion gave information that we have no reason to disbelieve because it is confirmed in the Bible."[89] Consider that of all the angels, only one-third fell away; two-thirds are good angels who serve God according to the divine will. They would obscure two suns! We have double the spiritual power!

God's provision for His soldiers includes the gift of spiritual garments. You must decide whether to accept Christ's endowment. In exorcism cases, many people seeking liberation from evil spirits had long ago ceased to wear God's armor. They had put on a different garment. Some clothed themselves, knowingly or not, in garments fashioned by the world, accommodating the flesh, or crafted by the devil. God's armor is not "in fashion" today. But to the Catholic soldier, it is the most glorious garment of all. Its fabric is fashioned with the white threads of divine love interwoven with the crimson threads of the Blood of the Lamb. It's a garment not of this world, and the soul who wears it confirms his call to be in the world, but not of the world (see John 17:16). The disciple dressed in the armor of God enjoys an esprit de corps

---

88 Ibid., 18.

89 Ibid., 17.

with the Church Militant and the Church Triumphant.

The Old and New Testaments teach of the blessedness of God's armor and our need for its protection. Let's proudly wear the uniform that God offers our families.

The Belt of Truth (Eph. 6:14)

"Jesus then said to the Jews who had believed in him, 'If you continue in my word, you are truly my disciples, and you will know the truth, and the truth will make you free'" (John 8:31–32). The girdle or belt is the center piece of a soldier's armor. The belt ties the clothing to the soldier's body. It holds his sword and adds soundness to his uniform.

Our beliefs and actions must be consistent with the truth of the Word of God (Acts 17:11). Anti-truth is the spirit of lies. Demons are liars: they contradict all truth, twisting it for their purposes. Sometimes, we are as gullible as Adam and Eve in Eden. During exorcisms, demons must concede to the truth proclaimed in the Rite, and they are tormented by it.

As soldiers for Christ, we are trained to resist lies and falsehoods and live without compromise to the truth. Otherwise, we are vulnerable to sin and evil. When the belt of truth is wrapped around us, we can leave no room for falsehood. In the family, we must remove all masks and false identities and call for authenticity. We must have a firm determination to speak the truth in charity. The following Scriptures apply:

- I am the way, and the truth, and the life (John 14:6).
- Jesus came into this world to bear witness to truth (see John 18:37–38).
- Jesus declared the truth will set you free (see John 8:32).

The Breastplate of Righteousness (Eph. 6:14)

This part of the armor of God characterizes personal sanctity. The most valuable treasure a person can have is a life of righteousness, a pure heart, and a godly mind. Jesus came to this world to fulfill all righteousness (Matt. 3:15). We were all stuck in sin, without any righteousness of our own. The righteous One came to free us from sin so that we may be righteous in Him.

Pilate and his wife Claudia called Jesus Christ a just man (Matt. 27:19, 24). When you maintain a pure conscience, a demon has no power over you. When you fall, as we all do, repent quickly, confess sincerely, and repair whatever may have been damaged. Pay the debt that is due. Sometimes, during exorcisms, demons call out a debt that the person never paid. The devil is an accuser—and that's why the breastplate of righteousness is vital for protection.

Exorcists teach that during an exorcism, the demon may call out our sins—past or present, real or false. We must not become flustered, but stay focused on prayer. Within the family, be aware of accusatory tones or judgmental attitudes.

Have faith in the sacrament of Reconciliation. Resist the devil when he reminds you of your confessed sins and taunts you. Immediately place yourself in the merciful Heart of Jesus; have confidence in the truth of divine forgiveness of confessed sins.

One who wears the breastplate of righteousness needn't fear the devil. The breastplate safeguards him. The life of a righteous person stands as a challenge to sinners. Remember also that the kingdom of heaven belongs to those who are persecuted for the sake of righteousness (Matt. 5:10).

St. Paul writes about the powerful weapon of righteousness:

> As servants of God we commend ourselves in every way: through great endurance, in afflictions, hardships, calamities, beatings, imprisonments, tumults, labors, watching, hunger; by purity, knowledge, forbearance, kindness, the Holy Spirit, genuine love, truthful speech, and the power of God; with the weapons of righteousness for the right hand and for the left; in honor and dishonor, in ill repute and good repute. We are treated as impostors, and yet are true; as unknown, and yet well known; as dying, and behold we live; as punished, and yet not killed; as sorrowful, yet always rejoicing; as poor, yet making many rich; as having nothing, and yet possessing everything. (2 Cor. 6:4–10)

The righteous are not afraid even of death. The martyrs and saints witness to this. The devil tested many saints, but failed to penetrate their breastplate of righteousness.

Feet Shod with the Equipment of the Gospel of Peace (Eph. 6:15)

A soldier marching into battle won't get far without the proper footgear. We might advance well for a while, but then quit because we are not properly outfitted with the gospel of peace. How do we march into war with the devil to make peace, then? The ultimate aim of proclaiming the gospel is to foster peace among peoples, societies, and nations (see Rom. 10:15, Isa. 52:7). Shod with the equipment of the gospel of peace, which St. Paul exhorts us to proclaim, we embark on this journey. When we are impregnated with the gospel, we walk in peace with God and others.

God's peace should permeate family life. Christ's peace is distinctive; as St. Augustine says, it is the tranquility of order.[90] Peace is the sum and substance of salvation. How often the Church prays for her deceased, "Rest in peace." It is this peace that only Christ can give that demons hate and plot to destroy. Demons push our buttons (which they know well) to disturb our peace of soul in any way possible.

To live Christ's peace requires the practice of prayer and virtue. This helps us to be better discerners and soldiers. The devil is a bully, and when he fails to rob us of our peace of soul, he flees. If demons can cause you to lose peace of soul, they'll persistently exacerbate your turmoil. Guard your peace of soul.

Watch out, too, for loved ones who lose their peace of soul. We need to stand firm when the enemy attacks our families. With feet properly outfitted with the gospel of peace, we're ready to do two lifesaving things: to flee from anything that is contrary to the gospel, and to stand firm in what is true and good. We should be prepared to push back against sin and evil.

Readiness also means that we are ready to be *led* by the Holy Spirit, that we can *wait* on the Lord's promptings. We do not move ahead of our Captain.

Imagine standing next a soldier in combat who's so nervous that his sword is shaking uncontrollably. When an evil spirit observes you "shaking in your boots," he'll likely mock you more. St. Paul teaches us to stand firm and be at peace. When we internalize the gospel, we stand on solid ground with peace of soul.

---

90 Augustine, *City of God*, chap. 13, quoted in Aquinas, *Summa Theologica* II-II, q. 29, art. 1.

The Shield of Faith (Eph. 6:16)

Scripture teaches that "faith is the assurance of things hoped for, the conviction of things not seen" (Heb. 11:1). St. Paul instructs, "Take up the shield of faith, with which you can quench all the flaming darts of the Evil One" (Eph. 6:16). St. Peter teaches that faith in God shields us (1 Pet. 1:5). Faith isn't static; it grows through time and experience. It's built up each time God carries us through trials and tribulation. Faith saves, heals, and shields us. Faith is both an offensive and defensive weapon of spiritual combat. It not only shields us from the devil's darts: it *quenches* them.

One evening, at our home, I hosted a dinner party for several priests, including the diocesan exorcist. During dinner, one of the newer priests asked the exorcist: "Please tell us what really drives the demons out of a possessed person. Is it the prayers of the Rite, or the power of Latin prayers?"

All eyes were on the exorcist, a very discerning priest with a reputation for sanctity. He considers himself no expert, but a pupil of the Chief Exorcist.

The exorcist responded, "It is personal and communal faith that drives demons away."

Recall the paralyzed man lowered through the roof of a house where Jesus was: "They came, bringing to him a paralytic carried by four men. And when they could not get near him because of the crowd, they removed the roof above him; and when they had made an opening, they let down the pallet on which the paralytic lay. And when Jesus saw *their* faith, he said to the paralytic, 'Child, your sins are forgiven'" (Mark 2:3–5, emphasis mine). Let your faith be dynamic, always increasing in your heart and family so your home can be a sanctuary of living faith that protects. As a family, take loved ones who need healing to the Lord in faithful intercessory prayer.

Lively faith in God is not naïve. It's not simply comforting thoughts and feelings. It's not a refusal of reality and the raw facts of life. Faith is not a kind of can-do attitude with which we simply "will" ourselves to believe what is not actually the case. Faith is not the decision to live by mythological fantasy. Faith is an act of trust. Trust in God goes beyond appearance and feelings. Faith is trusting that what has been revealed to us by God is true. It's believing in God's plan of salvation.

How do you release the power of faith? Fr. James Dominic Brent, O.P., explains:

> Faith is the supernatural ability to make contact with Jesus. According to St. Thomas Aquinas, each and every time you and I turn to Jesus and say to him, "Jesus, I believe in you," we make supernatural contact with Jesus. When we make such contact with him, heavenly power flashes forth from Jesus and touches us deep within our souls. When I say, "Jesus, I believe in your love," a flash of light to know his love is given to me. When I say, "Jesus, I believe in your power to heal me," a fresh application of divine medicine is applied to me. In each and every act of faith we spiritually touch Jesus, and Jesus spiritually touches us by releasing the grace of the Holy Spirit into our hearts.[91]

---

[91] Fr. James Dominic Brent, O.P., Angelic Warfare Confraternity Newsletter, Fall 2015.

The Helmet of Salvation (Eph. 6:17)

This piece of armor protects our head and our mind so that we take hold of the salvation that Christ won for us. Salvation saves us from death. The goal of faith is to receive the salvation of our soul (1 Pet. 1:9). St. Paul tells us, "Now is the day of salvation" (2 Cor. 6:2). In spiritual combat, our battle cry is, "I am not ashamed of the gospel: it is the power of God for salvation to every one who has faith" (Rom. 1:16).

As we defend our families from evil spirits, the more we are convinced that "there is salvation in no one else [but Christ], for there is no other name under heaven given among men by which we must be saved" (Acts 4:12), the more we will be confident in our defense and offense against demonic temptations and attacks. When we put on the helmet of salvation, we can experience what St. Paul taught: "If any one is in Christ, he is a new creation" (2 Cor. 5:17), redeemed and anointed. We can think in communion with the beautiful mind of Christ.

Here's a powerful anecdote about thinking with the mind of Christ:

> St. Anthony the Great was a pioneer among the ancient fathers of the desert, a champion in spiritual warfare who endured horrific demonic attacks. He once reported a vision. "I saw all the Devil's traps upon the earth," he recalled, "and I groaned and said, 'Who do you think can pass through them?' And I heard a voice saying: 'Humility.'" Like soldiers crawling under a barbed wire fence, we can crawl right under the Enemy's snares by lowering ourselves through humility.[92]

---

92 Quoted in Thigpen, "Know Your Commander."

The virtue of humility is to be cultivated in family life. It's not easy to resist worldly pride, but loved ones can learn to appreciate the blessing of humility over the ugliness of pride. According to St. Paul, it was by the humility of Christ that the devil was defeated (see Phil. 2:3–11).We humble ourselves knowing that God lifts us up to His victory (see James 4:10).

The Sword of the Spirit, Which Is the Word of God (Eph. 6:17)

"For the word of God is living and active, sharper than any two-edged sword, piercing to the division of soul and of spirit, of joints and of marrow, and discerning the thoughts and intentions of the heart" (Heb. 4:12). During the Rite, we witness how demons are tormented by God's Word. The prologue of John's Gospel is especially effective as a weapon and is often proclaimed during an exorcism. At home, I sometimes read John's prologue aloud if I'm experiencing a diabolical attack. Praying with the Word of God is necessary for a well-trained soldier. "Let the word of Christ dwell in you richly" (Col. 3:16). The sword of the Spirit is an offensive weapon—it cuts through darkness with the light of truth. The book of Revelation describes this sword: "I saw... in the midst of the lampstands one like a Son of man... from his mouth issued a sharp two-edged sword" (1:12, 13, 16).

Demons know the Scriptures. They know how much Jesus Christ loves and chooses us—over them. They hate us (which is an understatement) because the place where they once dwelled in heaven is now the place where lowly humans will someday exist eternally—near the throne of God. Demons know their place is hell, where they face an eternity of torment.

When the devil tempted Jesus in the desert, Christ used the Word to resist Satan's temptations. Jesus said, "Man shall not live by bread alone, but by every word that proceeds from the mouth of God" (Matt. 4:4). To live by "the word that proceeds from the mouth of God" is to abide in His love. When we live in the Word, it changes us; it animates our life, vocation, service, and relationships. We become who we are called to be by living the Word of God.

Pray at All Times in the Spirit (Eph. 6:18)

St. Paul writes: "Pray at all times in the Spirit, with all prayer and supplication. To that end keep alert with all perseverance, making supplication for all the saints" (Eph. 6:18). Prayer is sometimes considered the seventh piece of God's armor. All the pieces of God's armor coalesce through prayer, which not only threads the pieces together, but also makes them come to life in spiritual combat. "The prayer of a righteous man has great power in its effects" (James 5:16). That's why, when the Lord Himself taught us to pray, He included the petition "Deliver us from evil," which can be translated, "Deliver us from the evil one," that is, the devil.

In the Gospel, when the Canaanite woman pleaded with Jesus to heal her demon-possessed daughter, He didn't answer her. The disciples wanted to send her away, but the mother persisted, "Lord, help me!" Christ told her that it wasn't right to take the children's bread and toss it to the dogs. The mother wasn't offended or angry—she humbly responded, "Yes it is Lord: even the dogs eat the crumbs that fall from the master's table." In response, Jesus affirmed: "Woman, you have great faith. Your request is granted" (see Matt. 5:22–29). Then, the woman's daughter was healed!

Persistent, faith-filled, humble, and precise intercessory prayer is a weapon that moves the Heart of God. If the woman had been proud and had taken offense at Christ's initial response to her, her daughter might not have been delivered from the demon.

Without prayer, we can neither discern the spirits properly nor hear the heartbeat of our divine Captain, from whom we receive our marching orders. Without prayer, we sabotage ourselves and our families; without prayer, we are simply incapacitated in spiritual combat.

The spiritual master Fr. Jacques Philippe addresses a particular aspect of prayer for spiritual warriors:

> Faithfulness in prayer involves a painful confrontation with what we have in our hearts. There we find things that weigh us down, tangled things, dirty things. But the day comes when, deeper down than our psychological wounds, even deeper than our sins and dirt, we reach a pure spring, the presence of God in the depths of our hearts, enabling our whole selves to be purified and renewed, "He who believes in me, out of his heart shall flow rivers of living water" (Jn 7:38). Human beings are not purified from the outside inwards, but starting from within. Not so much by a moral effect we make, but by discovering a Presence within us and letting him act freely. By faithfulness in prayer, we find within us a space of purity, peace, and freedom. The center of the soul is God, says St. John of the Cross.[93]

---

93 Jacques Philippe, *Thirsting for Prayer* (New York: Scepter Publishers, 2014), 62.

The kind of prayer St. Paul exhorts us to pray at all times is the prayer of the heart. Throughout the day, we lift up our hearts to Jesus, saying: *With every beat of my heart, your holy name is praised; with every beat of my heart, I proclaim my love for you. With every beat of my heart, I long for you. With every beat of my heart, I trust in you.*

The prayer of the heart is a perpetual vigil. In the midst of spiritual combat, we still lift up our hearts: *Lord, the fiery darts of the devil are assailing me, but I know that you are my defender; the liar is tempting me to doubt and discouragement, but I will hope in you; Lord, my family is attacked from all sides, but I know you will carry us through the fire.*

Of course, the highest prayer we can pray is the communal prayer of the Church, the Holy Sacrifice of the Mass. Our personal prayer life grows through liturgical prayer as well as mental, meditative prayer, including the Rosary, Lectio Divina, and prayer of the heart.

Dressing the Family in God's Armor: Receiving Our Spiritual Inheritance

In the family, children should be taught about the garment of God's armor. They can act out the process of putting on the armor—placing a helmet on their head and a belt around their waist; putting on shoes for the gospel of peace; and raising a rubber sword to show that they're ready to stand for Christ.

Dressing in the whole armor of God empowers us to pick up our daily cross as required for discipleship. I have learned the hard way how necessary it is for a family not to rebel against a cross that God allows. In the long run, that cross can serve to sanctify the members of the family. In hindsight, we can see His grace, but not always in the midst of the trial. That is why we must persevere through the darkness toward the light of the resurrection.

> We are faced with a specific request from God that is among the clearest in the New Testament. It is an obligatory path: If we do not begin to walk on it, we will not move toward God but rather toward ourselves and our own whims. In fact, we will move toward spiritual defeat. The gift of God, which is the Holy Spirit, requires free acceptance—precisely because He is a gift—just as the marital gift of the bridegroom requires a free "yes" from the bride. But our "yes" is not genuine or profound unless it has been declared by way of the cross.[94]

Our yes to God is genuine when declared by way of the Cross. Demons tempt us to run from the Cross, to throw it away, to avoid it and resent it. That's what demons do because it's by the Cross that they're defeated. And it is by the Cross that we are lifted up above the world, the flesh, and the devil to sing praises to our victorious King. That Good Friday kiss that we place on the crucifix should be repeated daily in prayer.

In my opinion, dressing the family in God's armor is an inheritance that has passed through generations of Catholics. The Virgin Mary wore God's holy garments, as did St. Joseph and all the saints throughout the ages. This inheritance has supplied for

---

[94] Raniero Cantalamessa, O.F.M. Cap., *Sober Intoxication of the Spirit* (Cincinnati: Servant Books, 2005), 10.

countless families. We pass down this holy garment to the next generation of spiritual warriors.

I never met my mother's cousins who died in World War II; they drowned in maneuvers at sea. Their mother, my mother's aunt, received an inheritance—their military pensions for the rest of her life—since the war claimed two of her beloved sons. The military pension provided her enough money to pay for the Catholic education of her sister's children. Therefore, my mother received a Catholic education that her parents could not afford. In turn, my parents made big sacrifices to send their five children to Catholic schools. Mom was always aware that she was the beneficiary of the inheritance of the two fallen soldiers in our family. She passed on the gift that she had received to my siblings and me by prioritizing our Catholic education.

My point in sharing this story is that God's armor is not only a living garment but also a perpetual education. It's a gift from God that has been passed down through generations. Some souls—Catholic martyrs—literally laid down their lives for love of God and future generations of believers. May God strengthen Catholic families to persist in passing down the gift of faith. May we never be afraid or ashamed of wearing the very unfashionable but holy garment of God's armor. "You received without pay, give without pay" (Matt. 10:8).

Demons Fear You

For a Christian, fear of the devil is completely unjustified, for if you stand firm in Christ, demons fear you. As a child, St. Therese of Lisieux had a dream, which she relates in her autobiography, about how devils feared her.

One night I dreamed that I went out for a walk alone in the garden. Arriving at the stairs that had to be climbed so as to get to the garden, I was frozen to the spot with fright. In front of me, near the bower, there was a barrel of lime and on the barrel two horrible looking little devils were dancing with surprising agility, given they had irons attached to their feet. Suddenly, their inflamed eyes looked towards me and then instantly showing themselves to be much more scared then I, they jumped off the barrel and went to hide themselves in the clothes room that was there in front. Seeing that they were not very brave, I wanted to see what they were going to do, and so I approached the window. The poor little devils were there, running over the tables not knowing how to hide from my sight. Sometimes they came close to the window looking with suspicious to see if I was still there, and upon seeing me they began to run desperately around the place again. Certainly the dream was nothing of the extraordinary. But I believe nevertheless that God allows this dream to be remembered always to show me that a soul in the state of grace has nothing to fear from demons, who are cowards capable of running away from the look of a child.[95]

St. Therese, Little Flower, please assist us
in being fearless and faithful in spiritual warfare.

[95] St. Therese of Lisieux, *Story of a Soul*, chap. 1, quoted in Fortea, *Interview with an Exorcist*, 26, Kindle.

6

FAMILY COVENANT OF PROTECTION

Strategies: The Ten Commandments, the Beatitudes, Blessings

> The cultivation of all that is good, progress in the spiritual life and growth in love are the best counterbalance to evil. . . . Christian triumph is always a cross, yet a cross which is at the same time a victorious banner, borne with aggressive tenderness against the assaults of evil.[96]

Moses said to the Israelites, "The LORD will fight for you, and you have only to be still" (Exod. 14:14). In the context of this Scripture, the Israelites, in "great fear" of the approaching Egyptian army, wanted to turn back (Exod. 14:10). Just before they witnessed the great miracle that God ordained for them, they wanted to retreat back into slavery. Moses counseled the terrified Israelites to be still, at peace, because God would do battle for them.

Why is it hard to believe that God cares this much for you?

---

[96] Pope Francis, Apostolic Exhortation *Gaudete et Exsultate* (March 19, 2018), no. 163.

The Holy Trinity cares about the details of your life. So great is Jesus' care for you and the salvation of your family that He descended into the abyss of sin and evil on Good Friday. He loved you enough to pin Himself to the Cross at Calvary—beaten and bloodied, stripped of everything. He became utterly vulnerable, had His Sacred Heart pierced, so that you would know that you are lovable, redeemed.

You have only to believe in God, obey His commandments, and let go of a life of slavery to the world, the flesh, and the devil. God fights for you by the power of the Holy Spirit. St. John wrote, "Little children, you are of God, and have overcome them [the enemies of Christ]; for he who is in you is greater than he who is in the world" (1 John 4:4). God fights for you as He did for the Israelites. He moved the mind and heart of Pharaoh to fulfill the divine will. He fights for you by providing a hedge of protection around you, assigning angels and saints to guard you, and fortifying you with gifts and graces to "fight the good fight" *with* Him. When you are defending your family, fighting for your marriage and children, the Lord is at work in you. You make a beautiful team.

History has proven that God constructed the family to be durable. We marvel at enduring stories of individuals who suffered trauma or abuse in dysfunctional families or experienced other painful, oppressive circumstances. These individuals courageously pressed onward and did not allow tragedy to define them. They became admirable persons of virtue and influences for good. Tried in the crucible of suffering, they never gave up. They allowed God to fight for them. God fights for you and your family in creative, surprising ways.

God's plan for the family includes purification by fire and sanctification by trials and temptations. What the devil intends for evil, God uses for good. We are assured that "in everything God works for good with those who love him, who are called according to his purpose" (Rom. 8:28).

Strategy: Family Protection: Keep the Ten Commandments

One exorcist's advice for restoring the family is to *begin with yourself*! If you work first on becoming the best version of yourself, then you'll inspire loved ones in an organic manner. Fr. Bill Watson advises: "We must never confuse the true peace of following the Lord with the false peace or shallow happiness of clinging to beliefs and practices that, even though familiar, are not serving our true freedom. We must shoulder the discomfort of spiritual growth that brings us freedom and thank the Lord for calling us to live authentically."[97]

When a person seeks liberation from evil spirits, immediate consideration is given to the doorway by which the spirit entered his life. We hold the door open for evil spirits by living a worldly life of sin: "For all that is in the world, the lust of the flesh and the lust of the eyes and the pride of life, is not of the Father but is of the world" (1 John 2:16). Sin's stench is attractive to demons: they flock to it.

Over the years, I've noted a consistent pattern: a doorway for evil is opened when a person in the family habitually breaks one

---

97 Fr. Bill Watson, Sacred Story Institute Newsletter, July 2, 2020.

or more of the Ten Commandments. Keeping the Ten Commandments secures our well-being:

> You shall diligently keep the commandments of the LORD your God, and his testimonies, and his statues, which he has commanded you. And you shall do what is right and good in the sight of the LORD, that it may go well with you, and that you may go in and take possession of the good land which the LORD swore to give to your fathers by thrusting out all your enemies from before you, as the LORD has promised. (Deut. 6:17–19)

St. Thomas Aquinas taught: "Obedience unites us so closely to God that in a way [*sic*] transforms us into Him, so that we have no other will but His. If obedience is lacking, even prayer cannot be pleasing to God."[98] The evil spirits militate against the Ten Commandments because these statutes are God's law of love. "If you would enter life, keep the commandments" (Matt. 19:17).

Most of us memorized the Ten Commandments when we were children. Perhaps we know them superficially as a set of rules that we must keep. Here, I offer a reflection on how keeping the Ten Commandments provides real protection from demons. *When we break a commandment, we break God's Heart.* God spoke all these commandments for our good, that we may be protected and righteous before Him to enjoy intimate communion.

God told Moses: "Thus you shall say to the people of Israel: 'You have seen for yourselves that I have talked with you from

[98] Quoted in "Obedience Quotes," *The Catholic Reader* (blog), December 20, 2012, http://thecatholicreader.blogspot.com/2012/12/obedience-quotes.html.

heaven. You shall not make gods of silver to be with me, nor shall you make for yourselves gods of gold'" (Exod. 20:22–23). Like the Israelites, we are tempted to make idols of persons and things to worship alongside God. We relate to Jesus' words to the apostles: "The spirit is indeed willing, but the flesh is weak" (Matt. 26:41). God instructs us as a Father does a child that our hearts will be free to love and serve Him and souls.

The devil presents many false loves and fleeting pleasures that tempt us to break the Ten Commandments. Pope Francis puts it this way: "When the evil spirit is able to anaesthetize the conscience, we can say that this is his real victory: he becomes the master of that conscience."[99] Vigilance in families is necessary because a conscience can easily be anesthetized. And this is a principal aim of demonic activity.

Parents, when you make rules for your household, you do so to protect good order, to prevent obstacles from getting in the way of joy, peace, and love. We all need boundaries. God gave His children boundaries for the boundless good of preserving us from sin and evil.

The Ten Commandments (Exod. 20), and Their Diabolical Counterparts

1. I am the Lord your God, who brought you out of the land of Egypt, out of the house of bondage. You shall have no other gods before me. (Exod. 20:2–3)

In the book of Exodus, the Lord reminds His people of the marvels of His love: He freed them from Egyptian slavery. He reveals

[99] Pope Francis, "The well-mannered evil one."

that He is a jealous God. True love demands that the Israelites worship no person, place, or thing above the Lord. He promises to bless them and protect them from enemies. He warns about idolatry because He is erecting a covenant of love and mercy with His people. He promises steadfast, protective love to those who honor Him and His commandments. You are radically protected when Jesus is Lord of your life.

Diabolical counterpart: idolatry. Satan tempts us to worship false gods. He is seductive, always seeks to be idolized. He strikes subtly or blatantly at our weaknesses (or those of a family member). If we are not vigilant about selfish indulgences and disordered attractions, or if we veer into areas of pride, control, and lies, God is eclipsed from our minds, hearts, and lives.

Often, when people first seek liberation from evil spirits, they have many demonic ideas, musings, and fears occupying their thought life. Christ has faded to the background, and devils have come forward. It's challenging for them to stop thinking of their pain, wounds, *and demons*. It's necessary to reset their lives and focus on the supreme goodness of God. In your Morning Offering or evening examination of conscience, prayerfully consider what or who has eclipsed God on that day. Virtue is built one well-lived day at a time.

2. You shall not take the name of the Lord your God in vain. (Exod. 20:7)

The Lord's name is holy, kingly, worthy of highest reverence and authentic worship. When God revealed His name, He made it possible for us to know Him at a deep level. Our highest duty is to worship, praise, thank, and honor the name of God. In the depths of our hearts, we should prostrate ourselves humbly before the glorious Trinity. In the family, reverence for God should be diligently cultivated. Families should love the Most Holy Trinity with humility, awe, and gratitude.

Diabolical counterpart: blasphemy. Speaking sacrilegiously about God or sacred things signals disrespect for God and people. Demons gloat when we join their camp by blaspheming God's holy name. Evil spirits are attracted to vulgar speech and lewd acts because these are contrary to God's purity and beauty. Demons mock God when His disciples behave more like devils than saints. We mock God when we are irreverent toward Him.

During exorcisms, demons sometimes speak through the possessed person, yelling out a horrific chain of vulgar blasphemies about God, the Virgin Mary, saints, and people. Demonic manifestations are downright ugly and animalistic. A spiritual warrior's tongue should be bridled by the Holy Spirit. Be mindful that every spoken word goes into the air. What we say may be used against us if it is not honorable to God.

3. Remember the sabbath day, to keep it holy. (Exod. 20:8)
"So God blessed the seventh day and hallowed it, because on it God rested from all his work which he had done in creation" (Gen. 2:3). If we treat Sunday like any other day of the week, we deprive ourselves of its special blessing. Disobedience signals weeds of disrespect and indifference. The *Catechism* explains the importance of observing the Sabbath: "God's action is the model for human action. If God 'rested and was refreshed' on the seventh day, man too ought to 'rest' and should let others, especially the poor, 'be refreshed.' The sabbath brings everyday work to a halt and provides

a respite. It is a day of protest against the servitude of work and the worship of money" (CCC 2172). Some essential workers, such as doctors, nurses, firemen, policemen, and priests, have no choice but to work on Sundays, but for most of us, keeping this commandment is possible, if we prioritize it. Make Sunday a family day of worship to celebrate God's goodness together.

Diabolical counterpart: indifference. Demons tempt us to trivialize the Lord's Day. Satan would deprive us of the liturgical blessing of the Holy Sacrifice of the Mass and Holy Communion. Why? The diabolical aim is to make us indifferent to God and His law of love. Disobeying this commandment can be a gateway to general indifference and cessation of prayer. We can be led into a dangerous state of apathy about God and the worship due Him. Demons attempt to keep us bound by the yoke of busyness. Not keeping the Lord's Day holy can quickly become a bad habit. Consider whether your family needs to check its hierarchy of values.

4. Honor your father and your mother, that your days may be long in the land which the LORD your God gives you. (Exod. 20:12)

This is the first commandment with a promise. It reveals that we owe a duty of gratitude. The *Catechism* explains:

> God has willed that, after him, we should honor our parents to whom we owe life and who have handed on to us the knowledge of God. We are obligated to honor and respect all those whom God, for our good, has vested with his authority....
>
> Observing the fourth commandment brings its reward....

> Respecting this commandment provides, along with spiritual fruits, temporal fruits of peace and prosperity. Conversely, failure to observe it brings harm to communities and to individuals. (CCC 2197, 2200)

For most of us, honoring our parents is a privilege and joy. Jesus honored Mary and St. Joseph with obedient love. Keeping this commandment should be like breathing for those of us who cherish our parents.

Diabolical counterpart: parental disrespect. In the family, demons militate against this commandment to break down the bonds between parents and children. Our decision to dishonor this commandment can have dire consequences emotionally and spiritually. Children, too, are harmed when parents set a bad example and break this commandment. Some people have been wounded or neglected by parents who abused or abandoned them. Separation from a disordered parental relationship does not necessarily mean we are dishonoring our parents. We must always *will the good* for our parents, as God does, and we must pray for their eternal salvation.

5. You shall not kill. (Exod. 20:13)

"Human life is sacred because from its beginning it involves the creative action of God and it remains for ever in a special relationship with the Creator, who is its sole end. God alone is the Lord of life from its beginning until its end: no one can under any circumstance claim for himself the right directly to destroy an innocent human being" (CCC 2258). We battle for life from the womb to the tomb. Families should strongly resist anything to do with the culture of death, including practices such as abortion, contraception, euthanasia, suicide, and murder.

Diabolical counterpart: murder. Life and death—here is the crux of spiritual combat. The arena of life and death is our battlefield. Demons are dealers of death; they thirst for it and seek to bring it about. The degree of diabolical hate for human life is unimaginable. Satanists carry out child sacrifice aggressively. Violent deaths and suicides are increasing today. In sharing with international audiences my testimony about the murder of my father-in-law, I discovered that not a few families have also experienced the murder of a loved one.

On June 19, 2020, Pope Francis declared that Sr. Maria Laura Mainetti, an Italian sister killed by three teenage girls as a satanic sacrifice, was a martyr for the Catholic Faith. Catholic News Agency described the murder as follows:

> The 60-year-old Sister of the Cross was in 2000 stabbed to death by three teenage girls in a park in Chiavenna, Italy. Mainetti's killers were convicted and imprisoned. The girls knew the religious sister because she had taught them catechism. They lured her to the park by claiming that one of them needed to talk, because she has been raped and impregnated and was considering an abortion. The three girls originally said the murder was "for a game," but later admitted they killed her as a demonic ritual.[100]

[100] Hannah Brockhaus, "Pope Francis declares Catholic sister killed in Satanic ritual a martyr," Catholic News Agency, June 19, 2020, https://www.catholicnewsagency.com/news/pope-francis-declares-sister-maria-laura-mainetti-killed-in-satanic-ritual-a-martyr-72635.

This heinous reality occurs more often than people realize.

6. You shall not commit adultery. (Exod. 20:14)
Chastity is a beautiful, godly gift worth the effort to protect. The *Catechism* explains:

> Chastity is a moral virtue. It is also a gift from God, a *grace*, a fruit of spiritual effort. The Holy Spirit enables one whom the water of Baptism has regenerated to imitate the purity of Christ....
>
> *Lust* is disordered desire for or inordinate enjoyment of sexual pleasure. Sexual pleasure is morally disordered when sought for itself, isolated from its procreative and unitive purposes. (CCC 2345, 2351)

We know chastity is spiritually powerful because demons war against it.

Diabolical counterpart: adultery. Vices against chastity include anything that fails to reflect the capacity for authentic self-gift or allows one's reason to be conquered by sexual feelings.

The inordinate desire for sexual pleasure (lust) is the root of a host of other vices, including masturbation, fornication, pornography, and rape. The use of pornography is an assault against God's design for chastity in marriage. When the sin of lust is constant and not subjected to self-control, demons are drawn in. Adultery is a serious sin that needs to be confessed and renounced. Healing of the marriage may require professional counselors or good spiritual direction from a priest.

7. You shall not steal. (Exod. 20:15)

"The seventh commandment forbids *theft*, that is, usurping another's property against the reasonable will of the owner" (CCC 2408). Stealing signals disrespect for others and may develop into disordered ideas of entitlement.

Diabolical counterpart: thievery. "The thief comes only to steal and kill and destroy. I came that they may have life and have it abundantly" (John 10:10). If you have ever suffered the injury of being robbed, you comprehend the violence that is done. A thief should make restitution as soon as possible. "Zacchaeus stood and said to the Lord, 'Behold, Lord, the half of my goods I give to the poor; and if I have defrauded any one of anything, I restore it fourfold'" (Luke 19:8). Often, demons lay claim to someone because of his *unconfessed sins* and *unpaid debts*. Stealing is what demons do.

8. You shall not bear false witness against your neighbor. (Exod. 20:16)

"The eighth commandment forbids misrepresenting the truth in our relations with others. This moral prescription flows from the vocation of the holy people to bear witness to their God who is the truth and wills the truth. Offenses against the truth express by word or deed a refusal to commit oneself to moral uprightness: they are fundamental infidelities to God and, in this sense, they undermine the foundations of the covenant" (CCC 2464).

Diabolical counterpart: lying. "You are of your father the devil, and your will is to do your father's desires. He was a murderer from the beginning, and has nothing to do with the truth, because there is no truth in him. When he lies, he speaks according to his own nature, for he is a liar and the father of lies" (John 8:44). When we lie, we cross into the devil's kingdom. Small white lies can lead to habitual lying. Lies, no matter how small, are not in the realm of God. To walk in the Spirit as soldiers of spiritual combat, we must secure the belt of truth around our waist and shun falsehood. In the family, great care is needed to cultivate an environment of truth. A young child who gets away with lying may develop a lifelong habit of telling lies, to his detriment. Evil spirits tempt us away from truth by seducing us with lies and falsehood.

9. You shall not covet your neighbor's wife. (Exod. 20:17)
On this commandment, the *Catechism* teaches:

> The ninth commandment warns against lust or carnal concupiscence. The struggle against carnal lust involves purifying the heart and practicing temperance. Purity of heart will enable us to see God: it enables us even now to see things according to God. Purification of the heart demands prayer, the practice of chastity, purity of intention and of vision. Purity of heart requires the modesty which is patience, decency, and discretion. Modesty protects the intimate center of the person. (CCC 2529–2533)

Diabolical counterpart: lust. Carnal concupiscence is a diabolical specialty. Many obsession cases began with unruly lusts, which lead to habitual sexual sin. Addiction to pornography is a diabolical scourge on marriages. Many men who receive exorcisms or deliverance share that they first encountered pornography as young children, when they found their fathers' pornographic magazines. Increasingly, women also now watch pornography. A priest invited me to lead a parish mission for women to address this issue. Sadly, the demon of lust is sometimes rampant within Catholic homes. Sweep the house clean with Mother Mary's help.

10. You shall not covet your neighbor's house . . . or anything that is your neighbor's. (Exod. 20:17)

> The tenth commandment unfolds and completes the ninth, which is concerned with concupiscence of the flesh. It forbids coveting the goods of another, as the root of theft, robbery, and fraud, which the seventh commandment forbids. "Lust of the eyes" leads to the violence and injustice forbidden by the fifth commandment. Avarice, like fornication, originates in the idolatry prohibited by the first three prescriptions of the Law. The tenth commandment concerns the intentions of the heart; with the ninth, it summarizes all the precepts of the Law. . . .
>
> The tenth commandment forbids greed and the desire to amass earthly goods without limit. It forbids avarice arising from a passion for riches and their attendant power. (CCC 2534, 2536)

Diabolical counterpart: envy. Satan and his cohorts tempt us to inordinate attachment to riches, fame, honor, and every worldly thing. We acquire a taste for such things if we do not hold our desires in check by prudence, humility, and moderation. Not a few people have sold their souls to the devil—literally—to attain riches, prosperity, fame, and honor. Such pacts are real, and they corrupt the soul if repentance and reparation are not done. Lust of the world is problematic and very seductive and needs to be diligently resisted. "When the demon enters so gently, politely, and takes possession of our attitudes, our values shift from service to God towards worldliness."[101]

The Prison of Unwilling: "Lord, Make Me Want!"

> Sin is precisely this: that I do not want what God wants. And I can't see how this opposition on my part could be broken. I can't see how this prison wall which holds me captive could be pierced through.... I know precisely what I ought to do. You've often told me yourself, the priest has told me, I have told myself. This, then, is not what is lacking. The will is lacking: the being able to want. There is a will in me that wants, and there is another will in me (the same one!) that does not want. "I do not understand what I do. For what I want to do I do not do, but what I hate to do...for I have the desire to do what is good, but I cannot carry it out.... What a wretched man I am! Who will rescue me from this body of death?" (Romans 7) Thus it is that I am rent apart in my innermost will, and the same thing in me that wants is precisely what does not want. And this is why I cry out to you from the depths of my Prison of Unwilling: Make Me Want![102]

---

[101] Pope Francis, "Vigilant against worldliness," Morning Meditation in the Chapel of Santa Marta, October 13, 2017.

[102] Hans Urs von Balthasar, "Jailhouse and Cocoon," chap. 8 in *Heart of the World*, quoted in Most Rev. Robert J. Carlson, Bishop of Saginaw, *Jesus Christ, the Divine Physician: Pastoral Letter on Penance*, 2nd ed. (Saginaw, MI: Catholic Diocese of Saginaw, 2008), 18, http://www.laluzestaencendida.com/pdfs/BishopCarlson_PastoralLetterOnPenance.pdf.

STRATEGY: THE BEATITUDES, BLESSINGS IN THE FAMILY

The word *beatitude* means "supreme blessedness." Christ's Sermon on the Mount instructs us in the godliness that begets blessedness. The Beatitudes call for spiritual maturity, since they require a profound conversion of heart. Fr. Jacques Philippe teaches that although the Beatitudes "first [concern] the individual" they also have a "community dimension." Father continues: "The family is the first and most essential of all Christian communities. Where can we better experience our own poverty and that of others than in the closely shared life of a couple and family members?"[103]

The Beatitudes and Their Diabolical Counterparts

Jesus' sermon on the Beatitudes (Matt. 5:1–12) reads as follows: "Seeing the crowds, he went up on the mountain, and when he sat down his disciples came to him. And he opened his mouth and taught them, saying":

1. *Blessed are the poor in spirit, for theirs is the kingdom of heaven.* Poverty of spirit helps us to rely on God, not ourselves. This is critical for participating in Christ's victory. Since Christ became an icon of spiritual poverty, His disciples must do the same.

   Diabolical counterpart: pride, egoism, irreverence, worldliness, envy, and the loss of heaven through our choice to separate ourselves from God.
2. *Blessed are those who mourn, for they shall be comforted.* A soldier for Christ will mourn appropriately, know God's comfort, and

[103] Fr. Jacques Philippe, *The Eight Doors of the Kingdom* (New York: Scepter Publishers, 2018), 18, Kindle.

persevere through grief to grace. Remember that Jesus wept after seeing those He loved in anguish (see John 11:32–36), when He saw the sins of humanity (see Luke 13:34; 19:41–42), and in Gethsemane before His crucifixion (see Heb. 5:7). Christ knows our need to be comforted during mourning.

Diabolical counterpart: eternal grief resulting from separation from God, resentment toward His divine will, and refusal to grieve for offending God. Demons mock our mourning and despise that God comforts us.

3. *Blessed are the meek, for they shall inherit the earth.* Christ, our Captain, meek and humble of heart, is a fierce warrior against sin and evil. He forms His soldiers accordingly.

   Diabolical counterpart: pride, mean-spiritedness, disrespectfulness, arrogance, and loss of the divine inheritance. It seems that demons fear the meek because God prefers and protects them.

4. *Blessed are those who hunger and thirst for righteousness, for they shall be satisfied.* Righteousness is the breastplate of God's armor. Clothed in God's righteousness, we are protected, able to walk on the steep and narrow path to victory.

   Diabolical counterpart: proclivity for wickedness, egoism, and selfishness; spiritual blindness; inordinate appetites; hunger for vice.

5. *Blessed are the merciful, for they shall obtain mercy.* Christ's soldiers must be as merciful as the Lord of Mercy, having received the gift of His merciful love.

   Diabolical counterpart: wrath, unforgiveness, jealousy, and false judgments. Demons vehemently militate against forgiveness and persistently remind us of our wounds to keep us mired in a "victim attitude." When we are vessels of divine mercy, we become victors with Christ.

6. *Blessed are the pure in heart, for they shall see God.* A soldier for Christ first experiences God's victory in his heart, purified by grace. Then, the soldier's eyes are opened to behold Incarnate Love.

   Diabolical counterpart: immorality, impurity, hypersexuality, and absence of God in one's heart. Demons are the epitome of the defiled, debased, dirty, and inharmonious.

7. *Blessed are the peacemakers, for they shall be called sons of God.* A spiritual warrior promotes God's peace—the tranquility of order—and identifies as God's beloved child.

   Diabolical counterpart: one who disrupts peace; has a controlling, disordered spirit; incites warlike chaos; and acts like an orphan instead of a child of God. Demons militate against peace by promoting conflict, noise, and irritation.

8. *Blessed are those who are persecuted for righteousness' sake, for theirs is the kingdom of heaven.* The valiant warrior is farsighted enough to see all the way through the valley of combat and perceive in the distance the longed-for eternal paradise.

   Diabolical counterpart: persecuting others to promote suffering and despair; unbelief; rejection of the Cross of Jesus. Demons deal in persecution of the righteous to mock the Righteous One who makes us righteous. That heaven is open to us, and not them, draws their wrath.

When you make the effort to practice the Beatitudes in the family, God meets you with grace to build a hedge of protection. The fruits of grace will be realized in the home through the enjoyment of family wisdom, peace, joy, and goodness. Fr. Cantalamessa teaches:

> The real metanoia, that is, change, occurs when we abandon our way of thinking and receive God's way of thinking, when we put aside our judgement and take on God's judgement. This is where the leap occurs. To repent means to take a running leap into the abyss of God's judgement.... Seen in the light of the immense love of the Father, sin appears for what it truly is: a betrayal of his immense love, "crucifying again the Son of God and...holding him up to contempt" (cf. Heb 6:6).[104]

Change my heart, O *God* is the heart-cry of a spiritual warrior. Several times a day, I pray: *Jesus, save me from myself!* In my family, when I'm challenged to love beyond my capacity, I pray: *Lord, please fill me with your love; give me your Heart, so I won't harm this person in any way.*

Strategy: Speaking Blessing in the Family

Fr. Salvatore Canals encourages: "If you know how to speak without wounding, although you may have to correct or reprimand, hearts will not close themselves to you. The seed will fall on truly fertile ground and the harvest will be plentiful."[105] In the domestic church, spoken words can be life-giving or life-taking. Fr. Jim McManus explains: "Why do words have such power in our lives? The reason is that on the deep, personal level, our spiritual level, we yearn for meaning and we live by the word that conveys meaning

---

104 Cantalamessa, *Sober Intoxication*, 137.

105 Salvatore Canals, *Jesus as Friend*, 4th ed. (New York: Scepter Publishers, 1997), 33.

to us. We form our self-image through that meaning. We are not born with a self-image: it is formed by the word that is spoken to us."[106]

In retreat work, I meet people in their seventies who have carried for fifty years the deep pain of ill-spoken words of a parent, spouse, teacher, or child! Families are meant to speak blessing upon another. Evil spirits tempt us to have ill will, even toward family members, which gives way to curses rather than blessings.

Caution: The New Idolatry

The *new idolatry* consists in hyper-egocentrism and the hyper-sexualization of men, women, and children. Society deceptively idolizes sex as the highest form of ecstatic pleasure and happiness. This affects couples and families because compulsive sexual behavior has the potential to negatively impact a person's physical and mental health, relationships, quality of life, and safety. It can be the cause of familial tension and personal despondency. Unfortunately, demons are quick to seduce a person into believing that hypersexuality equals happiness. Personal and familial vigilance is necessary to avoid being seduced into sexual sin. Beware of the grand illusion of the "gray area," which the devil uses to play games regarding human sexuality. The bad fruit of the hyper-sexualization of society can be seen in the lives of victims, who often experience low self-esteem, impulsive aggression, and hopelessness.

At the same time, idolizing hyper-egocentrism, society de-

[106] Jim McManus, C.Ss.R, *True Self-Esteem: Precious in the Eyes of God* (Liguori, MO: Liguori Publications, 2005), 21.

ceptively presents self-image and power as the new fulfillment of human desire. Christians are called to resist the vanities of the world that worship at the altar of "me, myself, and I." It takes courage to resist the relativism that preaches against absolute truth. Narcissism has torn apart many marriages and families with its bad fruit of power-grabbing, entitlement, and lack of empathy. Where there is egocentrism, the devil is close by.

Our response to the new idolatry is to counteract hypersexuality and hyper-egocentrism. We can resist the former by practicing and promoting personal and familial chastity, and the latter by cultivating personal and familial humility, simplicity, generosity, and magnanimity.

The new idolatry mocks the first commandment. It's not uncommon to erect idols that eventually erode our devotion and replace our love for God and family.

Caution: Universal Demonic Strategy

The devil has more than one way to destroy a family. Fr. Robert Spitzer, S.J., gave a conference on the following tactics of our ancient foe:

- deconstruction of transcendence (attacks on God, Jesus, and the soul)
- deconstruction of happiness (attacks against authentic freedom, love, and redemptive suffering)
- deconstruction of evil, sin, virtue, and redemption (attacks against truth)
- deconstruction of religion, the Church, marriage, family, and the priesthood (attacks against the divine will)

The *deconstruction of transcendence* related to God, Jesus, and the soul seduces people to reject God's omnipotence, beauty, and truth. The aim is to erase faith in Jesus Christ so that our hope is blotted out also. Deconstructing the *transcendence* of the human soul means reducing it to a base or nonexistent thing that does not require divine care.

The *deconstruction of happiness* involves rejection of the Christian teaching on freedom in Christ, doubt about the divine law of charity, and loss of the meaning of suffering. If we reject these, we can entertain the demonic idea of happiness that amounts to this: there is no God, the idea of God is oppressive, and you are your own god, in control of your own destiny.

Demons tempt us to reject the Christian idea of authentic freedom by misconstruing it as slavery. Remember, demons specialize in inverting the truth. They tempt us to associate God with condemnation, rejecting the truth that He redeems us. They aim to convince us that God does not want us to experience happiness. If we believe that following God means giving up happiness, the devil has a hook to catch us and convince us to accept his style of happiness—freedom to be our own god and to do whatever we want without consequences: no sin, no suffering. All of this is a lie, of course.

The diabolical undermining of Christian teaching on sin and evil aims to desensitize us, such that we believe everything is good and nothing is evil—in other words, to each his own. Think of the ramifications for the family. Shamefully, in the world's opinion, abortion is good, not evil, and having many children is a burden, not a blessing. Do you see the diabolical inversion?

This generation of Catholic families must resist sin and evil; push back the darkness. We must heed Scripture's many warnings:

"There are those who rebel against the light, who are not acquainted with its ways, and do not stay in its paths" (Job 24:13); "Some sat in darkness and in gloom, prisoners in affliction and in irons, for they had rebelled against the words of God, and spurned the counsel of the Most High" (Ps. 107:10–11); "Sons have I reared and brought up, but they have rebelled against me" (Isa. 1:2). If we accept the demonic lies and temptations in our families, evil spirits enter our camp. Instead, we must resist them: "Because the LORD your God walks in the midst of your camp, to save you and to give up your enemies before you, therefore your camp must be holy, that he may not see anything indecent among you, and turn away from you" (Deut. 23:14).

THE WEAPON OF RECONCILIATION

About the importance of Confession, Fr. Jose Fortea teaches:

> As human beings, we are dazzled by that which is the most spectacular to our eyes. Confession is not very spectacular; its work is very quiet and discreet. Nevertheless, confession is a divine gift much greater than exorcism. Exorcism only drives out a demon from one's body; confession drives out evil from one's soul. Confession destroys our attachments to iniquity and gives us sanctifying grace. Confession not only forgives but heals our soul and fills it with light. Frequent confession strengthens us with sanctifying grace and is a powerful force in helping us resist temptation (see CCC 1458).[107]

[107] Fortea, *Interview with an Exorcist*, 70, Kindle.

The deliverance power of the sacrament of Reconciliation cannot be sufficiently stressed. A thorough Confession is often the key to complete liberation from evil. Going to Reconciliation is something families may enjoy together as a healthy means of spiritual protection.

The *Catechism* quotes St. Ambrose's teaching on God's mercy: "The Lord who has taken away your sin and pardoned your faults also protects you and keeps you from the wiles of your adversary the devil, so that the enemy, who is accustomed to leading into sin, may not surprise you. One who entrusts himself to God does not dread the devil. 'If God is for us, who is against us?'" (CCC 2852).

The Weapon of Fasting

"Throughout scripture, we find that when God's people fast, the power of their prayers is increased, especially when they are engaged in special warfare. In the Old Testament, the Lord told Isaiah that a fast properly undertaken would 'loose the bonds of wickedness . . . undo the throngs of the yoke . . . let the oppressed go free' (Is 58:6)."[108] I've discovered the efficacy of even a small fast. God appreciates our efforts, no matter how small.

When spiritual combat is intense and prolonged, we must employ the weapon of fasting. "In the New Testament, we find that Jesus fasted for forty days and nights in the wilderness in preparation for this battle with Satan, who came to tempt him (Lk 4:1–2). And on one occasion, when Our Lord's disciples failed to cast out a demon from a possessed boy, he told them that 'this kind cannot

---

[108] *Spiritual Warfare Bible*, 636.

be driven out by anything but prayer and fasting' (Mk 9:29)."[109] If you combine prayer and fasting for your family, you will supercharge your intercessory power for the protection and holiness of loved ones.

Once, a demon, speaking through a possessed person, yelled out: "Ha! You didn't fast! You didn't fast!" Evidently, evil spirits can tell whether we fast. This shows what a difference fasting makes. If demons acknowledge our fasts, surely heaven must as well.

Holy Spirit, I implore you to consecrate my loved ones in the truth so we will keep the commandments and live the Beatitudes, that we may enjoy the beauty of life well lived in Christ. Amen.

[109] Ibid.

7

ENGAGING YOUR WEAPONS: HOLY DARING

Marriage Strategy: Stay in Love
Family Strategy: Building a Eucharistic Heart and Home

God alone knows how to create harmony from differences. But if God's love is lacking, the family loses its harmony, self-centeredness prevails and joy fades. But the family which experiences the joy of faith communicates it naturally. That family is the salt of the earth and the light of the world, it is the leaven of society as a whole. Dear families, always live in faith and simplicity, like the Holy Family of Nazareth![110]

The unmistakable sign of God's love for the family is that Jesus Christ was born into a human family. He had a mother and a father—the Virgin Mary and St. Joseph—and for thirty years, He lived in their home and obeyed them. How remarkable! Jesus' family life reveals how much God values families and devotes Himself

[110] "Homily of His Holiness Pope Francis," Holy Mass for the Family Day on the Occasion of the Year of Faith, October 27, 2013.

to them. While Scripture is mostly silent about Jesus' hidden life in Nazareth, we can draw a few conclusions:

1. The Holy Family were so *ordinary* that they remained unknown for thirty years.
2. They were so *humble* that they were content to be unknown and hidden.
3. They *grew in love* through obedience to the Father and service to one another.
4. They *prayed* and *worked* together, honoring one another.
5. They *made a home*, creating a loving sanctuary of peace.

We can imagine the exalted beauty of their family prayer—the Virgin Mary, St. Joseph, and the Child Jesus lifting their hearts to Abba, the Father. Did the angels visit them? How did the Holy Family play together; what made them laugh? How did they pray? Obviously, their family life took place before the institution of the Mass or the Rosary. Likely, their prayer life included the Hebrew Scriptures, since it is written of Mary: "Since Mary was born into Judaism, she experienced the Hebrew Scriptures both in her prayer and her mode of life as a woman of Nazareth."[111]

During His public ministry, Jesus entered the lives of many families. He performed His first miracle at Cana on behalf of the family (John 2:1–11). He healed Peter's mother-in-law (Matt. 8:14–15). He brought Lazarus back from the dead at the request of his family (John 11:1–44). Christ healed a possessed boy at the request of his father (Mark 9:14–29). Jesus brought a girl back from

---

[111] Bertrand Buby, SM, *Mary of Galilee, Volume II: Woman of Israel – Daughter of Zion* (New York: Alba House, 1995), 6, quoted in Sr. M. Danielle Peters, "Jewish Identity of Mary: The Jewishness of Mary," University of Dayton, December 2002, https://udayton.edu/imri/mary/j/jewish-identity-of-mary.php.

the dead at the behest of her parents (Luke 8:40–42, 49–56). He was sympathetic to families. He wept with them; He entered their homes; He shared meals with them and delivered them from evil spirits. He still shares our family's joys and sorrows to bless, heal, strengthen, and deliver us from evil.

Family: Messy, Miraculous Love

Exorcist Msgr. John Esseff once led a two-day retreat for the clergy and faculty of the Pope Leo XIII Institute. To preface the retreat, he asked us to consider the ways we were formed by our families. He began by sharing personal reflections about his family: "I was deformed by my family. I love them. They love me. But I was deformed by their thinking about certain things." It was evident that he truly cherished his parents and siblings; he loved them deeply. Yet they had raised him to have certain prejudices against families and religions unlike theirs. But even within this environment of conflicting family opinions about religion and ethnicity, heroic love was born.

Monsignor's younger sister became very ill. As her disease worsened and became life-threatening, she prayed to the Lord to take her life as an offering for her brother John's special mission. She sensed that John was called to the priesthood. When she was close to death, she finally told Monsignor about her prayer. Immediately, he became angry and yelled: "What did you do that for? No, you should not have done that! No!" Shortly afterward, his sister died.

As he shared the story of his sister's sacrificial offering of love, Msgr. Esseff's voice quivered and glistening tears streamed from his eyes. For Msgr. Esseff, his sister embodied the words of Jesus:

"Greater love has no man than this, that a man lay down his life for his friends" (John 15:13). We read about such stories in the lives of the saints. Monsignor's story demonstrates that God is still forming heroic and saintly people within our imperfect families.

Monsignor told another memorable story, this time about his mother. When he went to visit his parents, his mother took him aside to share an experience she had in a dream. In the dream, she was kissing the corpus of Jesus on the crucifix. She was adoring Jesus and thanking Him for His Passion. She asked Jesus what she could do to love Him more. Then, Jesus took on the image of her husband and said to her, "To love me more, love your husband."

A pregnant silence filled the room.

Listening to Monsignor's reflections, I observed a communal sigh of relief that a priest was speaking frankly about the imperfection and beauty of his family. He had given us permission to admit that our families are imperfect and our upbringing was perhaps a little warped, or even disordered. Yet, mysteriously, love weaves itself around family members to produce good fruit in due season. Grace leads us to the beautiful discovery of our human dignity. In families, we begin to realize there is something greater than ourselves at work. God is with us.

Families are messy and miraculous for many reasons. A prayerful gaze at the bloodied body of Christ hanging on the Cross or a reflection on the seven-times-pierced heart of Mother Mary reveals that agape love is not nice and neat. These icons of love teach us that suffering is part of the weight of sacrificial love. Pondering the life of the Holy Family can form and fortify us for spiritual combat. Transformation into the likeness of the Holy Family is an arduous process. We should pray daily for the patience, courage, humility, generosity, and grace to become the best versions of ourselves and our families. We make every effort; God controls every outcome.

Strategy: Holy Daring

The book *Holy Daring: The Fearless Trust of St. Therese of Lisieux* highlights the Little Flower's bold confidence in divine love and the courage with which she selflessly put that trust into action. Holy daring is faith and fortitude in action. The lives of the saints radiate this holy confidence. We find a striking example of holy daring in the words of Job: "Naked I came from my mother's womb, and naked shall I return; the Lord gave, and the Lord has taken away; blessed be the name of the Lord" (1:21). Stop and think about the holy daring of Job's proclamation.

I once worked with a woman, the wife of a deacon. When she received word that her only child was killed in an accident, she immediately proclaimed Job's daring words. I doubt that I could spontaneously demonstrate that deep a faith if I had lost my only child.

The Old Testament offers us another example of holy daring in the book of Genesis, when the Lord tests Abraham by asking him to sacrifice his son Isaac as a burnt offering (22:1–19). Abraham set out to fulfill the Lord's command. He built an altar, arranged the wood on it, bound his son Isaac, and laid him on the altar on top of the wood. But then, an angel of the Lord called out to Abraham: "Do not lay your hand on the lad or do anything to him; for now I know that you fear God, seeing you have not withheld your son, your only-begotten son, from me" (22:12). The Lord richly rewarded Abraham's faith: "I will indeed bless you, and I will multiply your descendants as the stars of heaven and as the sand which is on the seashore" (22:17). Did the Lord not require a radical test of faith for poor Abraham? God acted in holy daring, and Abraham responded likewise.

In the New Testament, the Virgin Mary and Jesus Christ are the ultimate icons of holy boldness. We see the holy daring of divine love on Good Friday and even more so on Easter Sunday. Today, we need families whose lives radiate the beauty of holy daring. We need families formed in revolutionary, radical faith to hold up the Cross of Jesus against people who throw it away, against demons who would bury it in hell.

Rooting out sin and evil that infiltrate our marriages or our children requires holy daring. Be brave and bold in defense of your family. The rebellious teenager who is accessing pornography or the daughter in high school who wants birth control pills must be accompanied, loved, prayed for, taught, and wisely led away from diabolical persons, places, or things. The husband who had a one-night affair, repents, begs forgiveness, and asks for another chance, should be treated the way Jesus approached the woman caught in adultery (see John 8:1–11). This is holy daring—the boldness of unbounded love and mercy. Holy daring is bold in faith, hope, and love. These theological virtues anchor us in Christ and ready us for spiritual combat. Faith, hope, and love empower our family life to be fruitful, fearless, and fearsome.

In his *Letter to Families*, Pope St. John Paul II expounds on the power of hope:

> Dear families, you too should be fearless, ever ready to give witness to the hope that is in you (cf. 1 Pet 3:15), since the Good Shepherd has put that hope in your hearts through

> the Gospel.... Immeasurably greater than the evil at work in the world is the power of the *Sacrament of Reconciliation*, which the Fathers of the Church rightly called a "second Baptism". Much more influential than the corruption present in the world is the divine power of the *Sacrament of Confirmation*, which brings Baptism to its maturity. And incomparably greater than all is the power of the Eucharist.
>
> The *Eucharist* is truly a wondrous sacrament.... *It is for you, dear husbands and wives, parents and families!*[112]

God has showered us with every gift and grace through the sacramental fountains of the Church. Prioritize, protect, and persevere in the sacramental life—and you'll be a real threat to the kingdom of darkness.

Strategy: Engage Your Weapons

The weapons to defend yourself and your family from evil spirits include the following:

1. *The weapon of the sacraments.* By frequenting Confession and Mass, you are fortifying your spiritual armor. These sacraments, weapons of defense and offense in spiritual battle, are essential to the spiritual life of a soldier for Christ.
2. *The weapon of Scripture.* Prayerfully read the Bible as a family if possible (even for only fifteen minutes a day). Memorize short Scripture verses to use in spiritual combat. Jesus Christ chose the weapon of Scripture to defeat the devil, who tempted Him

[112] Pope John Paul II, *Letter to Families*, 94–95.

in the desert (Matt. 4:1–11). Use Scripture to "talk back" to diabolical temptation. This does *not* mean dialoguing with demons, which must never be done. To talk back means to wield the sword of the Spirit: "For the word of God is living and active, shaper than any two-edged sword" (Heb. 4:12).

3. *The weapon of sacramental spousal authority.* Husbands and wives, pray blessings over one another; pray deliverance prayers for one another.
4. *The weapon of parental authority.* Pray blessings and deliverance prayers for and with your children. Make the sign of the cross on their foreheads often. Pray daily the Auxilium Christianorum prayers of protection.[113]
5. *The weapon of prayer.* The domestic church should be permeated by prayer. Praying as a family is not only a weapon of protection; it's an occasion for family intimacy. Even fifteen minutes of family prayer produces amazing fruit. Create an oratory in your home—a space dedicated to family prayer that is considered holy ground. Make it the place where family members go to pray alone as well as the gathering place for family prayer. Keep it simple but beautifully adorned with a blessed candle, a cross, a Bible, prayer books, images or statues of saints, and a rosary. Please pray for vocations. Write prayer petitions and place them in a prayer box.
6. *The weapon of God's armor.* God's armor is a garment of grace for victorious spiritual combat. As stated in chapter five, dress family members in the six pieces: the belt of truth, the breastplate of righteousness, the equipment of the gospel of peace,

---

[113] Located at http://auxiliumchristianorum.org/prayers/.

the shield of faith, the helmet of salvation, and the sword of the Spirit: the Word of God.

7. *The weapon of fasting.* The Lord Himself gave us an example of fasting. Foster the practice of offering up little sacrifices in reparation for sins—yours and those of others. Demons despise the spirit of fasting. Fight against the devil of indulgence. "In the Old Testament, the Lord told Isaiah that a fast properly undertaken would 'loose the bonds of wickedness... undo the throngs of the yoke... let the oppressed go free' (Is 58:6).... When Our Lord's disciples failed to cast out a demon from a possessed boy, he told them that 'this kind cannot be driven out by anything but prayer and fasting' (Mk 9:29)."[114]
8. *The weapon of sacramentals.* Keep sacramentals on your person and throughout your home. Sacramentals must be used with faith—not superficially, like a talisman. The *Catechism* states: "These [sacramentals] are sacred signs which bear a resemblance to the sacraments. They signify effects, particularly of a spiritual nature, which are obtained through the intercession of the Church" (CCC 1667). Examples of sacramentals include the following: making the sign of the cross; giving blessings to family members; and using blessed objects such as holy water, oil, salt, candles, incense, rosaries, crucifixes, scapulars, religious images, St. Benedict Medals, and Miraculous Medals. Sacramentals used during exorcisms are proven effective for helping to drive out evil spirits.
9. *The weapon of Catholic communities.* Find your group of like-minded spiritual believers, warriors, and families. Faith-filled

[114] *Spiritual Warfare Bible*, 636.

fellowship strengthens family members and is helpful for growth in knowledge. It's also enjoyable. Share the joy of the Lord together. Holy communities uphold their members, creating spiritual hedges of protection.

10. *The weapon of Catholicism.* Order your family and home to Catholicism. Create a peaceful refuge. Keep it undefiled—free from literature, art, artifacts, or games that would be offensive to God. Our God is a God of order. The devil is a promoter of disorder. Develop Christocentric problem-solving practices to defend yourselves from diabolical division and anger. Engage Catholic remedies as needed, and resist religious syncretism.
11. *The weapon of forgiveness.* Practice the art of forgiving love. Be quick to forgive yourself, your spouse, and your children. Be aware of hurt feelings in the family so that resentment doesn't develop. Don't leave room for an evil spirit to enter through a wound of unforgiveness, but rebuke this poison through prayer. Unforgiveness is a great obstacle to healing and deliverance.
12. *The weapon of communication.* Take great care to dialogue with each family member. Make every effort to keep communication lively. Engage the shyer members also. Stay interested in one another's daily lives. Bring everything to the light. Resist delaying or denying problems that need to be addressed. Ask the Holy Spirit to be your divine counselor.
13. *The weapon of virtue.* Virtue is the habit that protects the powers of the soul and disposes you to do good. Examples of virtues are chastity, temperance, charity, diligence, patience, kindness, and humility. Practicing these virtues arms

us against temptations to the seven deadly sins (pride, envy, gluttony, greed, lust, sloth, and anger). Grace is required for the practice of virtue; we can't be virtuous of our own volition. Be proactive in the family to deplore vice and cultivate virtue.

An Exorcist on Praying with Your Spouse

Exorcist Fr. Amorth advises that young married couples do two things:

> The first is to develop immediately the habit of praying together. This will lead to greater harmony and will keep away many evils. The second is to extend this good habit to your children and bring them to church—even when they are little and even if they cry and run around the church. One is educated in the church through osmosis. They will be grateful when they are grown, and so will you. And one must not omit—even if it is difficult—the desire of pardon toward the one who has acted wickedly against him.[115]

Often, a demonic attack on families begins with an attack against spouses. Demons despise the life-giving reality of the marital act. The blessing of marriage is realized in its fullness if the conjugal act is performed purely and in right relationship with God.

Demons will take advantage of the weaknesses (wounds) of a husband and wife:

---

[115] Amorth, *Exorcist Explains*, 91.

- Demons can act on the imagination to influence negatively the spouses' perception of one another.
- Demons may sow division and incite anger by altering your perspective of situations in your family.
- Demons may stir up lust. An evil spirit of lust is not confined to adultery or blatant acts of infidelity. The spirit of lust may enter through the couple's use of pornography, contraception, or aggressive control. Demons tempt couples to obsess about matters other than their spousal relationship and to remove God from the equation.
- Demons of the air hear the words families speak. Practice custody of the tongue, and speak blessings, not curses, even during disagreements.
- Demons aim at the weakest link. They know your weaknesses and those of your spouse and children. If one spouse is living a duplicitous secret life or the other ceases to pray, the devil will likely attack these weaknesses. Strive diligently to convert your vices to virtues.

God's Expectation for Marriage versus Its Diabolical Corruption[116]

God's Expectation

1. Ontologically equal (equal by nature)
2. Heterosexual
3. Monogamous
4. Patricentric

---

[116] These lists are taken from Fr. Robert Spitzer's presentation at the 2016 Pope Leo XIII Summer Conference at Mundelein Seminary.

5. Permanent
6. Made one flesh
7. Covenantal
8. Sexual
9. Fruitful
10. Life-giving

Satan's Corruption of Marriage

1. Spouse as property
2. Homosexual
3. Polygamous/polyamorous
4. Matricentric
5. Subject to divorce
6. Adulterous or "open"
7. Unholy/contractual
8. Celibate due to false asceticism
9. Fruitless
10. Deadly

Strategy for Marriages: Staying in Love

Obstacles that increase marital vulnerability to demonic attacks include the following: (1) having a confused idea of Catholic marriage; (2) misunderstanding the importance of self-giving love (perhaps woundedness makes a sincere gift of self impossible); and (3) not grasping each spouse's respective vocation within sacramental marriage.

I propose the following marital strategy of *staying in love*, articulated by Deacon James Keating:

> Beholding your spouse, listening to your spouse, and forgiving your spouse is the way to *stay in love*. Beholding God in prayer, listening to God in prayer, and repenting when something other than prayer has guided your judgement is the way to *stay in love* with God. The goal for both of these interpenetrating relationships is to desire, and then welcome, the object of your love, God and spouse, as the reigning presence in your heart. When this happens, you have internalized your beloved and you begin to think *like a spouse*; or in the case of your relationship with God, you begin to think *in prayer*. If you pray and if you internalize your spouse in your heart, you will become one who thinks in love, and to become such a person is to live in reality. If you stay in love, then all your decisions will flow from that love.[117]

Having been married for forty years, I know the power of sacramental grace for upholding spouses through every challenge. Archbishop Fulton Sheen's book *Three to Get Married* rightly teaches that God is faithfully present and available to spouses. Spousal wounds are crosses for us, but for God, they can provide space for Him to intervene—to heal with divine love.

One lesson I've learned is that a sense of humor goes a long way in marriage! Sometimes, a really good laugh fixes things as nothing else can. I've heard that evil spirits cannot mock authentic joy. The Scripture passage "The joy of the Lord is your strength"

---

[117] Deacon James Keating, PhD, *Spousal Prayer: A Way to Marital Happiness* (Omaha: IPF Publications, 2013), 44–45.

(Neh. 8:10) reminds us that joy strengthens us in spiritual combat. Find the joy in your marriage, and protect it as a precious gift. Even if spouses are estranged, willing the good for one another is necessary by God's law of love.

Pope St. John Paul II delivered the following message for spouses:

> Dear spouses, the gap you perceive between the Father's attention and your poor responses must not paralyze you but make you even more dynamic. You have been promised Christ's love, you belong to one another in this love. This love is not only a distant ideal but a present reality when you are united in the Lord, when you pray together, when, like the first time, you move toward one another, when at every moment you say "yes" to his will, when now you invoke him and you ask him, "Be stronger, you in us and between us, stronger than we are by ourselves." Though you, the power of divine love wills to be made present.[118]

Make an effort to create a beautiful life at home—simple, but beautiful. "Creating a beautiful life at home requires consistent attention to mastering little details. This is not the stuff of perfectionism, which rigidly sets unrealistic standards only to become discouraged and ineffectual when they are not met. Rather, this is a realistic optimism that is flexible and quick to begin again, day

[118] Quoted in *The Magnificat Adoration Companion* (Yonkers, NY: Magnificat, 2020), loc. 555–564 of 2846, Kindle.

after day, striving for the consistency of effort that an ordered life demands."[119]

Strategy: Building Eucharistic Hearts

Seven Characteristics of a Eucharistic Heart

1. *Incarnational love.* "This is my body which is given for you" (Luke 22:19).
2. *Resurrected life.* "I came that they may have life, and have it abundantly" (John 10:10).
3. *Humble service.* "If I then, your Lord and Teacher, have washed your feet, you also ought to wash one another's feet" (John 13:14).
4. *Grateful heart.* "We always thank God, the Father of our Lord Jesus Christ, when we pray for you" (Col. 1:3).
5. *Abiding presence.* "Behold, I am with you always, to the close of the age" (Matt. 28:20).
6. *Merciful communion.* "He who eats my flesh and drinks my blood abides in me, and I in him" (John 5:56).
7. *Victorious witness.* "And they have conquered him [the accuser of our brethren] by the blood of the Lamb and by the word of their testimony" (Rev. 12:11).

When we make every effort to live a eucharistic life, Christ helps us to become what we receive, and fashions our heart to be eucharistic.

Pope St. John Paul II taught that we need silent Adoration to

---

[119] Carrie Gress, Noelle Mering, and Megan Schrieber, *Theology of Home: Finding the Eternal in the Everyday* (Charlotte, NC: TAN Books, 2019), 115.

resist worldly temptations. Since God created us for beauty, we need to be in communion with the Beautiful One. This is the antidote to the ugliness that parades before our eyes. In the silence of Adoration, we enter into the beauty of God, who strengthens us for the good fight. Thus, we become a blessing to our families.

> The call to holiness is accepted and can be cultivated only *in the silence of adoration* before the infinite transcendence of God: "We must confess that we all need this silence." . . . It is also necessary to recognize and overcome certain temptations which sometimes, by diabolical deceit, present themselves under the appearance of good. . . . The praiseworthy desire to become close to the men and women of our day, believers and non-believers, rich and poor, can lead to the adoption of a secularized lifestyle or the promotion of human values in a merely horizontal direction.[120]

The "adoption of a secularized lifestyle" has undermined many Christian couples and families. Prudence is needed to live in the world and not become "of the world."

Strategy: Building a Eucharistic Home

A eucharistic home is the natural extension of a eucharistic heart. Through a eucharistic life celebrated with liturgical seasons, the home becomes a sanctuary imbued with eucharistic qualities.

---

[120] Pope John Paul II, Post-Synodal Apostolic Exhortation *Vita Consecrata* (March 25, 1996), no. 38.

1. *Holy ground.* Ask a priest to bless your home and consecrate it formally to the Sacred Heart of Jesus. Teach that the home is considered holy ground, where the gospel is upheld.
2. *Safe refuge.* Teach that everyone is safe at home. Create a refuge from the world, where everyone feels protected and nourished.
3. *Intimate communion.* Teach that just as Jesus faithfully communes with us in the Eucharist, we are committed to be faithful to each other in love and gratitude.
4. A *joyful place.* Teach that Jesus remains on earth in the Eucharist, giving us abundant joy in His abiding presence, protection, peace, and plenitude.
5. *Sacrificial offering.* Teach that because Jesus laid down His life in the service of others, we, too, must serve one another by making sacrifices of lasting love.
6. *Affirming dignity.* Teach that loved ones are cherished in the family for their God-given dignity. Nurture individual gifts and talents.
7. *Growing love.* Teach that God's love is alive, ever new, and creative; therefore, in the family, love is not stagnant, but grows every day through each member.
8. *Christocentric problem-solving.* Teach that Jesus told us that we would experience problems in the world and that we must solve them in a manner worthy of God's disciples, with peace and justice.
9. *Family meals.* Prioritize the family meal. At meal time and during the preparation of meals, be mindful of the parallels with the Last Supper. Remember the Lord's heart for feeding the apostles, lovingly preparing a meal for them—for exam-

ple, breakfast on the seashore after His resurrection (John 21:9–14). Remember that hungry stomachs are only part of the equation. The deeper hunger is for love. Make family meals a time for laughing, learning, loving, and even arguing constructively.

10. *Attendance at Holy Mass and Adoration.* Be a eucharistic family by prioritizing the reception of the Eucharist at Mass. Worship and praise together. Make family visits to the Blessed Sacrament—even very brief ones.

In his *Letter to Families*, Pope St. John Paul II wrote: "The Last Supper and the words he [Jesus] spoke there contain all the power and wisdom of the sacrifice of the Cross. No other power and wisdom exist by which we can be saved and through which we can help to save others.... The *educational power of the Eucharist* has been proved down the generations and centuries."[121] Similarly, the Lord told St. Faustina, "In the Host is the power; it will defend you always."[122] Let us unleash the educational power of the Eucharist in our families.

St. Peter Julian Eymard tells us, "The Eucharist is the work of a measureless love that has at its service an infinite power: the omnipotence of God." And he declares, "We must return from that Table like lions breathing fire, having become terrifying to the Devil!"[123]

In our eucharistic hearts and homes, we should be mindful that there are growing numbers of demonic agents who are

---

[121] Pope John Paul II, *Letter to Families*, 96.

[122] St. Faustina, *Diary*, no. 616.

[123] *Spiritual Warfare Bible*, 640.

enemies of the Eucharist. I encourage families to offer reparation for the demonic desecration of the Blessed Sacrament, which, tragically, is more widespread than we realize. What is reparation? The *Catechism* teaches that every offense committed entails the duty of reparation, even if its author has been forgiven (see CCC 2412, 2454, 2487, 2509). St. Therese of Lisieux said the best reparation she could ever make for sin was attending Holy Mass and worthily receiving Holy Communion.

Weapon: Family Intercessory Prayer

Intercessory prayer is a weapon against sin and evil. The *Catechism* defines *intercession* as follows: "Intercession is a prayer of petition which leads us to pray as Jesus did. He is the one intercessor with the Father on behalf of all men, especially sinners. He is 'able for all time to save those who draw near to God through him, since he always lives to make intercession for them.' The Holy Spirit 'himself intercedes for us . . . and intercedes for the saints according to the will of God'" (CCC 2634). A hallmark of an intercessor is that "he who prays looks 'not only to his own interests but also to the interests of others,' even to the point of praying for those who do him harm" (CCC 2635). The scope of intercessory prayer knows no bounds.

Intercession could be understood as the prayer that especially moves God's Heart. "But Moses implored the Lord his God saying, 'O Lord, why does your wrath burn hot against your people...? Turn from your fierce wrath, and repent of this evil against your people....' And the Lord repented of the evil which he thought to do to his people" (Exod. 32:11, 12, 14). This passage shows three dimensions of intercession: *action, prayer,* and *offering*. Moses took action, standing between a sinful people and their angry God. He prayed that God would relent, and he offered himself as a living sacrifice to do whatever God commanded. This is the essence of intercessory prayer. This is how we pray for loved ones: by taking action and standing between God and our spouses or children, be they faithful or prodigal. When I pray for a loved one, I like to imagine that I become a vessel of prayer, taking hold of Christ's hand with my right hand and extending my left to the person for whom I'm interceding.

I know of a lady who interceded unceasingly for her child, who was addicted to drugs. Then, suddenly, the child was arrested, convicted of a drug-related crime, and sentenced to prison for a few years. While there, the child stopped taking drugs, overcame his addiction, and developed a close relationship with Christ through a Bible study at the prison. Now, the child evangelizes inmates. The mother's intercessory prayer was answered—not as she envisioned, but God knew the best way to rescue this child. She is very grateful that God answered her prayer.

Christians are called, consecrated, and commissioned as intercessors with Christ. We pray, act, and ask for the grace and miracles that families need.

Eternal Father, graciously cleanse, heal, restore,
and liberate from evil our loved ones, whom we
commit to your merciful Heart. Amen.

8

UNMASKING DANGEROUS DIABOLICAL DISGUISES

Our Commander, the Lord Jesus Christ, the Conqueror of hell and death, calls us to battle alongside Him against the Enemy so that we can have a share in His victory. To fight the good fight, however, we must know not only our adversary and his strategies; we must also know the comrades that our great Commander has given us.[124]

To destroy the works of the devil, we must recognize the hidden evil that cleverly weaves in and out of our daily lives, families, and culture. Since demons are masters of disguise, we need godly masters of detection. Good discerners move in heavenly wisdom (see James 3:17) against sin and evil.

Many Catholic families are already engaged in pushing back the darkness by faithfully loving and serving each other as the Holy Family did. Whenever you surrender to God's will for your loved ones, you are overcoming demonic disobedience in the world. Every time you unite your suffering to Christ's, you are sending light into the darkness. Whenever you protect the innocence of your children and cherish the love God established between you

[124] *Spiritual Warfare Bible*, 376.

and your spouse, you are proclaiming God's victory. Whenever your family's heart is pierced in communion with the Lord's sorrowful Heart, you are building up God's kingdom.

With every act of love and service to God and family, you push back demonic deconstruction of faith and family. Keep making a difference.

Families are invited into the loving joy of the Holy Family's home in Nazareth. The mysterious years of hidden acts of love, joy, prayer, meals, and work contain a secret to happiness. It is from the Nazareth home that Jesus, St. Joseph, and Mother Mary went forth into public life, battle, and victory for the salvation of the world. Is that not the blueprint for today's Catholic families also? Did not the happy memory of their Nazareth years greatly sustain Mother Mary and Jesus Christ when their hearts received the sword that broke them wide open? That sword of love must pierce our hearts to release the power of the Cross in a world seemingly gone mad.

And don't forget St. Joseph, a powerful companion in our fight against Satan. In his book *Consecration to St. Joseph*, Fr. Donald Calloway, M.I.C., quotes Blessed Bartolo Longo, who once was involved with the occult and spiritualism. Suffering from demonic oppression, Longo turned to a Dominican priest for help and renounced spiritualism. Grateful for his deliverance, he became a Third Order Dominican and was deeply devoted to the Virgin Mary and St. Joseph. Longo especially appreciated St. Joseph's title "Terror of Demons" and penned the following:

> The fatherhood of St. Joseph terrorizes the devil.
> The humility of St. Joseph terrorizes the devil.
> The charity of St. Joseph terrorizes the devil.

The poverty of St. Joseph terrorizes the devil.
The purity of St. Joseph terrorizes the devil.
The obedience of St. Joseph terrorizes the devil.
The silence of St. Joseph terrorizes the devil.
The suffering of St. Joseph terrorizes the devil.
The prayer of St. Joseph terrorizes the devil.
The name of St. Joseph terrorizes the devil.
The sleep of St. Joseph terrorizes the devil. . . .
All fatherhood is a threat to Satan.[125]

Our families truly need St. Joseph's intercession and protection. When my marriage was going through a very rocky time, I wrote my husband's name on a sticky note, which I then folded up and tucked into the hand of a St. Joseph statue in the Adoration chapel. I told no one except my confessor. St. Joseph definitely worked wonders for us.

In spiritual combat, when you stay close to your Commander and your comrades the saints, there is nothing to fear. Experience God's victory each day by noting the little ways that loving acts *prevent*, *protect*, and *prevail* over evil.

Strategy: Unmasking Diabolical Disguises

This book can neither contain a complete inventory of diabolical disguises nor go into the details of each, but I'll list the most common threats to families, especially (but not exclusively) to young people.

---

[125] Donald H. Calloway, M.I.C., *Consecration to St. Joseph: The Wonders of Our Spiritual Father* (Stockbridge, MA: Marian Press, 2020), 220–221.

Teens and preteens are being pulled into diabolical things on the Internet. Recently, a priest shared that an eight-year-old girl caused her family's house to become diabolically infested. The little girl and her friend were online when they came across a video on how to summon a demon. The two girls followed the directions on the video, and within twenty hours, the home was plagued with manifestations of evil spirits: lights in the home turned on and off by themselves, doors and drawers opened and shut on their own, stenches filled the place. The entire family was frightened. The two little girls believed they were just playing around, but summoning a demon is not a game. Demons are quick to oblige disordered curiosity.

Be aware of what your children see online; police them well. The dark web is a free-for-all. It is the hyper-curious, naïve, or desperate person who seeks the services of psychics and fortune-tellers, reads horoscopes and tarot cards, and is pulled into online occult how-to videos. For kids, this is make-believe. As adults, we have a responsibility to teach the truth about the dangers these things present to their pure souls. We mustn't be afraid or naïve about these things, only vigilant. Educate your children, pray daily deliverance prayers, and, if needed, call a priest.

Pornogrind

Pornogrind is a genre of heavy metal music often defined by its sexually violent lyrics. Fr. Gabriele Amorth writes about the dangerous effects of pornogrind music on the minds of listeners:

> Records consecrated to Satan are based on the following four principles: beat, volume intensity, subliminal signal,

> and ritual consecration of every recording during a black mass. The first important item is the rhythm, called beat, which mimics the sexual act. Abruptly the listeners are caught up in a frenzy designed to produce a sort of hysteria. It's a result of the sexual instinct which is aroused through the use of beat. Secondly, the volume is deliberately set to at least seven decibels above the tolerance level of our nervous system. Prolonged exposure to such a noise level induces a type of depression, rebelliousness, and aggression. Thirdly, subliminal signs are transmitted at such a high pitch that we are unable to hear them. The signal is meant to disorient; at an intensity of 3,000 kilocycles per second, it acts on our unconscious, but our ears cannot capture it precisely because it is supersonic. Unknown to us, the brain produces a natural drug as a result of the stimuli it receives, and it disorients us. Suddenly, we feel strange. The strange feeling induces us to seek real drugs and drug addicts to increase their intake. Finally, before each record is released on the market, it is consecrated to Satan through a ritual that is a true black mass.[126]

Some serial killers have admitted to being into pornogrind music. For example, according to *USA Today*, twenty-four-year-old Connor Betts, who killed nine people in Dayton, Ohio, was the lead singer in a pornogrind band.[127]

---

[126] Fr. Gabriele Amorth, *An Exorcist: More Stories* (San Francisco: Ignatius Press, 2002), 73.

[127] Rachel Berry et al., "Dayton shooting gunman who police say killed 9 was in a 'pornogrind' metal band," *USA Today*, August 5, 2019, https://www.usatoday.com/story/news/nation/2019/08/05/connor-betts-dayton-gunman-pornogrind-metal-band/1926467001/.

Santa Muerte

Santa Muerte means "St. Death," or "Holy Death," and is a religious cult that is extremely popular in Mexico. The cult includes some aspects of witchcraft and Satanism combined with Catholicism. Santa Muerte has its own priests and holds religious services to obtain favors, which happen to come from demons.

The image of Santa Muerte is a female grim reaper commonly seen on clothing, tattoos, storefronts called botanicas, and media. Practitioners pray to St. Death to seek various favors, such as financial prosperity, success in love, protection from wrongdoing, or revenge against enemies. It's common knowledge that drug cartels, gang members, and criminals pray to her to keep them safe or to help them profit from their crimes.

Church officials in Latin America regularly rebuke the practice of Santa Muerte, but their counterparts in the United States have been slow to do so. Among the few U.S. Catholic bishops to have denounced Santa Muerte are Santa Fe Archbishop John Wester, El Paso Bishop Mark Seitz, and San Angelo Bishop Michael Sis. According to *Crux*, "Sis said La Santa Muerte is 'spiritually dangerous' and has no link to Catholicism. 'It should be completely avoided. It is a perversion of devotion to the saints.'"[128]

De-baptism

It's become increasingly popular for baptized Christians to undergo a "de-baptism." One organization that promotes the prac-

---

[128] Russell Contreras, "New Mexico archbishop again denounces 'Santa Muerte,'" *Crux*, March 25, 2019, https://cruxnow.com/church-in-the-usa/2019/03/new-mexico-archbishop-again-denounces-santa-muerte/.

tice is the National Secular Society in London, England. Here is a sample of the text printed on the society's official certificate:

> I ______ having been subjected to the Rite of Christian Baptism in infancy (before reaching an age of consent), hereby publicly revoke any implications of the Rite and renounce the Church that carried it out. In the name of human reason, I reject all its Creeds and all other such superstition in particular, the perfidious belief that any baby needs to be cleansed by Baptism of alleged ORIGINAL SIN, and the evil power of supposed demons. I wish to be excluded henceforth from enhanced claims of church membership numbers based on past baptismal statistics used, for example, for the purpose of securing legislative privilege.[129]

The person, along with a witness, signs the certificate, which is then sealed by the National Secular Society.

That demons seduce souls into "de-baptism" is a backhanded testimony to the deliverance power and protection of sacramental Baptism. As one Aleteia article explains: "A pastor is not able to remove a person from their baptismal registry because of the permanent nature of baptism. Atheists and Satanists who repent of their sins are gladly welcomed back into the fold of Jesus Christ and do not need to be baptized again."[130]

---

129 "Atheist group sells certificates of debaptism," Catholic News Agency, April 3, 2009, https://www.catholicnewsagency.com/news/atheist_group_sells_certificates_of_debaptism.

130 Philip Kosloski, "Can a Catholic be 'de-baptized'?," Aleteia, August 20, 2019, https://aleteia.org/2019/08/20/can-a-catholic-be-de-baptized/.

Magic

According to the *Catechism*, "all practices of *magic* or *sorcery*, by which one attempts to tame occult powers, so as to place them at one's service and have a supernatural power over others—even if this was for the sake of restoring their health—are gravely contrary to the virtue of religion" (CCC 2117). Fr. Amorth explains:

> The definition of magic tells us two things. Above all, it has ambition—through the utilization of evil spells, the evil eye, charms, magic filters, rituals, invocations, cursed foods and drinks ingested by the victims, crystal balls, et cetera—to modify and foretell the course of human events, and to utilize the preternatural (demonic) powers to make a person fall in love, be cured of an illness, be dismissed from a job, kill someone, provoke atmospheric events, et cetera. In other words, magic is a practice to do evil things and to influence people and the reality by the devil. This is also valid for the rites that are commonly called "white magic" and that are done for the good.... Magic is seriously contrary to the First Commandment: "You shall have no other gods before me" (Exod. 20:3).[131]

Divination: Ouija Boards, Tarot Cards, Pendulums

The *Catholic Encyclopedia* defines *divination* and explains its demonic origins as follows:

> From a theological standpoint divination supposes the existence of devils who have great natural powers and who,

[131] Amorth, *Exorcist Explains*, 38, 39.

> actuated by jealousy of man and hatred of God, ever seek to lessen his glory and to draw man into perdition, or at least to injure him bodily, mentally, and spiritually. Divination is not... foretelling what comes from necessity or what generally happens, or foretelling what God reveals or what can be discovered by human effort, but it is the usurpation of knowledge of the future, i.e. arriving at it by inadequate or improper means. This knowledge is a prerogative of Divinity and so the usurper is said to divine. Such knowledge may not be sought from the evil spirits except rarely in exorcisms. Yet every divination is from them either because they are expressly invoked or they mix themselves up in these vain searchings after the future that they may entangle men in their snares. The demon is invoked tacitly when anyone tries to acquire information through means which he knows to be inadequate, and the means are inadequate when neither from their own nature nor from any Divine promise are they capable of producing the desired effect. Since the knowledge of futurity belongs to God alone, to ask it directly or indirectly from demons is to attribute to them Divine perfection, and to ask their aid is to offer them a species of worship; this is superstition and a rebellion against the providence of God Who has wisely hidden many things from us.[132]

The *Catechism* explicitly condemns divination and offers examples of this dangerous practice:

---

[132] Edward Graham, "Divination," in the *Catholic Encyclopedia*, vol. 5 (New York: Robert Appleton Company, 1909), https://www.newadvent.org/cathen/05048b.htm.

> All forms of *divination* are to be rejected: recourse to Satan or demons, conjuring up the dead or other practices falsely supposed to "unveil" the future. Consulting horoscopes, astrology, palm reading, interpretation of omens and lots, the phenomena of clairvoyance, and recourse to mediums all conceal a desire for power over time, history, and, in the last analysis, other human beings, as well as a wish to conciliate hidden powers. They contradict the honor, respect, and loving fear that we owe to God alone. (CCC 2116)

Ouija board. A Ouija board is a means of divination that uses a board with an alphabet and other things printed on it and a planchette—a flat, heart-shaped piece of plastic with a window in it. Two people place their hands on the planchette. It moves and gives yes/no answers or spells out an answer. The movie *The Exorcist* features a Ouija board as the means by which the character Regan is courted by the demon who possesses her. People have become demonically afflicted after playing with a Ouija board. Repent, renounce, and confess sacramentally if you have played with a Ouija board, please.

Tarot cards. Tarot cards are a deck of cards with symbolic pictures on them used to determine the future. The cards are laid in a particular pattern, and the relationship between them communicates things about a person's life and future. These and other means of divination involve the invocation of spirits. This is a way to allow a demon access to a person's life. Even if the user believes that the information comes from a universal energy field, that does not preclude the involvement of a demon providing the information.

Pendulum. A pendulum is an object hanging from a string that is swung to find the answer to questions, for example, concerning the location of lost objects or good places to perform a magic ritual; or inquiries into health, gambling, relationships, and the like.

New Age Terminology

New Age ideas are addressed in the Church document *Jesus Christ, the Bearer of the Water of Life.*[133] Much of the doctrine of the New Age is the antithesis of Christianity. There is no sin, no guilt. Suffering and sickness do not really exist. There is no need for redemption or redemptive suffering or sacrifice. Christ is interpreted as a transpersonal being that everyone is. Forgiveness is not needed: no one is permanently damned or punished. All will reunite with God. I've heard heartbreaking stories about families torn asunder by New Age lies.

A few popular New Age ideas are as follows:

- *Chakras.* This term is used to describe seven doors in the human body that must be aligned for healing to take effect.
- *Soul tie.* Soul ties describe how a "bridge into our souls" can be created through our consent, directly or indirectly. As such, the souls of two people can become "knit" together through holy friendship (see, for example, the friendship of David and Jonathan, 1 Sam. 18:1–3). But there can also be unhealthy soul ties, created through fornication or adultery, for example. A soul tie can also

[133] Pontifical Council for Culture, Pontifical Council for Interreligious Dialogue, *Jesus Christ, the Bearer of the Water of Life: A Christian Reflection on the New Age* (February 3, 2003).

be created through engagement in other evil acts, such as New Age and occult activities, which make one a partner in evil and iniquity.

- *Energy*. This can include "universal" energy, chi (also spelled "qi" or "ki"), or prana depending on the New Age practice or therapy. It is pantheistic[134] and therefore opens doors to the demonic.
- *Karma*. The Hindu or Buddhist concept of karma is the idea that our actions in former lives determine our destiny. It therefore espouses reincarnation.

Witchcraft

The *Catholic Encyclopedia* offers the following explanation of witchcraft:

> It is not easy to draw a clear distinction between magic and witchcraft. Both are concerned with the producing of effects beyond the natural powers of man by agencies other than the Divine. But in witchcraft, as commonly understood, there is involved the idea of a diabolical pact or at least an appeal to the intervention of the spirits of evil. In such cases this supernatural aid is usually invoked either to compass the death of some obnoxious person, or to awaken the passion of love in those who are the objects of desire, or to call up the dead, or to bring calamity or impotence upon enemies, rivals, and fancied oppressors. This is not an exhaus-

[134] The *Catechism* defines *pantheism* as the belief that "everything is God, that the world is God, or that the development of the world is the development of God" (CCC 285).

> tive enumeration, but these represent some of the principal purposes that witchcraft has been made to serve at nearly all periods of the world's history.[135]

Religious Syncretism

Bernard D. Green defines *syncretism* as follows:

> The syncretistic tendency can be defined as the attempt to appropriate ideas and practices from a variety of spiritual traditions without any attempt to discriminate their truth or value on the basis of Catholic faith. One way in which the equality and compatibility of various religions is justified is by subsuming their various dimensions under generic categories. So, the writings of different religions are all put on the same level by being labeled "sacred." Similarly, different deities are subsumed under the general category of the Transcendent, and various rituals are all considered to serve the same function of contacting and establishing unity with the Transcendent.[136]

This à la carte approach to religion is on the rise in the United States:

> The religious beliefs and practices of Americans do not fit neatly into conventional categories. A poll by the Pew

---

135 Herbert Thurston, "Witchcraft," in the *Catholic Encyclopedia*, vol. 15 (New York: Robert Appleton Company, 1908), https://www.newadvent.org/cathen/15674a.htm.

136 Bernard D. Green, "Catholicism Confronts New Age Syncretism," *New Oxford Review* 61, no. 3 (April 1994), https://www.ewtn.com/catholicism/library/catholicism-confronts-new-age-syncretism-11322.

> Research Center's Forum on Religion & Public Life finds that large numbers of Americans engage in multiple religious practices, mixing elements of diverse traditions. Many say they attend worship services of more than one faith or denomination—even when they are not traveling or going to special events like weddings and funerals. Many also blend Christianity with Eastern or New Age beliefs such as reincarnation, astrology and the presence of spiritual energy in physical objects. And sizeable minorities of all major U.S. religious groups say they have experienced supernatural phenomena, such as being in touch with the dead or with ghosts.[137]

Syncretism, however, must be rejected by all Catholics:

> Catholicism is not a syncretistic religion, but a synthetic one, always seeking to bring forth something new as it learns from its interactions with every culture and religion. Because it is Catholic, it does not wish to overlook anything in other traditions which is good and touched by grace. It enters into cultures and seeks to preach the Good News to all peoples through their own language and cultural forms.[138]

We simply can't mix the Rosary with a witch's incantations, potions, or spells and call it Catholic.

---

137 "Many Americans Mix Multiple Faiths," Pew Research Center, December 9, 2009, www.pewforum.org/2009/12/09/many-americans-mix-multiple-faiths.

138 Green, "Catholicism Confronts New Age Syncretism."

Superstition

The following passage from the *Catechism* summarize the Church's teaching on superstition:

> The first commandment forbids honoring gods other than the one Lord who has revealed himself to his people. It proscribes superstition and irreligion. Superstition in some sense represents a perverse excess of religion. . . . Superstition is the deviation of religious feeling and of the practices this feeling imposes. To attribute the efficacy of prayers or of sacramental signs to their mere external performance, apart from the interior dispositions that they demand, is to fall into superstition. (CCC 2110, 2111)

There is no such thing as benign superstitious practices, such as checking horoscopes, because these practices can form an attitude or habit of seeking something other than God and not walking in faith.

Santeria

The BBC offers the following overview of Santeria:

> The religion focuses on building relationships between human beings and powerful, but mortal, spirits, called Orishas. An Orisha is a manifestation of Olodumare (God). Followers believe that these spirits will give them help in life, if they carry out the appropriate rituals, and enable them to achieve the destiny that God planned for them before they were born. This is very much a mutual relationship as the

> Orishas need to be worshipped by human beings if they are to continue to exist. Orishas can be perceived in the physical universe by initiates, and the whole community can share in their presence when they possess a priest during some rituals.[139]

In his book *The Devil in the City of Angels*, Jesse Romero describes Santeria as "a mixture of Catholicism and polytheistic African beliefs, but they practice stuff like magic, luck, consulting spirits, and other things that the mainstream Catholic Church does not practice. These are called sins of superstitions, which are a violation of the first commandment." He continues: "The term botanica also comes from Santeria, but it has come to serve as a catch-all name in this country for any occult shop in a Hispanic neighborhood selling orthodox and not-so orthodox religious goods. These stores tend to be run by folk healers who have a clientele that they help with a number of personal and spiritual problems."[140]

Wicca

Wicca, also known as the Craft, is a modern, neopagan religious movement whose participants seek to be in tune with the forces of nature, which it identifies with God. Wiccans form covens. Each coven has a high priest and priestess. Wiccans celebrate rituals, sometimes in the nude; use magic; cast spells; and invoke gods and spirits. They often perform their activities within a circle after

[139] "Santeria deities," Religion and Ethics, BBC, last updated September 15, 2009, http://www.bbc.co.uk/religion/religions/santeria/beliefs/orishas.shtml.

[140] Jesse Romero, *The Devil in The City of Angels* (Charlotte, NC: TAN Books, 2019), 90.

drawing a pentagram. They do not worship Satan. They do not cast spells to harm others, since their basic law is "do not harm." They also specialize in herbal and other alternative medicines. Not all witches are part of Wicca.

Wiccans invoke powers and spirits to achieve their magical purposes, which can be an opening for demonic activity. They can become addicted to the power that their magic seems to give them, which can lead them to pursue other occult activities and even black magic.

Church teaching on Wicca is taken from the Bible and the *Catechism:*

> There shall not be found among you any one who burns his son or his daughter as an offering, any one who practices divination, a soothsayer, or an augur, or a sorcerer, or a charmer, or a medium, or a wizard, or a necromancer. For whoever does these things is an abomination to the LORD. (Deut. 18:10–12)

> All practices of magic or sorcery, by which one attempts to tame occult powers, so as to place them at one's service and a have a supernatural power over others—even if this were for the sake of restoring their health—are gravely contrary to the virtue of religion. (CCC 2117)

Yoga

Many people believe yoga is just a stretching exercise, but this is not exactly true. The theory of yoga includes a powerful, non-physical force, which could be an opening to the demonic.

I'll start by sharing that, very recently, an experienced exorcist shared the following experience at a conference. He underwent major surgery, and before he was discharged from the hospital, a nurse handed him a piece of paper with yoga stretches to quicken his recovery. The priest politely said, "I do not do yoga." The nurse waved the sheet in the air and tried to hand it to him again. He repeated, "I do not do yoga." A third time, the nurse attempted to give Father the yoga instructions. A third time, the exorcist said, "I do not do yoga." Finally, the nurse opened another drawer and handed Father a different paper with stretching instructions unrelated to yoga.

If an exorcist priest won't do yoga, I'm convinced that it could be a doorway to demonic vexation.

Appendix B includes a registered nurse's story of how her life fell apart after she became a yoga master. She required many deliverance prayers, but finally, she renounced yoga, repented, and was liberated. She worked very hard to restore her finances, family relationships, physical health, and nursing career.

Here's an excerpt from Dominican friar Ezra Sullivan's excellent series on yoga:

> One indication of yoga's spiritual nature is the way it affects practitioners over time. *The International Journal of Yoga* published the results of a national survey in Australia. Physical postures (asana) comprised about 60% of the yoga they practiced; 40% was relaxation (savasana), breathing techniques (pranayama), meditation, and instruction. The survey showed very significant results: although most respondents commonly began yoga for reasons of physical health, they

usually continued it for reasons of spirituality. In addition, the more people practiced yoga, the more likely they were to decrease their adherence to Christianity and the more likely they were to adhere to non-religious spirituality and Buddhism.

In other words, whatever their intentions may have been, many people experience yoga as a gateway to a spirituality disconnected from Christ.

Doing justice to the complete nature of yoga, therefore, requires a more well-rounded definition: "A comprehensive system of human culture, physical, moral, and [psychological], and acting as a doorway on to the gently sloping paths that gradually lead up to yoga proper," that is, the spirituality of yoga founded in Hinduism.

Its aim is to control the body and the various forms of vital energy, with a view of overcoming physical impediments standing in the way of other, spiritual, forms of yoga. Its object is to ensure a perfect balance between the organic functions. Its ultimate goal and true end is to prepare man for the acquisition of that repose of spirit necessary for the realization of the "Supreme", or for "experiencing the Divine."

Yoga's religious and spiritual end is often forgotten or denied in a Western context; most people see it simply as a physical form of exercise. Such a simplification is unwarranted and dangerous.... Reducing yoga to a mere beautifying technique frequently creates ugly effects.[141]

---

[141] Fr. Ezra Sullivan, O.P., "What is Yoga? A Catholic Perspective (Part I)," *Spiritual Direction* (blog), January 29, 2014, www.spiritualdirection.com/2014/01/29/what-is-yoga-catholic-perspective-part-i.

Here are some facts and pronouncements from the Church. On October 15, 1989, the Congregation for the Doctrine of the Faith released its *Letter to the Bishops of the Catholic Church on Some Aspects of Christian Meditation*, warning about physical practices that are mixed with non-Christian teachings. The CDF noted, "The expression 'eastern methods' is used to refer to methods which are inspired by Hinduism and Buddhism, such as 'Zen', 'Transcendental Meditation' or 'Yoga.'"[142]

Some Catholic commentators say it is permissible to do the stretches and breathing exercises, so long as your teacher does not add any of the Hindu philosophy to his presentation. Caution is required, because sometimes the Hinduism is slipped in subtly. Christian alternatives include SoulCore or Pilates (not mixed with spiritual yoga). We are aware of Catholics, including clergy and nuns, who engage in yoga. But we don't know whether this is negatively affecting them or not. My guess is that some people do not connect the dots between yoga and negative experiences they may be having.

Some people connected yoga to their need for exorcism; others did not. In some cases, yoga became one problem among many that opened the doorway to demons. For the nurse who became a yoga master, yoga was the *only* identifiable doorway to the demonic destruction occurring in her life.

Here's a quote about yoga from an experienced exorcist: "I have one person who was deep into yoga and is oppressed severely; however, she got deep into its spirituality and started to live and

---

[142] Congregation for the Doctrine of the Faith, *Letter to the Bishops of the Catholic Church on Some Aspects of Christian Meditation* (October 15, 1989), n. 1.

work with those who practice the occult. From my personal perspective, I don't think someone who stretches on a mat in the morning yoga class is likely to become possessed, but those who enter deeply into its non-Christian spirituality have a problem." Please read in appendix B the testimony of the registered nurse who became a yoga master, and exercise good discernment.

Reiki

The USCCB has published guidelines on the evaluation of Reiki, an Eastern technique that purports to heal patients by manipulating their "universal life energy." The USCCB says that Reiki is neither scientific nor Christian. Rather, it is superstitious.

> Since Reiki therapy is not compatible with either Christian teaching or scientific evidence, it would be inappropriate for Catholic institutions, such as Catholic health care facilities and retreat center, or persons representing the Church, such as Catholic chaplains, to promote or to provide support for Reiki therapy.[143]

Curses

Exorcist Fr. Jose Fortea defines a *curse* as "an action that is done to harm another with the help of demons," for instance, "to kill, to cause one to be possessed, to make things go bad in business, to make someone sick." Of the remedies for curses, Father writes:

---

143 United States Conference of Catholic Bishops Committee on Doctrine, "Guidelines for Evaluating Reiki as an Alternative Therapy," March 25, 2009, http://www.usccb.org/about/doctrine/publications/upload/evaluation-guidelines-finaltext-2009-03.pdf.

> When people come to my parish saying that they are suffering from a curse, I tell them that it is impossible to prove demonic causality except in rare cases. But if they really suffer from a curse, the only remedy is to do the following: (1) Pray the Rosary, (2) Read the Bible, (3) Speak with God every day, (4) Attend Mass frequently, even daily, (5) Place a blessed crucifix and an image of the Blessed Virgin Mary in one's home, (6) Make the sign of the cross with holy water daily.[144]

Generational Curses

Fr. Amorth writes:

> Each exorcist develops a personal position [on generational curses] based on his considerable experience. I have had some cases in which persons suffering demonic possession had ancestors who practiced magic and witchcraft. Moreover, I have ascertained that a curse can be transmitted [from one generation to the next], particularly if it is issued by a father or a mother against a son, his marriage, and his future children.... Curses, which are wishes of evil, are extremely powerful, especially if they are made with real treachery by those who are related by varying degrees of kinship to the victim. But they can be conquered with blessings. Jesus said, "Bless those who curse you, pray for those who abuse you" (Luke 6:28).... My teacher, Father Candido Amantini, has serious doubts that sinful tendencies spread generationally.... But even with this doubt, I always advise

144 Fortea, *Interview with an Exorcist*, 110, Kindle.

> the afflicted to make whatever sacrifices are necessary to break each evil spell.[145]

In appendix A, you will find an exorcist's "Prayer to Remove Generational Spirits" that laypersons may pray to break a curse.

Satanism

There are two forms of Satanism: theistic and atheistic. Theistic Satanists believe that Satan is a real entity, either a person or an impersonal force, that needs to be acknowledged. They believe that their rituals and prayers are directed to a real being. They often practice magic. Satanists promote a self-focused morality that is hedonistic, power-seeking, and vengeful. Their main ritual is the black mass, which may involve the desecration of the Eucharist as well as various sexual activities.

The 1975 CDF document *Christian Faith and Demonology* addresses Satan and demons:

> The many forms of superstition, obsessional preoccupation with Satan and the demons, and the different kinds of worship of them or attachment to them have always been condemned by the Church. It would therefore be incorrect to hold that Christianity, forgetful of the universal Lordship of Christ, had at any time made Satan the privileged subject of its preaching, transforming the Good News of the Risen Lord into a message of terror.[146]

---

145 Amorth, *Exorcist Explains*, 60–61.

146 Congregation for the Doctrine of the Faith, *Christian Faith and Demonology* (June 26, 1975).

Satanism is briefly mentioned in *Jesus Christ, the Bearer of the Water of Life*.[147]

Freemasonry

The Church has persistently condemned Freemasonry and forbade Catholics to belong to a Masonic lodge.

> Of all the Papal condemnations of Freemasonry, Pope Leo XIII's 1884 Encyclical *Humanum Genus* stands unparalleled in strength and brilliance. A more complete and concise explanation and condemnation of the evils and errors of Masonry will not be found in any other magisterial pronouncement. Again and again in this encyclical, the Pope emphasizes that the goal of Freemasonry is nothing less than the utter destruction of the Church and Christianity. He writes, "No longer making any secret of their purpose, they are now boldly rising up against God Himself. They are planning the destruction of the holy church publicly and openly, and this with the set purpose of utterly despoiling the nations of Christendom, if it were possible, of the blessings obtained for us through Jesus Christ our Savior."
>
> Pope Leo explains that since Masonry is based on Naturalism, it is anti-Christian in its essence. Naturalism holds that human nature and human reason are supreme, and that there are no truths revealed by God that men are bound to believe. Naturalists deny the authority of the Catholic Church

---

[147] Congregation for the Doctrine of the Faith, *Jesus Christ, the Bearer of the Water of Life*, no. 2.3.4.1.

> as God's voice upon earth, and therefore, "It is against the Church that the rage and the attack of enemies (Freemasons) are principally directed." Pope Leo explained that one of their most powerful means of warring against the Church is their promotion of religious indifferentism—the idea that it really does not matter which religion one belongs to.[148]

The Church's most recent pronouncement against Freemasonry was the *Declaration on Masonic Associations*, published by the CDF in 1983. It states: "The Church's negative judgment in regard to Masonic association remains unchanged since their principles have always been considered irreconcilable with the doctrine of the Church and therefore membership in them remains forbidden. The faithful who enroll in Masonic associations are in a state of grave sin and may not receive Holy Communion."[149]

Video Games, TV, Media

Prudence is necessary regarding television, social media, the Internet, and magic or occult games. Demons attempt destruction of faith by esoteric (cryptic, secret, occult) practices aimed especially at young people. Professors have warned that evil spirits and curses can be associated with certain forms of entertainment.

I've been told by exorcists that it is difficult to liberate a person from addiction to video games. The following anecdote illustrates why:

---

148 John Vennari, *The Permanent Instruction of the Alta Vendita* (Charlotte, NC: TAN Books, 1999), 41–42.

149 Congregation for the Doctrine of the Faith, *Declaration on Masonic Organizations* (November 26, 1983).

A long-time video gamer and devout Catholic is sounding the alarm about a new breed of satanically-themed video games that target God and the Catholic Church, invite players to make pacts with the devil, and elevate Satan to hero status.

"This has been going on for the last 10 years, but especially in the most recent games," said Lance Christian, 32, of Alton, Illinois. "It wasn't until last month when I said, 'enough is enough!' I'm a gamer, but I'm deep into my faith and I think God is showing me this so I can make other people aware of it."

He has seen games gradually become more occult-based, promoting Satan and even the persecution of Christians. For instance, in one game, players kill the Archangels Michael, Gabriel and Raphael before going on to destroy God. Another game requires players to sell their soul to the devil and rewards them for "killing unbaptized infants."

All these games seem to have one central theme—God is the enemy and the devil is the hero. One game guide blatantly states: "The Judeo-Christian God is portrayed as the prominent villain in the series."

"This is just the tip of the iceberg in what I have discovered," Mr. Christian said. "I feel that the devil has a new tool to work with in this age of technology, and the majority of adults in a position of responsibility are left in the dark."[150]

---

[150] Susan Brinkmann, "Gaming for Satan: New Video Games Mock the Church and Glorify Satan," *Women of Grace* (blog), February 5, 2010, https://www.womenofgrace.com/blog/?p=3966.

Catholic versus Demonic Symbols

We Catholics use meaningful symbols, tokens, and signs to indicate our common Faith. In the *Catechism*, we learn about the Greek word *symbolon*, from which the word *symbol* originates:

> The Greek word *symbolon* meant half of a broken object, for example, a seal presented as a token of recognition. The broken parts were placed together to verify the bearer's identity. The symbol of faith, then, is a sign of recognition and communion between believers. *Symbolon* also means a gathering, collection or summary. A symbol of faith is a summary of the principal truths of the faith and therefore serves as the first and fundamental point of reference for catechesis. (CCC 188)

This information is relevant in spiritual combat because evil spirits erect their own system of symbols, tokens, and signs, which invert or pervert their Christian counterparts. These symbols indicate participation in the reality they symbolize. A symbol is a form of a spirit presence that is not neutral because, in the spirit world, there is no neutrality. The spirit is either of God, of the devil, or of a human.

I want to caution families about keeping non-Catholic symbols, tokens, and signs in the home. Exercise prudence, and be aware of a child's suspicious attachment to a sign or symbol. A person may be easily led into a relationship with that which the symbol represents. For example, I wear a crucifix around my neck every day as jewelry. But to me, it's not just a piece of jewelry: it symbolizes my association with Jesus Christ hanging on the Cross.

Witches, Wiccans, Satanists, and occultists have signs and symbols that are not benign. They "brand" a person, so to speak. In marketing, it is customary for companies to craft a logo to signal their identity and purpose. Demons are cunning marketers.

One popular common symbol in homes is a *dreamcatcher*. I've seen it on the walls of children's bedrooms. Here's what a dreamcatcher symbolizes:

> This tradition is part of the shamanistic beliefs of Native Americans. The original dream catcher is said to have originated with the Ojibway (Chippewa) tribe although other tribes such as the Lakotas also lay claim to the object. For instance, a Lakota legend says the dream catcher was given in a vision to a spiritual leader by a spirit named Iktomi, a searcher of wisdom, who appeared in the form of a spider. Using the leader's willow hoop, which was decorated with feathers and beads, Iktomi began to spin a web that represented the good and bad forces of life. When he was finished, he had created a web in the shape of a perfect circle with a hole in the middle. He gave it to the leader and told him to allow his people to use the web to achieve their dreams. If they believe in the great spirit, the web will filter their good ideas and trap the bad ones.
>
> Because Native Americans believe that the night air is filled with dreams, both good and bad, they would hang a dream catcher over or near their bed at night in order to filter their dreams.
>
> Obviously, this is a superstition based on a pagan belief system. Even though dream catchers (and anything Native

American for that matter) are all the rage these days, I would pass on decorating my house—or myself—with any of these symbols.[151]

Pornography

The USCCB writes:

> Pornography is a grave offense against God and His gifts to men and women. God created men and women "in His image" to share in His divine life. Rather than respecting and cherishing this image of God, pornography promotes a harmful and destructive anthropology (view of the human person). It teaches people to use others as "objects"—in this case, a means of selfish, lustful gratification. In addition, since pornography attacks sexual desire and the conjugal act itself, it wages war on marriage.[152]

The harmful effects listed below are only a small sampling of the many evils of pornography:

- harm to the soul
- harm to personal morality and chastity
- harm to public morality
- harm to marriage
- increased violence toward women

---

151 Susan Brinkmann, "What's Wrong with Wearing Occult or Native American Symbols?," *Women of Grace* (blog), July 14, 2011, https://www.womenofgrace.com/blog/?p=1187.

152 "Pornography," United States Conference of Catholic Bishops, accessed September 30, 2019, http://www.usccb.org/issues-and-action/marriage-and-family/natural-family-planning/resources/pornography.cfm.

- alteration of brain patterns (which is especially harmful to children)
- possibility of decreased brain matter[153]
- increased stimulation and perversity, which may lead to rape
- risk of contracting sexually transmitted diseases
- harm to innocent persons assaulted and murdered by those stimulated by porn, such as serial killer Ted Bundy, who admitted that he grew up consuming pornography

In November 2015, the USCCB formally approved *Create in Me a Clean Heart: a Pastoral Response to Pornography*. The document discusses Church teaching on human sexuality and chastity, explains why pornography is inherently sinful, examines the ways it harms individuals and society, and suggests a pathway for those who wish to break their addiction. "In our duty as pastors and shepherds to proclaim Christ," the bishops wrote, "we must state clearly that all pornography is immoral and harmful and using pornography may lead to other sins, and possibly, even crimes." Below are some highlights from the bishops' statement.

- "[Sexual] intimacy should not be put on display or be watched by any other person, even if that person is one's own spouse. Nor should the human body be unveiled or treated in a way that objectifies it sexually and reduces it to an erotic stimulant."
- Pornography is directly associated with "adultery, domestic violence, the abuse of children in child pornography, and

[153] Catholic News Agency, "Fighting the 'Porn Myth' with science," *Catholic World Report*, March 27, 2017, https://www.catholicworldreport.com/2017/03/27/fighting-the-porn-myth-with-science/.

sex trafficking. It also can be implicated in contraception use and abortion, given that it promotes and even celebrates promiscuity and a view of sexuality devoid of love or openness to new life."

- "Pornography use within marriage severely damages the spouses' trust and intimacy both because of the pornography use itself and because of the deception and lies usually involved in one spouse hiding his or her behavior from the other. It has been identified by divorce lawyers as a major factor in over half of divorces."
- Pornography can cause people to become "trapped in a cycle of fantasy, ritual, acting out and despair"—a cycle the Church can help to break through "ongoing support such as counseling, spiritual direction, coaching, accountability groups, couple to couple groups, conferences, and retreats for men and women."[154]

Summary

St. Paul cautions us: "Satan disguises himself as an angel of light. So it is not strange if his servants also disguise themselves as servants of righteousness. Their end will correspond to their deeds" (2 Cor. 11:14–15).

I've presented some prevalent demonic disguises to alert families.

---

[154] United States Conference of Catholic Bishops, *Create in Me a Clean Heart: A Pastoral Response to Pornography*, November 17, 2015, http://www.usccb.org/issues-and-action/human-life-and-dignity/pornography/upload/Create-in-Me-a-Clean-Heart-Statement-on-Pornography.pdf, quoted in Jim Graves, "4 Experts Offer Advice on How to Conquer Porn Addiction," *National Catholic Register*, January 24, 2018, https://www.ncregister.com/blog/jimgraves/4-experts-offer-advice-on-how-to-conquer-porn-addiction.

I'm not sure that my parents had to worry about such things, but today, Catholic families need to be forewarned. Our Catholic viewpoint on demonic tactics is antithetical to the world's. Christ told us, "They are not of the world, even as I am not of the world" (John 17:16). We are called to stand apart from the world, which will persecute us. The hidden saints among us will continue the Catholic tradition of reconstructing what the devil or man has deconstructed.

Loved ones who wander away from Christ and His Church, who practice witchcraft or are involved in the occult—they are not beyond God's reach! Stay in communion with the Holy Spirit to intercede for your family always. If you have already been doing this for years, keep going: don't give up. God does not ignore your good efforts—they will bear fruit in due season. So what if you are in heaven when a child returns to the Faith, or a wayward spouse converts? You will have done for your family what God asked of you.

Our marriages and children may face very difficult times. Thankfully, there will always remain a faithful flock of Catholic families to seed a fresh blossoming of family life. Thereby Christ's victory is magnified.

Lord Jesus, I trust in you, who are worthy of all my trust and love. Graciously grant an increase of faith, hope, and love in my family. Amen.

9

HEALING THROUGH DELIVERANCE MINISTRY

Strategies: Renewing Baptismal Promises, the Father's Blessing, Praying for Healing, and Offering Up Suffering

> The Church, as a mother, never abandons the family, even when it is downhearted, wounded and humiliated in so many ways. Neither when it falls into sin nor moves away from the Church; she will always do everything to try to care for and heal it, to call it to conversion and to reconcile it to the Lord.[155]

Blessing our children and spouses is a dynamic expression of our baptismal authority and priestly duty in the family. Fr. Gabriele Amorth exhorts us to exercise our baptismal priestly gifts:

> Parents, as the priest of their own family, always have the duty to bless their family members, even by the laying on of hands. Even more so, parents have the right and the duty to make the sign of the cross on their children, blessing them.

[155] Pope Francis, General Audience (March 25, 2015).

> A parent's blessing is very efficacious. When I was small, I did not go to bed without my mother's blessing. Also, reciprocal blessings of spouses are highly advisable, because there is an extremely strong sacred bond between them, created through the sacrament of Marriage.[156]

Blessings bestow God's grace, edifying both the giver and receiver of the blessing. At Baptism, we were baptized priest, prophet, and king. Laypersons are not part of the ministerial priesthood, but we exercise a priestly ministry within our respective vocations.

Exorcists agree that *deliverance ministry* is the means by which most people find healing and freedom. Deliverance ministry involves not only casting out any demons, but also taking back any authority we may have ceded to the enemy due to our woundedness or sin. Much of this work can be done within the Catholic family and with the help of parish priests, mental-health professionals, and lay ministries such as Unbound.

What Is Deliverance Ministry?

Neal Lozano, executive director of Unbound, defines *deliverance ministry* as follows:

> Deliverance ministry is a participation in the ministry of Jesus, who came to set the captive free, deliver us from the power of sin, and destroy the works of the devil. It is a

[156] Fr. Gabriele Amorth, *Father Amorth: My Battle Against Satan* (Manchester, NH: Sophia Institute Press, 2018), 49.

> ministry of love and mercy, a ministry of the whole Church. Often, people understand deliverance ministry specifically as a form of minor exorcism, because it is directed at driving out evil spirits. But the meaning of the word "deliverance" is much richer and deeper than the ministry of casting out evil spirits or even the remnants of their influence. To understand deliverance ministry, we need to first see deliverance ministry in its broader context.[157]

Lozano's book provides one woman's practical testimony of deliverance related to marriage:

> I have struggled with anger and criticism toward my husband that I have been unable to control for years. I understood the root cause, but was still unable to get a handle on it. At the [Unbound] conference, I repented and renounced everything having to do with that subject that I could. I forgave everyone I could think of, as well. I was not sure if anything significant had happened....
>
> On the drive home...I repented very loudly for withdrawing my heart from my father, from God, and from my husband. I broke down and started to cry for several minutes. I renounced, and took command and felt like a weight had been lifted off my shoulders.
>
> It wasn't long before my first test. The very next morning my husband and I began to argue. Normally, I would shout back and get defensive. Instead, for the first time in

[157] Neal Lozano, *Resisting the Devil* (Huntington, IN: Our Sunday Visitor, 2009), 41.

> my marriage, I actually cried! I told my husband that he really hurt me when he yelled at me. I could not believe it was me! For the first time in so long, I felt like my heart was opening to him.[158]

This testimony is a good example of how, through woundedness, we close our hearts to loving intimacy. Only when we expose our wounds to God's light of love can we experience healing. I recall how difficult it was for me to tell my husband how he had hurt me and for my son to tell me how I had hurt him. For healing, the pain had to be exposed and our relationships strengthened by communication.

Healing is the reordering of the faculties that have been damaged because of our sins and the sins of others. Healing reorients a person's heart and life so that nothing comes between him and God. Healing is being free enough to be receptive of God's love and convinced of our identity as His beloved children. Knowing our true identity frees us from lies, both diabolical and human.

Jesus Christ is the Healer. The scriptural emphasis on healing is unveiled in Jesus' first sermon after His Baptism, when He went to Nazareth to preach in the synagogue.

> He stood up to read; and there was given to him the book of the prophet Isaiah. He opened the book and found the place where it was written, "The Spirit of the Lord is upon me, because he has anointed me to preach good news to the poor. He has sent me to proclaim release to

[158] Ibid., 42.

> the captives and recovering of sight to the blind, to set at liberty those who are oppressed, to proclaim the acceptable year of the Lord." . . . And he began to say to them, "Today this Scripture has been fulfilled in your hearing." (Luke 4:16–19, 21)

A Catholic Warrior's Rule of Life

The Church has long recognized the benefit of a rule of life for all her faithful—not just priests and nuns. "Many Catholics throughout the centuries have found themselves seeking to live their lives more perfectly for God. They sought the wisdom of the spiritual leaders of their time who, to 'make their election complete' (2 Peter 1:10) wrote down the attitudes and behaviors that they believed formed a person in virtue in order to rise to divine heights in their faith."[159]

Furthermore, we read in the *Catechism*, "by virtue of their kingly mission, lay people have the power to uproot the rule of sin within themselves and in the world, by their self-denial and holiness of life" (CCC 943).

Here, I propose *a Catholic warrior's rule of life.* I encourage you to create a personal rule of life tailored to your situation. A Norbertine priest shared that persons who join the Norbertine lay order create an *individualized* rule of life, since the Norbertines don't expect a homeschooling mother of six to follow the same spiritual regimen as an elderly empty-nester.

---

[159] TJ Burdick, "What A Rule Of Life Is And Why You Need One," Epic Pew, January 17, 2018, www.epicpew.com/rule-life-catholic/.

To be effective spiritual warriors capable of wielding defensive and offensive weapons, we must lead an intentional, ordered spiritual life every day. Consider the ideas below.

1. *Sacramental life.* Receive the sacraments with great regularity. If daily Mass is offered, strive to attend.
2. *Scripture.* Daily read the Bible (even for a brief time); reflect on the Four Gospels; pray the Psalms; consider Lectio Divina.[160]
3. *Liturgical life.* If possible, pray the Liturgy of the Hours. If you can't pray the full Divine Office, consider using the shorter edition printed in *Magnificat*'s monthly booklet (https://us.magnificat.net/). Celebrate the liturgical seasons.
4. *Adoration.* Visit the Blessed Sacrament as frequently as possible: it is very efficacious for healing and holiness.
5. *Virtue.* Strive for growth in the virtues;[161] keep the Ten Commandments and the Beatitudes; prioritize faith and family.
6. *Catholic sacramentals.*[162] Keep sacramentals in your home and on your person. Use holy water, blessed salt, scapulars, a St. Benedict crucifix, and Miraculous Medals.

---

160 "The method of *lectio divina* follows four steps: *lectio* (reading), *meditatio* (meditation), *contemplatio* (contemplation), and *oratio* (prayer)." "Ever Ancient, Ever New: The Art and Practice of *Lectio Divina*," United States Conference of Catholic Bishops, September 20, 2009, usccb.org/beliefs-and-teachings/how-we-teach/catechesis/catechetical-sunday/word-of-god/upload/lectio-divina.pdf.

161 "Virtue is a habitual and firm disposition to do good" (CCC 1833).

162 The *Baltimore Catechism*, no. 1052, defines a *sacramental* as "anything set apart or blessed by the Church to excite good thoughts and to increase devotion, and through these movements of the heart to remit venial sin."

7. *Daily prayer.* Pray especially for the Lord to heal any area that may have been an entryway for evil spirits. For example, if addiction to pornography is your predominant sin, pray specifically for purity and chastity.
8. *Consecration to Jesus through the Virgin Mary, St. Joseph, and St. Michael.* Practice lively devotion to the Holy Family.
9. *Prudence.* Avoid the places and associations that were doorways to any demonic bondage.
10. *Home oratory.* Create an area of the home reserved for prayer, complete with holy articles, and consider it holy ground for prayer only.
11. *The father's blessing.* Fathers, bless your families. Pray for each family member to receive the Eternal Father's blessing.
12. *Home consecration to the Sacred Heart.* Exorcists highly recommend this consecration as protection for the home and family.
13. *Devotion to Our Lady of Sorrows.* For protection, some exorcists recommend praying the Rosary of the Seven Sorrows, also known as the Seven Dolors Rosary.
14. *Holy environment.* In your line of sight, place objects such as icons, crucifixes, and pictures of saints so that your heart is frequently lifted to God.
15. *Sacred music.* Some exorcists recommend playing sacred music such as Gregorian Chant in the background to help sanctify the home atmosphere.
16. *Auxilium Christianorum prayers (www.auxiliumchristianorum.org).* These include prayers to be said every day and others to be recited on specific days of the week.
17. *Fasting.* Incorporate some form of fasting into your spiritual life to cultivate a spirit of poverty and sacrifice.

These are time-tested methods that provide powerful protection for you and your family. The devil will tempt you to doubt the spiritual efficacy of Catholic practices in the home. Know that these same sacramentals and prayers are used together with the Rite to expel demons.

A Personal Healing Exercise: The Seven R's

Over my years of accompanying people, I've learned the efficacy of spiritual exercises for inner healing. I created these for a retreat, but they are well suited to a Holy Hour.

1. *Review.* Prayerfully reflect on your history. Ask the Holy Spirit to reveal how you may have opened yourself to sin and evil by choosing something or someone other than God. Search for a root cause. A fever in the body indicates infection. For example, an addiction to pornography *may* originate from a traumatic experience. Prayerfully take your insights to Jesus at Calvary. Gaze at the Crucified Lord, aware that He is gazing at you.

2. *Repent.* Repent of the wounds you may have inflicted on yourself or others through neglecting God, yourself, or your family. Humbly apologize to the Lord. Pray for an abundance of divine mercy. Make an appointment with a priest for Confession. If you have never made a general confession, know that it has been proven to be quite healing.[163]

---

[163] "Usually, the term 'general confession' refers to going to confession and confessing all the sins of one's past life (or of an extended period, like the past year) instead of just those sins committed since one's previous confession. Traditionally, making this kind of confession has been a recommended spiritual practice for moments of major life transition." Fr. John Bartunek, L.C., "What Is A General Confession?," *Spiritual Direction* (blog), September 27, 2018, https://spiritualdirection.com/2018/09/27/what-is-a-general-confession.

3. *Release and forgive.* Imagine yourself at the foot of the Cross. Gather all the harm that has been done to you and that you have done to others. Consider any unforgiveness in your heart—the times that you could not forgive others or yourself. Release this into the Father's Heart. Offer a prayer of release and forgiveness. For example:

> *Eternal Father, I have been carrying a heavy burden. Years of sin—mine and that of others—insults, and injuries weigh me down so that I'm chained by lingering grief, anger, unforgiveness, and pain. I release it to you, Heavenly Father. I release all unforgiveness; please take it through the merits of your Son's Cross. Please liberate me that I may be free to love and serve as you ask. Amen.*

4. *Renounce.* Offer to the Eternal Father a prayer of renunciation. For example:

> *Eternal Father, I renounce the ways I have given my sexuality to sin; I renounce my sexual sins. I give my sexuality to Jesus Christ to be an instrument of righteousness. I renounce the way I have given my appetite and my drinking to sin; I renounce my sins of drunkenness and gluttony. I give my appetite and my drinking to Jesus Christ that I may be healed. I consecrate my life to the rule of Jesus Christ, to be His and His alone. May the atoning Precious Blood of Jesus Christ cover my sins and cleanse me. May your Holy Spirit possess and transform me. Amen.*

5. *Renew baptismal promises.* Internalize these promises. Sometimes, alone in Adoration, I make these a personal prayer: *Father, I reject Satan, and all his works, and all his empty promises,* et cetera.

V. *Do you reject Satan?* R. I do.

V. *And all his works?* R. I do.

V. *And all his empty promises?* R. I do.

V. *Do you believe in God, the Father Almighty, creator of heaven and earth?* R. I do.

V. *Do you believe in Jesus Christ, His only Son, Our Lord, who was born of the Virgin Mary, was crucified, died, and was buried, rose from the dead, and is now seated at the right hand of the Father?* R. I do.

V. *Do you believe in the Holy Spirit, the holy Catholic Church, the communion of saints, the forgiveness of sins, the resurrection of the body, and life everlasting?* R. I do.

V. *God, the all-powerful Father of Our Lord Jesus Christ has given us a new birth by water and the Holy Spirit, and forgiven all our sins. May He also keep us faithful to Our Lord Jesus Christ for ever and ever.* R. Amen.[164]

For a family service, a parent leads the renewal of baptismal promises. The family members renew their baptismal vows and sprinkle themselves with holy water.

6. *Receive.* Internalize God's healing mercy for you. Receive the stirring of the Holy Spirit in you. Reflect on God's Word:

O LORD, you have searched me and known me! You know when I sit down and when I rise up; you discern my thoughts from afar. You search out my path and my lying

[164] "Renewal of Baptismal Promises," Catholic Online, accessed April 30, 2020, https://www.catholic.org/prayers/prayer.php?p=1653.

> down, and are acquainted with all my ways. Even before a word is on my tongue, behold, O LORD, you know it altogether. You beset me behind and before, and lay your hand upon me. Such knowledge is too wonderful for me; it is high, I cannot attain it.... For you formed my inward parts, you knitted me together in my mother's womb. I praise you, for I am wondrously made. Wonderful are your works! You know me right well; my frame was not hidden from you, when I was being made in secret, intricately wrought in the depths of the earth. Your eyes beheld my unformed substance; in your book were written, every one of them, the days that were formed for me, when as yet there was none of them. (Ps. 139:1–6, 13–16)

7. *Rejoice.* Look again at a crucifix. Praise and thank the Lord for saving and loving you. Rejoice in your identity as a child of God. Pray: "The LORD is my strength and my shield; in him my heart trusts; so I am helped, and my heart exults, and with my song I give thanks to him" (Ps. 28:7).

Strategy: The Weapon of Renewing Baptismal Promises

Through the sacrament of Baptism, you received the Church's deliverance ministry and entered the perfect love of the Trinity. Here's an anecdote about the exorcistic power of renewing baptismal promises.

I know of a situation that occurred at a parish during Confession. The priest was in a partitioned confessional when he heard a loud thump in the penitent compartment. Arising, Father opened the door to check if the penitent was okay. The penitent, crouched in the corner of the little compartment, lunged onto Father, grabbed him by the neck, and hung there. She was strongly manifesting evil spirits in plain sight of other parishioners who were lined up for Confession. People ran to help the priest. It took several parishioners to subdue the woman, whom they then gently placed upon the steps of the sanctuary. As the parishioners restrained the woman, the priest was inspired to lead her through the renewal of baptismal promises. With effort, she managed to follow the priest's lead through the renunciations. Then, the manifestations stopped. Father made an appointment to follow up with the woman. Later, it was discovered that the woman's relatives were practicing Santeria.

Unbound Deliverance Method

Unbound is a nonconfrontational lay ministry of deliverance and healing. To the best of my knowledge, it is widely appreciated by clergy in dioceses around the world.[165] The ministry offers numerous resources, including books and media. Unbound uses Five Keys to help a person gain freedom: (1) repentance and faith, (2) forgiveness, (3) renouncing the work of your enemies, (4) standing in the authority you have in Christ, and (5) receiving God's blessing of your identity and destiny. The idea is to close the entryways through which evil spirits gain access to your life.[166]

---

165 "Heart of the Father: Endorsements," Heart of the Father, accessed July 24, 2020, https://www.heartofthefather.com/about/endorsements/.

166 Neal Lozano, *Unbound: A Practical Guide to Deliverance* (Grand Rapids: Chosen Books, 2003), 54.

From a Priest: How to Prepare for an Unbound Session

If you know a priest or trained layperson in your parish or diocese who could lead you or a family member through Unbound deliverance sessions, please avail yourself of this ministry. It has been helpful for countless people and provides excellent results.

A priest shared the following spiritual exercises that he gives to persons prior to leading them through Unbound. With Father's permission, I share his reflections below. His spiritual exercises can be helpful on their own or in connection with Unbound.

> *Form of Prayer: Prayer of Personal Reminiscence.*
> This preparation consists of a series of meditations to be done separately. There is no time limit for each meditation. Take the time you need to prepare your small story to tell the priest or minister in the Unbound session.
>
> Place yourself in the presence of God and ask the Holy Spirit to help you recall memories (personal events of your life) that are significant to your life and have formed you into the person you are. There are good memories, for which we are grateful, and bad memories, for which we seek healing. When a memory arises, try to relive it in the presence of Christ. See Him with you in that moment. This will help you to reinterpret the memory in the light of God's providence and mercy. Ask the Holy Spirit to help you recall memories of God's blessings in your life, past hurts that need healing and forgiveness, and past sins that you need to repent of. Then, ask for the light to see the snares of the evil one who has held you bound by his lies and robbed you of your freedom in Christ.

First Meditation: The Father's Blessing.
Quietly reflect on the major events of your life when God blessed you. Think of the goodness that you have received from others who have made you joyful. At the time, you may not have been aware of God's presence, but He was there, blessing you through others. Examples may include joyful family events, your First Holy Communion, your Confirmation, or when you began to discern your vocation. Reminiscing about these events should fill you again with God's renewed blessing and a sense of gratitude. It should make you aware that the goodness you possess is a gift from the Lord.

Second Meditation: How You Have Blessed Others.
Our ability to bless others (pour goodness into them) comes from the fact that we ourselves have been blessed first. Reflect on your life and see how you have blessed others, that is, how you have brought goodness into their lives. We don't fully receive the Father's blessing until we give it away to others—even to our enemies (see Rom. 12:20).

Third Meditation: The Evil and Harm You Have Endured from Others.
This is a difficult meditation to undertake, and you should not begin until you have made the previous meditations and have been strengthened in the love and goodness of God. United to Christ Crucified, reflect on the crosses and misfortunes that have befallen you, the evil that you have endured from others. At the time, you may not have felt God's presence, you may even have wondered where He

was, asking, "My God, my God, why have you forsaken me?" (Matt. 27:46). But God was there watching over you, just as He was with His Son on the Cross. Remember the first words Christ spoke on the Cross: "Father, forgive them; for they know not what they do" (Luke 23:34). Then, list the people you need to forgive and what you need to forgive them for. Be specific.

Then, reflect upon how you have responded to those crosses and offenses, especially if they led you into sin or in any way limited your freedom and took you down the wrong path (through fear, depression, envy, pride, resentment, addictions, and so on). These are evil spirits that must be renounced in the name of Jesus Christ. Try to discover any of the devil's lies (deceptions) that have held you bound or any of his schemes that have tied you down and limited your freedom. Write them down so as to renounce them in the name of Jesus.

Fourth Meditation: Sins You Have Committed for Which You Wish to Repent.

Having experienced evil, we often let it enter our heart. In turn, we sin and hurt others. In this meditation, examine your life and see how you have returned evil for evil. Notice how you have hurt others and brought evil into their lives. Make a list of the specific sins for which you need to repent. Then, meditate upon Christ's Passion and see how your sins have hurt the Lord and broken the Father's Heart. Most of all, reflect upon the infinite love and mercy that flows from the Sacred Heart of Jesus.

Writing Your Small Story.

After you have made your meditations, write your story. It should be balanced, containing the Father's blessings in your life, your wounds and hurts, whom you need to forgive, and what you need to repent of. Make notes. It doesn't need to be written out in full. You should be able to deliver it orally to yourself in twenty minutes. It may take longer during the session, since the priest (or lay minister) may ask questions.

The Five Keys.

During the Unbound session, the priest or minister will help you tell the story you have composed using the four meditations. He will then lead you through the Five Keys, one at a time.

First key: repentance. In the name of Jesus, you will repent of the sins you have confessed in the session.

Second key: forgiveness. Neither is repentance complete nor is forgiveness fully received until you have forgiven those you need to forgive. Therefore, in the name of Jesus, you will forgive those who have harmed you for what they have done to you.

Third key: renunciation. Even after repentance and forgiveness, you will still have old wounds, bad habits, and temptations, which comprise the evil spirits we must wrestle with daily. Therefore, you need to name the evil spirits individually and renounce each one in the name of Jesus Christ.

Fourth key: taking authority. After you have renounced the evil spirits, the priest or minister will take authority over them and cast them out in the name of Jesus Christ.

Fifth key: the Father's blessing. Having repented of your sins, forgiven others, and renounced evil spirits, you are ready to receive more fully the Father's blessing. The priest will give you absolution and then will pray over you, asking the Father to bless you.

Strategy: The Weapon of the Father's Blessing

During Holy Week 2020, amid the COVID-19 pandemic, Msgr. John Esseff called me to catch up. Monsignor has been my friend since 2010, when we worked together for the Pope Leo XIII Institute. I said that I was writing this book, and he generously offered these comments, which I jotted down during our conversation:

> I believe that today, the deepest need of the family, for its protection, is the need to have a deep relationship with God the Father. Each family member is called to be another Jesus in the home. But if a person does not know God the Father, does not love Abba as Jesus loves Him, then how can that person be another Jesus? We are God's children. We need our Father. We need to be loved by our Father as Jesus was loved by His Father. We have the same Father.
>
> The father of the family must live and act with the Heart of the Father. We are given life from the Heart of the Father. What is our relationship with Him? We hold back...perhaps because of the way our earthly father treated us, without emotion, without affection; or perhaps he was disinterested in us. So we think that our Heavenly Father is like that also. We think that the Father doesn't care, or that

He will only punish us for being bad. Our family experiences of mother and father are deeply embedded within our heart. But our Heavenly Father is not like this. Jesus is the reflection of His Father. So families need to be in deep relationship with God the Father.

The human heart cries out "Abba!" Jesus taught us this. The mother and father of a family need to know that they can cry out "Abba!" and be heard, understood, known, and empowered to fulfill their vocation to marriage and family life. Only when they experience the fatherly tenderness needed by a child of God can they extend to one another the same tenderness of charity.

That relationship of love between the Father and a person is deeper than his masculinity or her femininity. It is the deepest part of a person's essence. You are the Father's beloved son or daughter. When you know this, you can begin to love as Jesus asks. So we pray: *Jesus, teach me to love the Father as you love Him, please. Lord, show me the Father, please—that I may become a true son or daughter, fully alive in the depths of His paternal Heart.*

What God is allowing in the world today is a purification of the human family. He isn't terrorizing humanity—that's the work of evil. God is repairing what has been broken for a long time.

He's reaching into the depths of the domestic church and repairing it, refining families and revealing what needs to be fixed. He's preparing us for the Father, now or later; He is allowing this time to align ourselves to the Father.

We must cry out to the Father of mercy. We can do so

with confidence because Our Father advances the salvation of His people. We can push back what is evil; what is of the devil we can stand against—destruction, despair, discouragement, disease, and death. But what Abba Father has allowed is to be received in peace, patience, perseverance—and with deeper prayer. Abba Father is revealing His love in the midst of this storm. Watch for it.

Thank God for Msgr. Esseff's paternal heart! Most of us know of families who are suffering from paternal abandonment. Men, I urge you to be the fathers we desperately need in the family. In an apostolic exhortation to the men of his diocese, Bishop Thomas J. Olmsted wrote:

> Today's attack on fatherhood, and by extension, motherhood, is multi-pronged and breathtakingly damaging. 41% of children are born into unmarried homes in our day, an increase of 700% from 1950, when the out-of-wedlock birthrate was a mere 6%. These children are not fatherless because of some sweeping physical conflict, like World War II, which caused many wounds of fatherlessness, but rather because, far worse, fathers' own willed absence is happening on a massive scale. It is not hard to see how men's fears of fatherhood find a legion of support in today's culture of self, encouraging men to flee from this beautiful gift in pursuit of their own desires. The child is forced to ask the question: "Where is my Daddy?" What then is the impact on a child's heart, on his or her understanding of the world, of love, and of the Heavenly Father, when the answer to this question is

"He left us," or "I don't know," or "From the sperm bank, and he left no contact address"?[167]

Similarly, Fr. Donald Calloway exhorts:

> The devil hates God the Father and every reflection of this fatherhood. This hatred incites the devil to destroy fatherhood in all men, laymen as well as priests. Demons have tremendous fear of zealous popes, priests, and the blood of martyrs, but he also greatly fears laymen who pattern their fatherhood off of St. Joseph. The last thing that devil wants is for men to be apparitions of St. Joseph, increasing the presence of St. Joseph in the world.[168]

Fathers, we need you to be brave versions of St. Joseph, please! Your leadership is vital and can make or break the family. By answering God's call to fatherhood, you build up God's kingdom in the domestic church. Fathers, God has entrusted the family to you and endows you with His paternal love.

The Weapon of Personal Prayer

Exorcist Fr. Paolo Carlin instructs:

> We often take for granted that we know what prayer is, but in reality we do not. From childhood, we were taught to say

[167] Most Rev. Thomas J. Olmsted, Apostolic Exhortation *Into the Breach* (September 29, 2015).

[168] Calloway, *Consecration to St. Joseph*, 222.

> prayers in the morning and in the evening, but perhaps we did not understand the value or the meaning of it.
>
> At the Last Supper Jesus said: "This cup which is poured out for you is the new covenant in my Blood" (Luke 22:20). With these words, Jesus is telling us that God the Father has established an eternal alliance with man, a relationship of faith founded on the sacrifice of Christ on the Cross. This alliance is maintained only if, through the Gospel, there is a response from man. This response occurs in prayer that has been stirred up by the teaching of the Word of God. To pray is to converse with God after having listened to Him. Jesus tells us: "You did not choose me, but I chose you" (John 15:16).
>
> Prayer is also praise and thanksgiving. This is the prayer that Jesus prefers: that He is thanked continuously for life, for what we are, and for what we have.[169]

Pray with confidence that God hears, cares about, and is moved by your prayer. Fr. Carlin reminds us that we must maintain our alliance with God; our hearts should be continuously stirred up by God's living Word.

If you must pray through tears, do so knowing that Christ considers it the most precious gift of all—the cry of your heart that is pure, contrite, suffering, believing, and reaching for Him. The Lord's Heart is so very tender, easily moved by the slightest sigh or tear of a pure heart.

---

169 Fr. Paolo Carlin, *An Exorcist Explains How to Heal the Possessed* (Manchester, NH: Sophia Institute Press, 2018), 71.

The Weapon of Praise and Gratitude

Recall that St. Paul and Silas were miraculously liberated from prison after they sang hymns to God:

> The crowd joined in attacking them; and the magistrates tore the garments off them and gave orders to beat them with rods. And when they had inflicted many blows upon them, they threw them into prison, charging the jailer to keep them safely. Having received this charge, he put them into the inner prison and fastened their feet in the stocks.
>
> But about midnight Paul and Silas were praying and singing hymns to God, and the prisoners were listening to them, and suddenly there was a great earthquake, so that the foundations of the prison were shaken; and immediately all the doors were opened and every one's chains were unfastened. (Acts 16:22–26)

Reflecting on this Scripture, Fr. Raniero Cantalamessa writes:

> With their clothes torn, covered in blows, and shackles on their feet, Paul and Silas did not pray to God to help them, but instead sang the praises of God.... We do not praise God for the evil that brings the whole of humanity to its knees; we praise Him because we are sure that He will be able to draw good out of that very evil, for us and for the world. We praise Him precisely because we are convinced

> that everything works for the good of those who love God, and above all, of those whom God loves![170]

In the first book of Samuel, we read how David responded to an evil spirit's attack on the king: "And whenever the evil spirit from God was upon Saul, David took the lyre and played it with his hand; so Saul was refreshed, and was well, and the evil spirit departed from him" (16:23). Here we have the weapon of praise and gratitude! Prayers of praise unleash tremendous spiritual power for the family. They also quickly correct temptations to self-pity or negativity because they miraculously refocus us on God, not the problem at hand.

When I intercede for my family, even in terribly upsetting situations, I have learned to praise and thank God ahead of time: *Thank you, Lord, for what you are doing through this trial, for the good that you will bring out of it. I believe that it is tailored to the salvation of my family. I believe that you are in the midst of this spiritual combat, fighting for us. Grant that I may cooperate with your grace, get out of your way, discern your will, and do whatever you tell me. I praise you; I love you, Lord, and I trust you.* Then, I pray the deliverance prayers. I've learned to resist being pulled into drama that isn't of God.

We find many descriptions of prayer throughout Christian history:

> "True prayer," wrote St. Augustine, "is nothing but love." Prayer should arise from the heart. "Prayer," said St. John

---

[170] Fr. Raniero Cantalamessa, O.F.M. Cap., "CHARIS' Message in Preparation for Pentecost 2020," *CHARIS Magazine*, no. 4. (May 2020): 12, https://www.charis.international/wp-content/uploads/fourth-issue-charis-magazine-english-1.pdf.

> Vianney, "is the inner bath of love into which the soul plunges itself." "Everyone of us needs half an hour of prayer each day," remarked St. Francis de Sales, "except when we are busy—then we need an hour." Definitions of prayer are important, but insufficient. There is a huge difference between knowing about prayer and praying. On this issue, the Rule of St. Benedict is clear, "If a man wants to pray, let him go and pray."
>
> St. John Damascene gave a classic definition of prayer: "Prayer is the raising of one's mind and heart to God or the requesting of good things from God" (CCC, no. 2559, citing St. John Damascene, *De Fide Orth.* 3, 24).[171]

Pope St. John Paul II describes the essence of family prayer this way: "Joys and sorrows, hopes and disappointments, birth and birthday celebrations, wedding anniversaries of the parents, departures, separations and homecomings, important and far-reaching decisions, the death of those who are dear, etc.—all of these mark God's loving intervention in the family's history."[172] Jesus beautifully weaves Himself into the fabric of family life.

Healing Wounds through Deliverance Ministry

Why would we need deliverance? Because we sin and have been wounded by our own imperfections or the imperfections of oth-

171 "Prayer and Worship," United States Conference of Catholic Bishops, accessed May 1, 2020, http://www.usccb.org/prayer-and-worship/index.cfm.

172 Pope John Paul II, *Familiaris Consortio*, no. 59.

ers. We hurt one another. Many of us have suffered something traumatic in our lives. Catholic life is healing, no doubt. The sacraments can keep us liberated. As you'll read in a priest's testimony below, sometimes, we realize there are obstacles getting in the way of deeper love and healthier relationships. Deliverance ministry can help to clear away any obstacles such as unforgiveness and disordered attachments.

A Priest's Testimony: Example of Deliverance Ministry

The following is Msgr. Charles Pope's story of deliverance and healing.[173]

> At a critical point in my life, I needed deliverance. Specifically, I experienced grave and increasingly debilitating bouts of severe anxiety.
>
> This significant torment began for me at about age 10, when I began to experience long periods of sleeplessness due to extreme worry. At the time, there were many crises underway in my family related to my sister's severe mental illness and my parents' struggles with alcohol. The episodes of extreme anxiety lasted for months at a time but were sporadic, coming and going somewhat mysteriously.
>
> Throughout my teenage years, the frequency and intensity of these episodes increased, eventually spurring my parents to place me in outpatient psychotherapeutic counseling, through which I was prescribed psychotropic

173 This testimony is reproduced here with Monsignor's generous permission.

medicines. This was somewhat beneficial and my college and seminary years were largely serene.

I experienced a major crisis at age 33 when, as a young priest, I was asked to take a very challenging assignment. While I initially agreed to it, I was soon assailed by debilitating anxiety, sleeplessness, panic attacks, and almost non-stop rumination and depression. I was certain that I was losing my mind. This led to brief hospitalization and the need to step back from the assignment.

However, my crisis only worsened, descending into post-traumatic stress syndrome and deeper, darker depression. I also began to experience a demonic presence. Even on sunny days my peripheral vision was shrouded in a palpable darkness. I experienced demonic presence in my bedroom, a dark, brooding presence that tormented me throughout the night. I found it necessary to sleep in my outer room with the door open for fear of this presence.

Knowing and seeing my declining condition, a brother priest prayed with me and insisted that I seek help. It was clear that I was in need of deliverance, that I was not living the normal and promised Christian life. I was tormented by fear and locked in depression and self-loathing. My accuser, the evil one, had shown his face and largely robbed me of the glorious freedom of a child of God. Deliverance was needed, but I knew it wasn't going to be easy.

More than twenty years later, I can tell you I have been delivered. Thank you, Jesus! I rarely worry about things now.

I also want to say that deliverance takes time and

involves a multidisciplinary approach. Unfortunately, most people just want relief. But God is in the healing business; healing takes time, courage, prayer, patience, and waiting for the Lord.

The elements of my deliverance and healing included daily Mass, daily prayer and reading of Scripture, spiritual direction, psychotherapy, group therapy, weekly Al-Anon meetings, weekly confession, deliverance prayers, and walking in fellowship with the people of God. Gradually, through all these means, the dark moments grew briefer and the light grew brighter. My priestly ministry also grew richer. I became more compassionate and more able to help others in their struggles.

One of the things I had to discover was that my deliverance was linked to uncovering and naming sinful drives and distorted thinking, which provided doorways for the devil to rob me of my freedom.

The primary sinful drive with which I struggled was that of control, which is a form of pride. Growing up in an often-troubled home, one of my survival strategies had been to carve out small areas in my life that I could strictly control. For example, I kept my bedroom very clean, even locking it when I was away from the house. There were many similar things that I did; the little areas of life that I could control gave me some sense of safety.

As I grew older and my responsibilities increased, I brought this desire for control into those areas and often insisted on being in control of things that could not reasonably be controlled. Finally, struggling in the face of this challenging assignment I was given, I realized that I could never possibly keep everything under control; I spiraled into great crisis.

Ultimately I needed to repent of my strong drive to control. I had to see it for the pride that it was. I needed to learn to rely more on God. But striving to rely on someone other than myself—even God—was terrifying. It took lots of repentance, growing self-knowledge, and learning "the moves" of pride and control. In addition, I had to develop better and more reasonable strategies for dealing with these situations, accepting the fact that there are many things I cannot control.

Through it all, there were great battles with Satan, who did not want to easily relax his grip on me. Thanks be to God, I had many helpers, counselors, and people who prayed for me. Deliverance did come, slowly at first, but with increasing speed as time went on.

This is deliverance ministry. It takes time and many helpers from many different disciplines. Sacraments are essential and fundamental, as are prayer and the Word of God, but in most cases deliverance cases also requires psycho-therapeutic and medical intervention. This was my journey to deliverance.

In my years as a priest I have also walked with others, slowly helping them to find serenity and to appreciate that there is a big difference between relief and healing. Little by little, building trust and striving to increase the "healing team," I have seen many make progress similar to my own—but it takes time; it is a journey. God proceeds very delicately and deliberately in these matters. Healing takes courage and God often waits until we are ready.

So, while recent interest in exorcism is encouraging, we must be careful not to focus too much on what is rare (demonic possession), overlooking what is often *more* necessary and applicable to most cases: deliverance prayer and ministry.[174]

Strategy: Praying for Healing and Offering up Suffering

In her book *Healing: Bringing the Gift of God's Mercy to the World*, Dr. Mary Healy writes:

> Why then, it must be asked, would we do so much on a natural level to heal sickness, and yet hesitate to seek supernatural healing? We understand that there is no contradiction between the redemptive value of suffering and our intense human efforts to bring healing. Why would we think there is a contradiction between the redemptive value of suffering and asking God for healing? What would you think of a doctor who, upon diagnosing a patient with cancer, says to him, "Sorry, I'm not going to treat you because it's better that you simply accept this cross in your life. Offer it up." He'd be fired on the spot! Why would any disciple of Jesus—one who has access to unlimited divine grace and power—upon hearing that someone is ill,

174 Pope, "Getting Unbound."

> respond in like manner? Ironically, Catholics faced with illness usually have no hesitation in seeking medical treatment, yet many are reluctant to ask God for healing. They assume God must want them to suffer. They go to the doctor, but not to the divine Physician. . . . Catholic theology is often a matter of both-and rather than either-or. Is Jesus Christ fully God or fully man? Both (cf. Phil 2:6–8). Is our faith based on Scripture or Tradition? Both (cf. 2 Thess 2:15). Are we justified by faith or works? Both (cf. Gal 2:15; Jas 2:24). Should we embrace our suffering in love, or pray for healing with expectant faith? *Both!* (cf. 1 Pet 4:13; Jas 5:16).[175]

Dr. Mary Healy's lesson leads us to pray for healing always! Offer up suffering always! This is the lesson of Calvary. Jesus offers His suffering to the Father for the redemption of the world, that we may be healed of sin. The Lord prays, suffers, and heals. Our homes should be places for healing prayer. And it's important that not one drop of suffering be wasted, that it instead be united to the suffering of the Lord Jesus on the Cross. "Heal me, O LORD, and I shall be healed; save me, and I shall be saved; for you are my praise" (Jer. 17:14).

On behalf of my family, I've pleaded, *Lord, we need a miracle, please!* We have been in situations where nothing short of a miracle would suffice to resolve our family crisis. As before, Dr. Mary Healy explains that God works miracles in *both* ordinary *and* extraordinary ways:

---

[175] Healy, *Healing*, 132.

> A miracle in the biblical sense, then, can involve natural as well as supernatural causes. It may involve God working though nature in ways that are mysterious and unknown to us. It may include an extraordinary coincidence, such as a chance encounter that leads to someone with a rare condition to just the doctor who can help. It may include the interactions of professional therapy with a divine work of inner healing that goes beyond what therapy can do.[176]

The book of Sirach expresses this balanced perspective:

> My son, when you are sick do not be negligent, but pray to the Lord, and he will heal you.... And give the physician his place, for the Lord created him; let him not leave you, for there is need of him. There is a time when success lies in the hands of physicians, for they too will pray to the Lord that he should grant them success in diagnosis and in healing, for the sake of preserving life. (38:9, 12–14)

What matters is that a person or a family is made whole. Then, with the man who was born blind, we will say, "One thing I know, that though I was blind, now I see." (John 9:25).

O Divine Physician, graciously heal our family from every wound, sin, and evil. With loving gratitude, we offer every suffering for your holy intentions. Amen.

---

[176] Ibid., 70.

10

WITH THE VIRGIN MARY AND THE ANGELS IN SPIRITUAL COMBAT

Strategies: Working with Mary, Devotion to Your Guardian Angel and St. Michael

> Till the end of time, Satan will never give up tempting men, setting up obstacles to their salvation, and combatting them; but he will do all this only within the limits allowed him by the Immaculata; this means, only in so far as this is necessary to enable us to reap the merits of our victory, which will be certain if we fight the battle under her standard, with her, through her, by her and in her. There is much evil in the world, but let us not forget that the Immaculata is more powerful yet, and that she will "crush the infernal serpent's head."[177]

It is breathtaking to witness the humble fierceness of the Blessed Mother in spiritual combat. She is the unfailing Lady of Victory, defender of souls, conqueror of demons. For spiritual combat in

[177] Letter of St. Maximilian Kolbe to Fr. Florian Koziura, March 2, 1931 quoted in Fr. H.M. Manteau-Bonamy, O.P., *Immaculate Conception and the Holy Spirit: The Marian Teachings of St. Maximilian Kolbe* (Libertyville, IL: Marytown Press, 2008), 86.

the family, the help of Mother Mary is necessary, effective, and humbling. That our triune God has given to you and me such a flawless, powerful Mother of Grace reflects the extravagance of divine love for poor creatures.

The Blessed Mother is perfectly attuned to the spiritual and temporal needs of families. Our gentle and fierce Mother, moved by the weight of divine love, blesses the domestic church with an abundance of grace. Always aware of the exalted role of the family, and knowing the manifold ways that Satan attacks it, Mother Mary watches over us. The Immaculate Heart is compelled to act in holy boldness on our behalf. Adorned with heaven's endowment, the Virgin Mary is the most powerful warrior in the Lord's entire army. Never doubt that God has anointed Our Holy Mother for spiritual combat and victory.

The New Eve's Obedience of Faith: A Weapon for Victory

Dr. Andrew Swafford explains the parallels between Eve and Mary: "Both Eve and Mary were approached by an angel (with Eve, a fallen angel); doubt crept into Eve's heart, whereas Mary's faith was steadfast (see Luke 1:45). Eve participated in the downfall of the first Adam, just as Mary participates in the victory of her Son, the New Adam (see Luke 2:34–35). In the words of the early Fathers, 'the knot of Eve's disobedience was untied by Mary's faith.'"[178] Whenever we imitate Mary's obedience of faith, we break any de-

---

178 Dr. Andrew Swafford, "Mary: The New Eve and Our Spiritual Mother," *Ascension Press Blog*, May 3, 2017, https://media.ascensionpress.com/2017/05/03/mary-new-eve-spiritual-mother/.

monic yoke of prideful disobedience in our heart. Here's how the *Catechism* defines *obedience of faith*:

> To obey... in faith is to submit freely to the word that has been heard, because its truth is guaranteed by God, who is Truth itself. Abraham is the model of such obedience offered us by Sacred Scripture. The Virgin Mary is its most perfect embodiment. (CCC 144)

With Mary's help, we will not echo Lucifer's prideful proclamation, "I will not serve!" (see Jer. 2:20). Rather, we will always say yes to whatever God asks or permits in our lives. Often, there's more pain in resisting God's will (turning away from it) than in surrendering to it.

To respond as did the Virgin Mary to God's divine plan for our lives can stretch us beyond our comfort zones. We've discovered that God's path is usually the harder, more uncomfortable, self-emptying one. God's standard is the Cross, after all. During exorcisms, when the priest commands a demon to look at the crucifix in his hand, it's torturous for the demon to obey. The devil is made to stare at the very instrument of his death and damnation. Evil pride is crushed.

We will embrace our family crosses more bravely and more gratefully if we realize that Jesus Christ is sharing a portion of the chalice of love that He drank. When we look back at the storms of our life, we see that carrying our crosses actually fortifies us. "Let no one be tired! Take your armor against your adversaries in the cause of the Cross itself. Set up the faith of the Cross as a trophy against the deniers.... Don't be ashamed to confess the Cross. Angels glory in it. . . . The Cross is a crown, not a dishonor."[179]

During the Good Friday liturgy, the Church leads us through the Veneration of the Cross. Then, we tenderly kiss the cross out of reverence. In family life, we reverence the Cross in our daily service to loved ones, in whom Christ dwells. The devil is threatened by this and retaliates against it because the Cross is the instrument of his eternal defeat.

The Virgin Mary's Role in Spiritual Combat

The Virgin Mary helps liberate us from evil spirits in the following ways:

1. Mary is the vessel—the mediatrix—of God's grace. God anointed her for spiritual warfare as the most powerful threat to Satan because of her extraordinary union with Jesus.
2. Because God chose the Virgin Mary to be the New Eve against demons, the name of Mary has a similar impact to the name of Jesus. This is seen during exorcisms.
3. Mary's holy, maternal presence is extraordinarily painful to demons. They know the efficacy of Marian intervention. The Incarnation—the undoing of the devil—was fulfilled in Mary.
4. Mary's virtues and union with the Holy Spirit make her a fierce destroyer of diabolical plots and tactics. Her life-giving love and defense of God's family are infuriating to prideful demons.

---

[179] St. Cyril of Jerusalem, Catechetical Lecture 13, 22, quoted in Mike Aquilina, *A Year with the Angels* (Charlotte, NC: Saint Benedict Press, 2011), 195.

At a spiritual warfare conference, Fr. Robert Spitzer, S.J., gave a presentation contrasting the logic of Satan with the logic of the Virgin Mary. Reflecting on this comparison, we learn the proper disposition toward God's will. Note the fruitfulness of Mary's logic versus the dire outcome of Lucifer's logic, which led Eve astray.

The Logic of Lucifer and Eve in Eden[180]

1. Ego-comparative
2. Indifference toward God
3. Dissatisfaction with what she has
4. Ingratitude
5. Disobedience, rebellion
6. Pride
7. Self-worship
8. Being a god over others through domination

The Logic of the New Eve, the Virgin Mary, toward Redemption

1. Contributive, transcendent
2. Interested in God's will
3. Satisfaction with what she has
4. Gratitude, praise
5. Obedience of faith, surrender
6. Humility
7. Worship of God
8. Leading others to God
9. Yes to the divine will

---

[180] These lists are taken from Fr. Robert Spitzer's presentation at the 2016 Pope Leo XIII Summer Conference at Mundelein Seminary.

In the family, Mary's rationality can be taught; we can train ourselves to imitate her *fiat* of love and service. When we choose to sin, we're operating by the logic of Eve and the devil. With Mary's help, we won't go astray!

Mary, Culture, Family, and Spiritual Warfare

Mary is the protector of the family and the culture of life. The universal Church is imbued with Mary's motherly character. Her motherliness is God's provision and blessing for the domestic church as well. When the family is attacked, you and I do not fight alone: we are accompanied by the best of soldiers—Jesus Christ, the Blessed Mother, the choirs of angels, and the saints. The challenge is to allow them into our battles, obey their strategies, and follow their lead. In combat, they guide us to know when to move defensively or offensively.

A challenge for modern families is the concept of living together with Mary and the Holy Spirit. This implies a trajectory away from a godless culture—we're marching counterculturally. We're challenging the deconstruction of transcendence, happiness, and morality. How? By building morally upright, happy, and spiritually thriving families. We rebuild our wavering marriages, and we never give up praying and fasting for our wayward children. Our families engage in the culture wars to build a culture of life and advance the divine concept of marriage and family. We saturate our minds and hearts with the beauty and truth of Catholicism. We strive to be converted daily to become ideal disciples. We renounce Satan and his empty promises. We rebuke sin. We never give up. We see the evil around us, but we see the great good that exists also.

"Heaven Is an Acquired Taste"

A challenge for families is that "desiring heaven is an acquired taste." Bishop Thomas J. Olmsted of the Diocese of Phoenix penned a thought-provoking article around this idea:

> Learning to desire and love heaven can be quite difficult. For we live in a world that is utterly upside down, a world that is not rich regarding what matters to God, a world that is obsessed over passing and trivial things and pays little attention to eternal and heavenly things. Therefore, to desire and love heaven means to be willing to go against the world's priorities and preoccupations. To be detached from all this and learn to love heaven requires a painful journey of sacrifice and self-denial. This is why the Lord has reminded us, "Enter through a narrow gate. For wide is the gate and broad is the road that leads to destruction, and many enter through it. But small is the gate and narrow is the road that leads to life, and only a few find it" (Mt 7:13–14). Our hearts are disordered; we easily desire not so much those things that are good and lasting, but those that are sinful and harmful. We seek after apparent goods instead of true goods. For this reason, learning to love heaven is an "acquired taste."[181]

The bishop's reflection is challenging especially as it relates to family life. What must be done to acquire a taste for heaven?

[181] Most Rev. Thomas J. Olmsted, "Desiring Heaven is an acquired taste," Four Last Things, *Catholic Sun*, April 17, 2018, https://www.catholicsun.org/2018/04/17/desiring-heaven-is-an-acquired-taste/.

How do we train our palate for holiness? A look at Church history, particularly the lives of saints, reveals the attractiveness of holiness. Most of us recall Pope St. John Paul II and St. Mother Teresa of Calcutta. Not long ago, these saints lived among us as lights in the darkness. Their works were great, but it was their personal sanctity that captivated us. It set them apart, made them attractive even to the secular masses. We marveled at them as icons of Jesus and Mary, as reflections of a greater light that shone through them. They had acquired a taste for heaven. By their witness, many of us also acquired it.

I've always appreciated how God uses one saint to help raise another one. Think of St. Teresa of Avila and St. John of the Cross, St. Francis and St. Clare, St. Benedict and St. Scholastica, St. Ambrose and St. Augustine and St. Monica. It is necessary to find your community of like-minded prayer warriors, families, parishioners, and clergy. Find the holiest people around you and befriend them. Help one another to acquire a taste for heaven.

We stand on the shoulders of saints, immersing ourselves in the beauty and joy of the Lord. In our home, we are vigilant about not indulging the flesh, the world, and the devil. The Church asks us to ponder the Four Last Things so that we acquire a taste for heaven.

Devotion to the Passion of Christ and the Sorrows of Mary

Some exorcists suggest the practice of daily devotion to the Passion of Jesus Christ by praying the Sorrowful Mysteries of the Rosary. They also suggest devotion to Our Lady of Sorrows. In the fourteenth century, it was revealed to St. Bridget of Sweden that devotion to the Virgin Mary's Seven Sorrows draws signal graces. The devotion consists in praying seven Hail Marys while meditating on the Seven Sorrows of Mary. The sorrows of Mary are as follows: (1) the prophecy of Simeon (Luke 2:34–35); (2) the flight into Egypt (Matt. 2:13–15); (3) the loss of Jesus for three days (Luke 2:41–52); (4) meeting Jesus on the Way of the Cross (Luke 23:26–31); (5) the Crucifixion (John 19:17–30); (6) Jesus' descent from the Cross (John 19:38–40); and (7) the burial of Jesus (John 19:38–42).

Daily reflection on the Passion of Christ and the Sorrows of Mary helps us to "be sober, be watchful" (1 Pet. 5:8). We become more aware of the price Christ paid to ransom us. When we enter the preternatural battle, there's a literal tug-of-war over our soul and the soul of the family. In spiritual combat, we go to Calvary with Jesus and Mary, where the climactic battle occurred and the devil was defeated. A warrior is familiar with going to Calvary and even feels at home there, since God's love is powerfully revealed on Jerusalem's hill.

Mary's Seven Sorrows reveal the truth about spiritual combat: it pierces hearts and raises us mystically to the Cross. Christ's love is incarnational: His Heart of flesh and blood suffered. Mary also experienced agony; she freely offered her Immaculate Heart to the sword seven times to suffer with Jesus as generously as possible.

Heaven is our calling. It is no wonder that demons seek to make us forget about our eternal reward. Theirs is lost. Ours can be secured if we do whatever it takes to "acquire a taste for heaven." God's providence will work this out if you offer the all-important yes to God's will.

Family Strategy: Working with Mary

> During the seventeenth-century beatification process for St. Francis de Sales, one of the Annecy Monastery Visitation nuns made a formal statement about an exorcism she had witnessed. A young man had been possessed by a demon for five years, and an exorcism was being performed in the presence of the relics of St. Francis by the Bishop Charles Auguste de Sales of Geneva, who was the saint's nephew and successor to the Episcopal see.
>
> According to her report, during one of the sessions the demon shouted furiously, "Why should I leave?"
>
> One of the Visitation nuns present, perhaps frightened, invoked the Blessed Virgin: "Holy Mother of God, pray for us!"
>
> On hearing these words, the demon screamed even more loudly: "Mary! Mary! There's no Mary for me! Don't say that name; it makes me shudder! If there were a Mary for me, as there is for you, I wouldn't be what I am! But for me there is no Mary! If I had one instant of the many instants that you people waste . . . ! Just one lone instant and a Mary, and I would not be a demon!"[182]

Our Holy Mother never ceases to amaze! Look at what Mary, Queen of Prophets, did at Guadalupe, Lourdes, Fatima—she crushed Satan and his plans. She heals the sick; defeats satanic sacrifices; guides us with messages of conversion and warning; and exhorts us to be virtuous and valiant in proclaiming Christ's victory.

---

[182] *Spiritual Warfare Bible*, New Testament, 63.

God knows that we desperately need a mother's love, wisdom, and protection. We cry out full throated for Mary's intercession in spiritual combat, quickly saying spontaneous prayers for help and protection: *Mother Mary, protect me. Mother Mary, help me. Mother Mary, please guide me. Mother Mary, pray for me.*

In my spiritual battles, I discovered a particular Marian action to be helpful for protecting my marriage and family: *pondering*. "Mary kept all these things, pondering them in her heart" (Luke 2:19). Pondering as Mary did means to recall, receive, and respond. The domestic church is well served when mothers can *recall* God's faithfulness as Mary does in her Magnificat; *receive* the gift of God to fill her with love; and *respond* with magnanimity to the needs of loved ones. In spiritual warfare, it's fruitful to remember the manifold ways that providence has carried you (and loved ones) through fiery ordeals and the attacks of enemies. Mary kept all these things in her heart, thereby honoring God and His designs. I think a woman who ponders and cultivates a Marian heart more easily obtains victory over evil spirits because by *recalling*, *receiving*, and *responding* she never loses sight of heaven for herself and her family. Then, whatever it takes to help get her family to heaven, she does because she's working with the Blessed Mother.

Mary's Rosary: A Mighty Weapon

Countless books, testimonies, and saints throughout Church history have proclaimed the miraculous power of the Rosary for conversion, healing, and deliverance. The Rosary is a Christocentric prayer in which we journey with Mary through the biblical mysteries of Christ's life. Through our praying the Rosary, Mary aids us to internalize our identity as soldiers for Christ.

Years ago, when one of my sons was troubled and seemingly being pulled into darkness, I prayed an intercessory Rosary for one year before liberation miraculously occurred. Since I write for Catholic Exchange, I published the following Rosary reflections that I composed. You may substitute the name of a loved one for "my son" when you say these prayers.

The Rosary for Healing and Deliverance

The Glorious Mysteries of the Holy Rosary

1. **The First Glorious Mystery:** The Resurrection of the Lord (Mark 16:1–8).
   Dear Lord, please let the grace of your resurrection penetrate my beloved son and bring him to new life in you. Raise him up above the dark pit that he's descending into. Grant resurrection of his true self because a false self is operating. Heal his heart, please. Be glorified in my son, and do not let the devil take him away from you. Release the grace of his Baptism to protect him from every evil. Amen.

2. **The Second Glorious Mystery:** The Ascension of the Lord (Mark 16:19).
   Dear Lord, please take hold of my son and pull him up from the darkness. Draw him toward you, toward heaven, toward the Father. Help him to transcend his current struggle and enter into your resurrected love. You said that you would not leave us orphans. Please do not let my son be an orphan. Grab him back from the

enemy of his soul. Detach him from any darkness, please. Raise him out of darkness into your great light. Amen.

3. **The Third Glorious Mystery:** The Descent of the Holy Spirit (Acts 2:1–4).
Dear Lord, the grace of the upper room at Pentecost is for all souls. I spiritually place my son near Mary in the upper room so he can experience a personal Pentecost. Come, Holy Spirit, fall afresh upon this young man; fan into flame the baptismal graces he received when you accepted him into the family of the Holy Trinity. Make him fully alive in the power of your Spirit. Consecrate him in the truth, and free him from the lying one. Amen.

4. **The Fourth Glorious Mystery:** The Assumption of the Virgin Mary (Jth. 15:9–10).

Dear Mary, I entrust to you my little son. Be his mother. I am at a loss. You know what to do. Mary, you are no stranger to suffering. Take him to your Immaculate Heart where he can be safe from harm. Mary, plead before the mercy seat of the Father who assumed you into heaven. Please ask for mercy upon my son so God will be glorified and the devil won't gloat about snatching him away. Mary, I have no more wine. Please ask your Son for a miracle of grace that supplies for our family's great lack.

5. **The Fifth Glorious Mystery:** The Coronation of the Virgin Mary (Rev. 12:1).
Dear Lord, with the coronation of Mary, you crowned the fulfillment of your glorious work. You desire each creature to reach

> *his fulfillment, to be crowned with everlasting glory. When you received my little son at Baptism, you took him into your house and gave the Blessed Virgin Mary to be his mother. I beg you to pour special grace upon my son through Mary's maternal heart. Let it penetrate him and change his direction. Set him on the right path: the straight, narrow, royal road to heaven. I will never cease to pray for my son until he receives his crown of glory, a gift of your merciful love. Rescue him, please. Amen.* [183]

Fifteen years later, I continue to receive testimonies from families who prayed with those Rosary reflections.

Recently, I received a letter from a woman who found these reflections on the Internet while she was in the hospital, awaiting the outcome of her son's attempted suicide. Below, you'll read her family story in her own words, with her permission. It's an edifying reflection.

A Testimony: The Rosary for Healing and Deliverance

From a non-Catholic wife, mother, and nurse, after her son's suicide attempt:

> I have recently been on a journey of grief. Your work has been a big part of my healing. I wanted to share with you the power of your meditation, *The Rosary for Healing and Deliverance*. This prayer has changed me forever as I prayed it for my son. I discovered the Rosary, and we were saved.

---

[183] Kathleen Beckman, "Praying the Holy Rosary for Healing and Deliverance," Catholic Exchange, May 21, 2010, https://catholicexchange.com/praying-the-holy-rosary-for-healing-and-deliverance.

In 2017, my fourteen-year-old, bright and talented son lay in the ICU. He had just come out of the operating room having had two brain surgeries in hopes of containing the damage of a self-inflicted gunshot wound from a few hours prior. His cranium was split down the middle and the left parietal bone removed to allow for swelling. Two drains were inserted into his brain to drain the blood; a third tube was inserted to measure pressure and drain cerebrospinal fluid. He was on a ventilator and in a medically induced coma. He had left home that morning happy and excited about his basketball game. Now twelve hours later our world came to a crashing stop.

Midnight, day two: I knew I had to pray but I could not. Beyond exhausted and running on pure adrenaline, I couldn't think. I could not put words together to make a sentence to pray. In the hospital lobby at midnight and alone (my husband and friends had left for a little break), I found myself googling the words "healing prayer." The first hit I found by divine providence was Kathleen Beckman's prayer for healing and deliverance.

This prayer was a lifeline, a cry of protection from a mother's heart to look after her son. The prayer called forth the power of the Holy Spirit, the protection from evil, and the surrender of her son to Jesus through Mary. These reflections were the very cry of my own soul. Here was this prayer that had all the intentions that I desperately wanted to articulate. It was embedded in the Hail Marys of the Catholic Rosary.

I knew very little about the Rosary except that it was

used by Catholics to help them pray. I had never said a Hail Mary. But it was right there for me. All I had to do was read the prayer. I did not have to think; the words were there for me. As I read the words and repeated the Hail Marys, I experienced great peace and assurance. I was finally able to pray again.

That night at midnight in the lobby of a hospital where my son was admitted after a suicide attempt, I found Mary! Here was a mother who understood. Here was someone, the Mother of Jesus, whose heart was pierced at the foot of the Cross. From the joy of His Conception and Birth, to the agony of the Crucifixion, Mary understands what it is to be a mother. Mary stood by Jesus as he was beaten, tortured, and finally murdered. Though her heart was pierced, she was present, always loving, always trusting. She modeled for me a mother's true surrender and humble yes to God—no matter what the circumstance. Here was someone who could ask for mercy for my son, for me, when I simply could not form the words.

The Rosary: A Prescription for Healing and Hope

I shared my experience with friends the next day. Within twenty-four hours I was the owner of a beautiful rosary, gifted to me by the monks of St. Gregory's in Oklahoma. In my mind, the rosary they gave to me was extra special because it was blessed by the pope. I continued praying the reflections for healing and deliverance with the Rosary even though this form of prayer was very foreign to me. Calling upon Mary as my advocate was a new experience. I was in no state to debate theology. I just knew that I found something that worked, and I could not let it go. I physically clung to the rosary. I knew the prayer pointed me to Jesus. I found great comfort in it. I repeated this prayer all day long.

Praying the Rosary made me feel very close to the Heart of God. The cadence and monotonous nature of the Hail Marys calmed my anguished soul. The extreme focus on the mysteries of Jesus kept my eyes on Him rather than on the horror of the situation. I felt protected and received hope that God was all over this situation for our family.

Rosary Prescription: 2–3 Rosaries a Day, as Needed for Anxiety

My overwhelming emotional response to my son's injury was undoubtedly that of anxiety. It was a very physical anxiety that I had never experienced before. I would awaken daily to a sore, aching body. My shoulders frozen tense in an "alert and flee" pose. My head pounding with tension.

As a nurse, I knew that my anxiety was critical, that typically individuals in like situations are given medications such as Valium to help reduce the symptoms and blur the horror of the reality. However, I had stumbled upon a powerful anti-anxiety agent in the Rosary. I found myself turning to the rosary every time my anxiety would increase. The Rosary, unlike prescriptions such as Valium, addressed the cause of my anxiety—that is, that I wanted to my son to be saved, healed, protected. The Rosary addressed this, so it was my anti-anxiety prescription. I didn't want to mask the trauma of what happened; I wanted my son and family to be healed and delivered.

My extreme anxiety continued for almost a year. It was undoubtedly situational anxiety. My son could not talk; he could not move. He had a helmet on his head to protect his exposed brain. Occasionally he would be "awake" and communicate with hand squeezes. It was simply terrible.

The mornings were the most difficult times for me. The thought of facing another day in this new paradigm was frightening. Had I not had the Rosary, then anti-anxiety agents or possibly hospitalization would have occurred for self-preservation. Physically clutching the beads brought relief. Within the first six months of this journey I had broken three rosaries. And yes, I had unfortunately broken the rosary blessed by the pope into three pieces.

Like medications, there were side effects to praying the Rosary, such as occasional narcolepsy. However, I found this side effect was quite tolerable, and often welcomed. Initially, I thought it was the repetitive prose of the Hail Mary that released the tension. But as time went on and I became more familiar with the Rosary, I believe that my focus on Jesus instead of my immediate world is what took away my fears. As I got better, I was able to reduce my prescription of the Rosary to once daily.

Looking back, my story is one of spiritual warfare. This should never have happened. There was evil all over the situation. There was a kid at school who had been kicked out of several other schools and had just joined my son's class. He spent the semester telling my son that he should kill himself because no one would care. After my son shot himself, the kid left the school the next day and never returned. We have no idea what happened to him. We have asked for it to be looked into, but nobody has. My son recalls holding the gun to his head, picking it up and putting it down several times repeatedly. Then he landed on the wrong decision.

My husband and I had gone through a rough patch in our marriage about two years before this happened, but we had some counseling, and were doing much better. Things were good. Then this happened. I think that when the devil could not break up the marriage, he attacked the family. My son is adopted. His mother chose not to abort him against much pressure from her parents. I think this speaks into our story. God spared my adopted son from being aborted by his birth mother. Now, God spared him from trying to kill himself. The devil didn't win. God wins. Thank you for helping us to be healed and delivered from evil.

May God be praised for giving us the wonderful gift of the Rosary!

Exorcists Testify: Mary and the Rosary

One exorcist testifies to the power of Mary:

> In another exorcism, a demon said, "When you say the Hail Mary, it is as if she takes your spirit and brings it each time to the Father. Because she loves you like no one else loves you, she takes you up there with her. And when you remember the life of That One (he is referring to meditation on the

> singular mysteries during the Rosary), for me, it is a torture to relive all the times that He did that (swear word).... You finish one and then begin another. It is an uninterrupted song in every part of the world. But, for us, it is a deadly backdrop. With all those (swear words follow) of the mysteries, you remind us each time that which he did, and it huuuuurts us!"[184]

This exorcist also shared stories of the devil's hatred of Fatima and the three visionaries:

> Concerning the triumph of the Immaculate heart of which Our Lady spoke at Fatima, a demon, pronouncing with tremendous effort the name of Mary, exclaimed, "You do not know, or you know it, but you do not believe it, or you do not have enough faith. It is the Immaculate Heart of Ma...ar...y that will save the whole world. Only her Immaculate Heart!"
>
> ...The memorial of Francisco and Jacinta Marto, two of the shepherd children at Fatima, is celebrated on February 20. During an exorcism that day, a demon that had possessed a person referred to Francisco when he exclaimed, "That little one gave me so many kicks with all those rosaries, so many!" Then, turning to Blessed Jacinta (not Saint Jacinta) with great trembling he said, "And that other one, the smallest of the three. She was the 'the worst.' She is the

[184] Francesco Bamonte, *The Virgin Mary and the Devil in Exorcisms* (Chicago: Pope Leo XIII Institute Press, 2014), 106–107.

one who said quickly, 'Yes! Yes! Take me with you. Cause me to suffer. It is enough that the others do not suffer!' That little, stupid one said that. How did she know that! Who had taught her those things? She was so transparent. I could not touch her, so transparent, almost like That One there."[185]

Here is another powerful testimony of Mary's love:

We were present [at the exorcism] and could see the reactions of the demon. We heard, "She is here, always her! She is the queen of my pain! She destroys me continually. She does nothing else but pray for you to her son. And all her prayers are answered. No human should have this power. Why did He humiliate us that way? He put us under everybody."[186]

Thanks be to God for Our Lady of Victory!

Fallen Angels: Your Enemy

Regarding the fallen angels who rebelled against God's will, their intellect knows the truth, but due to their rebellion against God, their will always inclines them to evil. The sin of the demon is his wound (pride, etc.). It's the source of his shame. Demons make rapid associations while we make

[185] Ibid., 154, 157.

[186] Ibid., 166.

> educated guesses. They have nemesis saints or angels whom they hate.[187]

I've seen this often during exorcisms when the priest calls upon the help of St. Michael, or a saint such as St. Gemma Galgani. Some demons react strongly to particular angels or saints that they hate because these holy warriors cause them to suffer more.

Our holy comrades in spiritual combat—Mary, the angels, and the saints—are ready to assist us to rightly exercise our free will in resisting sin and evil:

> Angels suggest, but we choose. Quoting two very early Christian writers, Origen tells us that an evil angel might suggest an evil thought, and a good angel a good thought. But in either case we have free will; we can choose to do evil or good.... For it is quite within our reach, when an evil power has begun to incite us to evil, to cast the wicked suggestions away from us, and to resist the vile inducements, and to do nothing that is at all deserving of blame. And, on the other hand, it is possible, when a divine power calls us to better things, not to obey the call. In either case, our own free will remains.[188]

Parents in particular must be aware that their decisions have consequences for good or bad. In the family, they bear responsibility

[187] My personal unpublished notes taken at the twelfth annual International Association of Exorcists course "Exorcism and Prayers of Liberation," Pontifical Athenaeum Regina Apostolorum, Rome, May 2017.

[188] Aquilina, *Year with the Angels*, 160.

for discerning choices. When I was a child, my parents taught me that there are good and bad angels and that I should not listen to the bad angels, but only to the good angels. This became a practical lesson from my youth. Children can grasp this, as I did.

When we fall short, we must not blame the devil for our sin:

> It is not an enemy from outside fighting with you, but a shoot of evil growing from inside you. Let your eyes look directly forward and lust does not exist. Keep what is yours and do not take what is someone else's, and there is an end to theft. Remember the judgment, and neither fornication, nor adultery, nor murder, not any other unrighteousness will prevail in you. But as soon as you forget God, you start to think up wickedness and do evil. But nature is not the only cause of evil. There is another who miserably urges us on to it—the devil. He urges everyone, but prevails only over those who listen to him. If you indulgently allow yourself to think of lust, through your imagination, it will strike its roots into you, and captivate your mind, and drag you down into the pit of evils. Don't let the seed in; it will break your faith in pieces. Root out the problem before it blooms, or, because you were lazy at the beginning, you may have to attack it with axes and fire later.[189]

Our focus should be on the good angels who not only defend us in spiritual combat, but also are messengers sent with good inspirations to follow Christ faithfully.

---

[189] St. Cyril of Jerusalem, quoted in Aquilina, *Year with the Angels*, 161.

Strategy: Devotion to Your Guardian Angel and St. Michael

St. Basil tells us, "Beside each believer stands an angel as protector and shepherd leading him to life" (quoted in CCC 336). In the nine choirs of angels, we glimpse the glorious logic of divine providence. How beautiful are God's designs for the human family. We can say that God thought of everything for love of us! Angels are all around us. "Christ is the center of the angelic world. They are *his* angels . . . they belong to him because they were created *through* and *for* him . . . they belong to him still more because he made them messengers of his saving plan" (CCC 331).

"The assistance of the angels that is given to the soul is to continue throughout the whole course of its life. Not even sins can suppress it. They can only sadden the angel of the soul. But angels do not merely protect the soul against the attacks of the devil; they also try to make it progress in the spiritual life. The angels, then, appear first of all as aiding the soul in its spiritual ascension."[190]

When a storm arises, and we're cast headlong into the middle of spiritual combat, the good angels lead us with inspirations to overcome evil with good. We need angelic help to conquer sin and evil and to heed the call to holiness. It takes continuous effort to build up a family, and, in one quick moment, a poor decision can tear the family asunder. The ripple effect can be devasting. Encourage each family member to develop a holy friendship with his guardian angel and the choirs of good angels.

Think of family members and their assigned guardian angel. When my son was away at college, I prayed that my guardian angel

---

[190] Jean Danielou, *The Angels and Their Mission* (Manchester, NH: Sophia Institute Press, 2009), 93.

would communicate with his guardian angel. This was fruitful. "What mother has not noticed the narrow escape of one or the other of her children from imminent danger, probably without thinking that it may have been through the intervention of its faithful Guardian?"[191]

Author Jean Danielou beautifully sums up our need for angelic assistance: "These guardian spirits have been sent to aid the human race. For our weakness is such that, if the guardian angels had not been given to us, we could not resist the many powerful attacks of the evil spirits. To this end, we had need of a higher nature. We know that this is so from the words with which the Lord strengthens Moses, trembling in his fear, 'My angel will go before thee.'"[192] Only in heaven will we know the countless times that our guardian angels, St. Michael, and the choirs of good angels saved us and our loved ones from grave harm.

St. Michael the Archangel

I could fill another book with stories of St. Michael's glorious intervention for me and my family. Like the two boys at the start of chapter one, since my childhood, I've been fascinated by and devoted to St. Michael, for whom we named our first son. Our home is filled with St. Michael statues, icons, and medals. Throughout the day, I invoke St. Michael and have unbounded confidence in his protection of all that is precious to God. During every minor or major exorcism, St. Michael is called upon, and the evil spirits manifest unique torment at the mention of his name.

---

[191] *St. Michael and the Angels* (Charlotte, NC: TAN Books, 1983), 52.

[192] Danielou, *Angels and Their Mission*, 82.

Commenting on invoking St. Michael, Fr. John Hardon, S.J., writes:

> We believe that St. Michael has extraordinary intercessory power with God. Two verbs we should always associate: to *invoke* and to *intercede*. We invoke St. Michael so that he may intercede for us with God. St. Michael's role has not changed, shall I say, over the centuries of both angelic and human history. He is now as he was when the angels were first tested. Michael was then the leader of the battling, warring angels. He is still their leader. What, then, are we begging St. Michael to obtain? We are asking that, through St. Michael, we might be protected from the second death, the death of our souls.[193]

A Prayer for Help from the Angels

Help, unity of the Trinity; have pity, Trinity of unity; help me I pray, thus placed as in the peril of a great sea, so that the plague of this year will not draw me with it, nor the vanity of the world. And this very prayer I make to the high powers of the heavenly warfare, that they will not leave me to be harried by enemies, but defend me with their strong armor, that before me in the battle will go those armies of the heavenly warfare, Cherubim and Seraphim with their thousands, Gabriel and Michael with the like ones. May Thrones, Powers, Archangels, Principalities, Dominions, Angels defend me with their thick array, and be strong to overthrow my enemies.[194]

---

193 Hardon, *Meditations on the Angels*, 150, 152.

194 St. Gildas the Wise, "Lorica," quoted in Aquilina, *Year with the Angels*, 209.

APPENDIX A

PRAYERS FOR FAMILY HEALING AND DELIVERANCE

Prayer to Remove Generational Curses

Lord Jesus Christ, Incarnate Son of God the Father, Thou who hast chosen to enter into human history by being carried in the womb of Thy Blessed Mother, grant I beseech Thee that any demons that may have been introduced into my generational line by any one of my ancestors may be blocked from passing to the subsequent generations. I ask Thee that if the evil spirits entered the generational line by the sin of one or more of my ancestors, that Thou wouldst pardon the temporal punishment due to their sin and free us from the demon's involvement in our lives. Blessed Virgin, we ask thee to offer the Precious Body, Blood, Soul and Divinity of thy Son to God the Father in reparation for the sins of those ancestors who may have introduced any evil spirits into my generational lines, as well as any subsequent sins that may have resulted from the evil spirits affecting those of the generational line. If any evil spirit has been introduced into my generational line as a result of a curse or malefice done by someone outside my family, I ask Thee to give me the grace to forgive them wholeheartedly and I ask Thee, Jesus, to break the curse or malefice, if it is still in place. God the Father, I forgive them for any of the effects of their sin that they may have committed against my family line and for any damage it may have caused. Jesus, I ask Thee to forgive me of any sins that may be the result of any generational spirits in my family and I ask Thee to block any power the evil spirits may have gained in my generational line as a result of my own sin. Heal any damage in the lives of the members of my family as a result of the generational spirit. I bind and completely and utterly reject, with full force of my will, any sin or spiritual defect of mine as well as any temptation, allurements or power that any generational spirit may have over me as a result of my sin or the sin of any other person. I do this in the Holy Name of Jesus and Mary and in the Name of the Father and of the Son and of the Holy Spirit. Amen.[195]

Prayer Against Every Evil

Spirit of our God, Father, Son, and Holy Spirit, Most Holy Trinity, Immaculate Virgin Mary, angels, archangels, and saints of heaven, descend upon me. Please purify me, Lord, mold me, fill me with yourself. Banish from me all the forces of evil, destroy them, vanquish them, so that I can be healthy and do good deeds. Banish from me all spells, witchcraft, black magic, malefic ties, maledictions, and the evil eye; diabolic infestations, oppressions, possessions; all that is evil and sinful; jealousy, perfidy, envy, physical, psychological, moral, spiritual, diabolical ailments. Burn all of these evils in hell, that that may never again touch me or any other creature in this entire world. I command and bid all the powers that molest me – by the power of God almighty, in the name of Jesus Christ our Savior, through the intercession of the Immaculate Virgin Mary, to leave me forever, and to be consigned into everlasting hell, where they will

[195] Ripperger, *Deliverance Prayers*, 26.

be bound by St. Michael, St. Raphael, and guardian angels, and where they will be crushed under the heel of the Immaculate Virgin Mary. Amen.[196]

Family Prayer for Protection

We bless your name, O Lord, for sending your own incarnate Son to become part of a family, so that, as he lived its life, he would experience its worries and its joys. We ask you, Lord, to protect and watch over this family, so that in the strength of your grace its members may enjoy prosperity, possess the priceless gift of your peace, and, as the Church alive in the home, bear witness in this world to your glory. We ask this through Christ our Lord. Amen.[197]

Intercessory Prayer for a Person under Demonic Influence

My Lord, you are all powerful, you are God, you are Father.
We beg you through the intercession and help of the archangels Michael, Raphael and Gabriel for the deliverance of our brothers and sisters who are enslaved by the Evil One.
All Saints of Heaven, come to our aid.
From anxiety, sadness, and obsessions, we beg you: free us, O Lord.
From hatred, fornication, envy, we beg you: free us, O Lord.

---

196 Archbishop Julian Porteous, *A Manual of Minor Exorcisms* (London: Catholic Truth Society, 2010), 62–63.

197 "Prayer for Families," United States Conference of Catholic Bishops, accessed April 20, 2020, http://www.usccb.org/prayer-and-worship/prayers-and-devotions/prayers/prayer-for-families.cfm. This prayer also appears in *Catholic Household Blessings and Prayers* (Washington, DC: United States Conference of Catholic Bishops, 2007).

From thoughts of jealousy, rage and death, we beg you: free us, O Lord.
From every thought of suicide and abortion, we beg you: free us, O Lord.
From every form of sinful sexuality, we beg you: free us, O Lord.
From every division in our family, and every harmful friendship, we beg you: free us, O Lord.
From every sort of spell, malefice, witchcraft and every form of the occult, we beg you: free us, O Lord.
Lord, you who said, "I leave you peace, my peace I give you," grant that, through the intercession of the Blessed Virgin Mary, we may be liberated from every evil spell and enjoy your peace always. In the name of Jesus Christ, our Lord. Amen.[198]

Prayer for Inner Healing

Lord Jesus, you came to heal our wounded and troubled hearts. I beg you to heal the torments that cause anxiety in my heart. I beg you to come into my life and heal me of the psychological harms that struck me in my early years and from the injuries that they caused throughout my life.

Lord Jesus, you know my burdens. I lay them all on your Good Shepherd's heart. I beseech you, by the merits of the great, open wound in your heart, to heal the small wounds that are in mine. Heal the pain of my memories, so that nothing that has happened to me will cause me to remain in pain and anguish, filled with anxiety.

Heal, O Lord, all those wounds that have been the cause of the evil that is rooted in my life. I want to forgive all those who have offended me. Look to those inner sores that make me unable to forgive. You who

---

[198] Porteous, *Manual of Minor Exorcisms*, 65–66.

came to forgive the afflicted of heart, please heal my own heart. Heal, my Lord Jesus, those intimate wounds that cause me physical illness. I offer you my heart; accept it, Lord, purify it and give me the sentiments of your Divine Heart. Help me to be meek and humble.

Heal me, O Lord, from the pain caused by the death of my loved ones, which is oppressing me. Grant me to regain peace and joy in the knowledge that you are the Resurrection and the Life. Make me an authentic witness to your resurrection, your victory over sin and death, your living presence among us. Amen.[199]

A Personal Prayer for Liberation from Evil

Lord, almighty, merciful and omnipotent God, Father, Son and Holy Spirit, drive out from me all influence of evil spirits. Father, in the name of Jesus Christ, I plead you to break any chain that the devil has on me. Pour upon me the most Precious Blood of your Son. May his immaculate and redeeming Blood break all bonds of my body and mind. I ask you this through the intercession of the Blessed Virgin Mary.

Archangel St. Michael, intercede and come to my help. In the name of Jesus, I command all demons that could have any influence over me to leave forever. By his scourging, his Crown of Thorns, his Cross, by his Blood and Resurrection, I command all evil spirits to leave me. By the true God, by the Holy God, by the God who can do all, in the name of Jesus Christ, my Savior and Lord, leave me. Thank you, Lord Jesus for your ministry of healing and deliverance. Amen.[200]

---

[199] Ibid., 64.

[200] Ibid., 62.

Pleading the Precious Blood of Jesus for Protection

Eternal Father, by the saving Blood of Jesus Christ, purge us of sin and darkness. The devil is defeated by the Blood of the Lamb (Rev. 12:11), so we ask that the Blood of Jesus cover all who are in need of protection (all church, civil, religious, and lay leaders; our families, friends, and enemies; all those for whom we have promised to pray; and ourselves). We plead the Precious Blood of Jesus Christ for our families, homes, schools, and places of employment. We plead the Precious Blood for our salvation, safety, marriage, children, relationships, health, vehicles, finances, Church, and country. May the water and blood that flowed as a fountain of grace from the throne of the Most High protect and heal us. Holy Spirit, fill us with your light and love. Amen.

A Prayer for My Spouse in Spiritual Combat

Lord Jesus Christ, thank you for the gift of my spouse, N., who is a blessing of divine providence. I beseech your grace and mercy upon N., who is struggling. I place N. in the chalice of your Most Precious Blood that is the divine blessing cup. Your Precious Blood is life-giving, life-changing, liberating, and healing. I implore special grace upon N. that our marriage will thrive in genuine self-giving love, according to the divine will. Your Sacred Heart is the hospital of the afflicted, where healing love and mercy minister to us. Please grant N. peace of soul, clarity of mind, liberation from evil, healing, and strength for the journey. Thank you, good and gracious Lord Jesus, for your loving attentiveness to the cries of my heart for my spouse. Amen.

Prayer to Break Inner Vows and Self-Cursing

Heavenly Father, I lift up to you all the difficult people in my life. In the Name of Jesus Christ, I forgive them for upsetting me, for rejecting me and for hurting me. I forgive them for making me feel so alone, so unloved, so guilty and for causing me so much pain. I forgive them for the horrible things they've said about me. I ask you, Father, to forgive them and bless them. Please forgive me for holding a judgement against each one and for trying to control my life's situation through inner vows and self-cursing.

Lord Jesus, please forgive me for making the following vows and curses when I said (N., i.e., If it hurts this much, I will never love again! If I want it done right, I have to do it myself! People will only let me down, I can't trust anyone! I'm so fat and ugly! I can't do anything right!). In the name of Jesus Christ, I renounce and break each of these vows and curses. I declare them null and void immediately, no longer able to influence me in any way. By the sword of the Holy Spirit, I cut myself free from each of these vows and curses, and from all their ill effects upon my life. In the Name of the Father, and of the Son, and of the Holy Spirit, Amen.[201]

Prayer of Someone Addicted to Pornography

Eternal Father, I am living in a fantasy world. My conscience is no longer pricked because it is numbed by sin and denial. I have betrayed

---

[201] Missionaries of the New Evangelization, *Deliverance Prayer Manual*, 44.

my humanity. Father, I repent of this addiction to pornography. It is alienating me from those I love, my cherished family and friends. Lord, it alienates me from you. I'm caught up in a lie, entangled in the chains of the devil, attached to my wound of sin. Father, graciously allow me to experience the redeeming power of the Precious Blood of your Son, Jesus. Please forgive me. Show me how to repent. I renounce the way I have misused my sexuality. Cast the devil far away from me, please. I desire to submit my sexuality to your holy standard. Lord, I need to be encouraged in this moment of truth. I am accountable to you. I need the grace of conversion. I implore that your Holy Spirit enter into me. Come, Holy Spirit, with a fresh outpouring of charity and truth. I require your help to control my base impulses. I desire the restoration of my dignity. Kindly enable me to rule over myself by clinging to your purity and holiness. Father, thank you for hearing my prayer. Amen.

A Parent's Prayer for a Child in Spiritual Combat

Eternal Father, we thank you for the gift of faith and family. Thank you for sending your beloved Son, Jesus Christ, to redeem us by His Cross and resurrection. We seek divine mercy for our family. We trust that you will never abandon us. We implore you to look with mercy upon our child, N., who is plagued with sin-sickness, health problems, and/or diabolical attacks. We entrust this child to you. Please take care of him (her) according to your perfect love, plan, and timing. We plead the Precious Blood of your Son to cover this child with spiritual protection. Father, please cut the chains that bind N. so he (she) is set free to live as your redeemed child. Guide N. to repentance for sin and renunciation of vice. By the infinite power of the Cross of your Son Jesus, please liberate and heal this child for the glory of your name. Amen.

A Father's Binding Prayer for His Family

Eternal Father, thank you for calling me to be the father of this family. In the name of your Son, Jesus Christ, and by the infinite power of His Precious Blood, and through the intercession of St. Joseph, I bind and cast out any evil spirits that may be in our home, or cars, or that are attacking any member of my family. I send them immediately and directly to the foot of the Cross to be judged, never to bother us again. Come, Holy Spirit, and descend upon our home and fill us (name loved ones) with your light and love. In the name of the Father, and of the Son, and of the Holy Spirit. Amen.

A Grandparent's Deliverance Prayer

Lord Jesus, thank you for the gift of becoming grandparents and for all the blessings bestowed upon us through the love of our children and grandchildren. Through the infinite power of your Precious Blood, and through the intercession of the Virgin Mary, we implore divine protection for our children and grandchildren. If there are evil spirits attacking them, we ask that you deliver them from all sin and evil. Amen.

A Deliverance Prayer for a Marriage

In the name of the Lord Jesus Christ, by the power of His Cross, His Blood, and His resurrection, I (we) bind you, Satan; the spirits, powers, and forces of darkness; the netherworld; and the evil forces of nature who are coming against my (our) marriage. By the power and authority of the Lord Jesus Christ, I (we) take authority over all curses, hexes, demonic activity, and spells directed against either or both spouses, our relationships, ministry, home, finances, and the work of our hands. I (we) break them in the name of Jesus Christ. I (we) bind all demonic interaction, interplay, and communications between spirits sent against me (us) and send them directly to Jesus Christ for Him to deal with as He wills. I (we) ask forgiveness and denounce all negative inner vows that I (we) have made with the enemy. I (we) ask that Jesus Christ, release me (us) from these vows and from any bondage in which they may have kept me (us). I (we) claim the Blood of Jesus, the Son of the living God, over every aspect of my (our) life for my (our) protection. I (we) pray all these things in the precious name of our Lord and Savior Jesus Christ. Amen.

Family Consecration to the Sacred Heart of Jesus and the Immaculate Heart of Mary

Most Sacred Heart of Jesus and Immaculate Heart of Mary, we consecrate our whole family to You. We consecrate all that you have given us: our lives, each member of our family, our gifts and talents, our sorrows and joys, our home and all our possessions. We beg You to use us to show forth Your love and Your glory. Help us in our weaknesses and selfishness, so that we may persevere, faithful to You, to the end of our lives. May we love You more each day and long to encounter You, Jesus, in the sacraments. May we serve You by serving one another, neighbor, and country. Accept, O Most Sacred Heart of Jesus and Immaculate Heart of Mary, our humble offering of our family to You.

Be with us always, in every trial, difficulty, and suffering. In You we hope. Amen.[202]

Prayer to Consecrate Your Memories to God

Most Holy Trinity, Eternal God, thank you for the gift of my life. Thank you for the many joyful memories throughout my lifetime. Thank you, also, for the moments when I cried with sorrow as a result of sin, whether mine or that of others. I desire to consecrate all of my memories to your honor and glory—the best of memories; the memories the devil holds over me; haunting memories of confessed sins; painful memories of other people's sins against me; memories wherein I felt rejection, scorn, or shame. I surrender these to you, Lord, as an offering of love. Grant that no memory will imprison me. I do not pray to forget painful memories, only that they would cease to hurt me and hold me back. Let me remember your tender mercies and love. Thank you, Lord, for redeeming and loving me from the beginning. Amen.

Prayer of Mothers at the Cross for Children Leaving the Faith

Lord Jesus, at the foot of your Cross, in the midst of your agony, stood your Immaculate Mother with her seven-times-pierced heart. At the Cross was heard the anguished cry of a Mother's heart for her Child, flesh of her flesh, bone of her bone. The Virgin Mary was your precious gift to me

[202] Composed by the Dominican Sisters of St. Cecilia, with the ecclesial approval of Most Rev. David R. Choby, D.D., J.C.L., bishop of Nashville, on December 9, 2014.

from the Cross when you said, "Behold, your Mother." Now I place myself at the Cross with Mary to draw closer to you in my anguish. My heart is pierced with sorrow for my children who are walking away from you and the Church. At the foot of the Cross, I deliver my ardent petition for my children to return to the Faith. Please never forget or forsake my children, even when they forget and forsake you. I shall do as the father of the prodigal son: trust and pray for the return of my children. By the infinite merits of the Cross, graciously guide my prodigal children back home to you. Lord Jesus and Mother Mary, my children are yours. Amen.

A Cleansing Prayer before the Blessed Sacrament

My Lord Jesus Christ, who for the love you bear for us remain night and day in this sacrament, full of compassion and of love, awaiting and calling and welcoming all who come to visit you: I believe that you are present in the Sacrament of the Altar. I adore you in the abyss of my nothingness, and I thank you for having given me yourself in the Blessed Sacrament and for having called me to visit you in this church. In your eucharistic mercy, tenderly cleanse me of any anger, impatience, lust, sadness, negativity, or discouragement that I may have picked up from negative influences. From anything that binds me from the true freedom of a child of God, liberate me that I may be truly free for loving and serving you and souls. Lord Jesus, please send your holy angels to minister to me and my family, and to guard and protect us from all sickness, harm, and accidents always. I praise you in the Most Blessed Sacrament and thank you forever.[203]

---

203 Adapted from St. Alphonsus Liguori's Prayer before the Blessed Sacrament.

A Renunciation Prayer for Liberation from Sin

Lord Jesus, I desire salvation so much that I renounce what is against you. Even though I am attracted sometimes to things that are not good for my soul, I am now making the conscious commitment to stay away from those things that will lead me astray. I renounce pride and I ask for humility. I renounce envy and I ask for gratitude. I renounce anger and I ask for forgiveness and/or patience. I renounce vanity and I ask for modesty. I renounce sloth and I ask for zeal for you. I renounce lust and I ask for chastity. I renounce greed and I ask for generosity. I renounce gluttony or drunkenness and I ask for temperance. Thank you, Lord, for hearing my prayer. I trust that you will give me the strength and encouragement as I desire to grow in virtue. Your will, not mine be done. Amen.[204]

Prayer to St. Joseph for the Salvation of a Soul

O wonderful St. Joseph, I earnestly recommend to your care the salvation of N. Jesus shed his blood for this person; let not the precious blood of our Savior have been shed in vain. Deliver N. from the snares of the devil, heal N. from the poison of the world, and, I beg you, do not stop interceding for N. until the gates of heaven are opened to their soul. Beg your spouse to place N. under her maternal mantle. While this soul lives on earth, grant them conversion, love of Jesus, Mary, and the Catholic Church, and a return to the full participation in the Sacraments. Where

[204] Magis Women, *Standing Firm: Arming Yourself in God's Mighty Power*, 28.

else can I turn but to you, my spiritual father? In you I have confidence. In you I have hope. Hear my prayer, my spiritual father, and take away my fears. God will listen to you. Ask him for me for the sake of the love you have for all of us. Amen.[205]

St. John Paul II Deliverance Prayer

Immaculate Heart! Help us to conquer the menace of evil, which so easily takes root in the hearts of the people of today, and whose immeasurable effects already weigh down upon our modern world and seem to block the paths towards the future!

From famine and war, deliver us.

From nuclear war, from incalculable self-destruction, from every kind of war, deliver us.

From sins against the life of man from its very beginning, deliver us.

From hatred and from the demeaning of the dignity of the children of God, deliver us.

From every kind of injustice in the life of society, both national and international, deliver us.

From readiness to trample on the commandments of God, deliver us.

From attempts to stifle in human hearts the very truth of God, deliver us.

From the loss of awareness of good and evil, deliver us.

From sins against the Holy Spirit, deliver us, deliver us.

Accept, O Mother of Christ, this cry laden with the sufferings of all individual human beings, laden with the sufferings of whole societies.

---

[205] Calloway, *Consecration to St. Joseph*, 246.

Help us with the power of the Holy Spirit to conquer all sin: individual sin and the "sin of the world," sin in all its manifestations.
Let there be revealed, once more, in the history of the world the infinite saving power of the Redemption: the power of merciful Love! May it put a stop to evil! May it transform consciences! May your Immaculate Heart reveal for all the light of Hope![206]

Praying the Spiritual Warfare Retreat[207] That Jesus Gave to St. Faustina

"My daughter," Jesus told St. Faustina, "I want to teach you about spiritual warfare." Below in bold are the Lord's words to St. Faustina. Comments in italics are mine.

Never trust in yourself but abandon yourself totally to My will.
My Lord Jesus, grant that I wisely distrust myself, reject the devil's lies, and place all of my trust in you, my deliverer. Your will, not mine, be done.

Do not bargain with any temptation; lock yourself immediately in My Heart.
My Lord Jesus, graciously help me to resist every evil temptation and demonic attack. To that end, I lock my heart in yours. Let nothing ever separate me from you whom I love above all else.

---

[206] Quoted in Philip Kosloski, "Prayer for Deliverance from Evil by St. John Paul II," Aleteia, October 17, 2017, https://aleteia.org/2017/10/17/prayer-for-deliverance-from-evil-by-st-john-paul-ii/.

[207] St. Faustina, *Diary*, no. 1760.

At the first opportunity, reveal the temptation to the confessor.
My Lord Jesus, in your tender mercy, you provide a physician for my soul to whom I can reveal my sin. Thank you for the priest through whom I receive the medicine of forgiveness and healing. Bless him and keep him from harm, please.

Bear with yourself with great patience.
Lord Jesus, please grant me the virtue of patience that I may be patient with every person, including myself. When the devil tempts me to impatience, help me to resist, please. Grant that I may never hurt anyone through my impatience. Thank you for being patient with me.

Do not neglect interior mortifications.
Lord Jesus, I beg you to aid me in making interior mortifications with prayer and fasting so I can resist every demonic dart and evil temptation. Grant me a spirit of sacrifice and the grace to discipline myself as you ask.

Shun murmurs like a plague.
Lord Jesus, I implore you to aid me to tame my tongue, weigh my words, and resist gossip and murmuring, so that I may never harm a person's reputation or be disturbed by false accusations against me.

Let all act as they like; you are to act as I want you to.
Lord Jesus, with your grace, I desire to stay focused on my vocation and mission without comparing them to those of others. Help me to

resist temptations and suspicions concerning the business of others. Protect me, please, from a spirit of curiosity or control.

Observe the rule as faithfully as you can.
Lord Jesus, graciously help me to resist all temptations to infidelity and all temptations to quit, seek an easier path, or rebel from the hard work of my vocation, so that I may never offend you and break our covenant of love or the promises I have made to others.

If someone causes you trouble, think what good you can do for the person who caused you to suffer.
Lord Jesus, grant that my heart will be quick to forgive. May I always exercise forgiveness and not be resentful or unforgiving. If someone has harmed me or wished me ill will, knowingly or not, I beg for the grace to pray blessing and forgiveness for that person.

Do not pour out your feelings.
Lord Jesus, I implore the grace to resist the temptation to pour out my feelings to others, to speak to people of the matters of my heart. To you alone does my heart belong. I desire to preserve my heart for you above all.

Be silent when you are rebuked.
Lord Jesus, graciously help me to remain silent and peaceful whenever I am rebuked by others in authority over me. Grant that I never give in to the temptation to be angry, resentful, or proud when I am rebuked, misunderstood, or maligned by others. Seal my lips; protect my heart.

Do not ask everyone's opinion, but only the opinion of your confessor; be as frank and simple as a child with him.

Lord Jesus, I humbly implore your help to resist temptations to seek the opinion and approval of others. The desire of my heart is to please you, my Lord. Thank you for my confessors who absolve my sins. Bless your priests. Please grant me the heart of a child, pure and simple.

Do not become discouraged by ingratitude.

Lord Jesus, you know that it hurts to be taken for granted and met with ingratitude or insensitivity. In your mercy, help me to resist discouragement when I'm not appreciated. I pray that my every act of love and service to others may be for the glory of your name.

Do not examine with curiosity the roads down which I lead you.

Lord Jesus, kindly allow me the grace to resist inappropriate curiosity about the future and where you are leading me. I beg you for deeper faith, not superficial faith; deeper prayer, not superficial, polite prayer. Jesus, I will trust in you.

When boredom and discouragement beat against your heart, run away from yourself and hide in My heart.

Lord Jesus, graciously come to my aid when the devil tempts me to be bored with the monotony of daily life. Assist me to appreciate the ordinary and the simple beauties of life on earth. Please strengthen me in the might of your Spirit, so that I may not enter the valley of discouragement and doubt.

Do not fear struggle; courage itself often intimidates temptations, and they dare not attack us.
Lord Jesus, help me not to be afraid of the daily battles and many temptations from within and without. You are my icon of courage; I implore you to give me a courageous heart, a servant's heart full of zeal for souls—a heart like yours, please.

Always fight with the deep conviction that I am with you.
Lord Jesus, you have asked me to fight with deep conviction that I can overcome myself and the devil who would terrorize my soul. Help me to wield the sword of your Spirit. Lord, stay with me, please: I will wander on wrong paths if you are not my soul's compass on the journey.

Do not be guided by feeling, because it is not always under your control; but all merit lies in the will.
Lord Jesus, grant me the strength to be guided by faith, not my feelings. I desire to offer the Trinity a sacrifice of praise, even in the storms of life. Not my will but yours be done always.

I will not delude you with prospects of peace and consolations; on the contrary, prepare for great battles.
Lord Jesus, thank you for teaching me the truth about spiritual combat, for calling and equipping me for the great battle between light and darkness, evil and good. I implore the grace to be a good and faithful servant soldier for my eternal King.

Know that you are on a great stage where all heaven and earth are watching you.
Lord Jesus, having called me to the great stage of life, your grace empowers me to fulfill the mission assigned to me. You anointed me for love and mission and called me to bear good fruit for the glory of your name. Fiat! *Yes, Lord!*

Fight like a knight, so I can reward you. Do not be unduly fearful, because you are not alone.
Lord Jesus, you have commissioned me to be fearless because you accompany me in spiritual combat. Therefore, I will do as you ask; I will fight like a knight in your army, in anticipation of the great victory that is, yours—forever. Amen.

A "Magnificat with Mary" Litany[208]

Mary, with your consent to become the Mother of God, torrents of grace poured forth upon the earth, opening up for me a path to follow.
In times of loneliness, Mary, be with me.
In times of turmoil and uncertainty, Mary, be with me.
In times of grief, loss, or illness, Mary, be with me.
In times of sadness or depression, Mary, be with me.
In times of lost plans and broken promises, Mary, be with me.
When I am anxious about the welfare of my family, Mary, be with me.
When a job or financial stress weighs heavily on my heart, Mary, be with me.

[208] Composed by the Sisters of Life, quoted in *Magnificat Adoration Companion*, loc. 1803–1857 of 2846, Kindle.

When I am discouraged by the weight of my sins, Mary, be with me.
When I am tempted, Mary, be with me.
When I am afraid, Mary, be with me.
When the Lord calls me to greater kindness and love, Mary, be with me.
When the Lord calls me to greater forgiveness, Mary, be with me.
When the Lord calls me to greater purity, Mary, be with me.
On the wings of your Fiat, *Mary, I proclaim mine. Together we sing a* Magnificat *of praise:*
For all the blessings in my life, I praise you, Jesus.
For the gift of today, I praise you, Jesus.
For the gift of loved ones, I praise you, Jesus.
For the gift of my life, I praise you, Jesus.
For creating me with a special purpose and plan, I praise you, Jesus.
For never giving up on me, I praise you, Jesus.
For your infinite love, I praise you, Jesus.
For never leaving me, I praise you, Jesus.
For your inexhaustible mercy, I praise you, Jesus.
For laying down your life for me, I praise you, Jesus.
For your presence in the Eucharist, I praise you, Jesus.
For the greater good you will bring out of everything, especially:
In moments when I feel helpless and vulnerable, I praise you, Jesus.
In the midst of uncertainty, I praise you, Jesus.
In the midst of humiliation, I praise you, Jesus.
In the midst of difficulty, I praise you, Jesus.
In the midst of what appears as failure, I praise you, Jesus.
For sending your Mother to me in both joyful and sorrowful moments, I praise you, Jesus.
With Mary I sing: The Almighty has done great things for me, and holy is his Name. Amen.

St. John Paul II Prayer for Families[209]

Lord, from You every family in Heaven and on earth takes its name. Father, You are love and life. Through Your Son, Jesus Christ, born of woman, and through the Holy Spirit, the fountain of divine charity, grant that every family on earth may become for each successive generation a true shrine of life and love.

Grant that Your grace may guide the thoughts and actions of husbands and wives for the good of their families and of all the families in the world.

Grant that the young may find in the family solid support for their human dignity and for their growth in truth and love.

Grant that love, strengthened by the grace of the sacrament of marriage, may prove mightier than all the weaknesses and trials through which our families sometimes pass.

Through the intercession of the Holy Family of Nazareth, grant that the Church may fruitfully carry out her worldwide mission in the family and through the family.

We ask this of You, Who is life, truth and love with the Son and the Holy Spirit. Amen.

Prayer to St. Joseph, Terror of Demons

Saint Joseph, Terror of Demons, cast your solemn gaze upon the devil and all his minions, and protect us with your mighty staff. You fled through the night to avoid the devil's wicked designs; now with the power

---

209 Quoted in Philip Kosloski, "Prayer of St. John Paul II for all families," Aleteia, December 31, 2017, https://aleteia.org/2017/12/31/prayer-of-st-john-paul-ii-for-all-families/.

of God, smite the demons as they flee from you! Grant special protection, we pray, for children, fathers, families, and the dying. By God's grace, no demon dares approach while you are near, so we beg you, always be near to us! Amen.[210]

Consecration to the Holy Family

O Lord Jesus, you lived in the home of Mary and Joseph in Nazareth. There you grew in age, wisdom and grace as you prepared to fulfill your mission as our Redeemer. We entrust our family to you.

O Blessed Mother, you are the Mother of our savior. At Nazareth you cared for Jesus and nurtured him in the peace and joy of your home. We entrust our family to you.

O St. Joseph, you provide a secure and loving home for Jesus and Mary, and gave us a model of fatherhood while showing us the dignity of work. We entrust our family to you.

Holy Family, we consecrate ourselves and family to you. May we be completely united in love that is lasting, faithful and open to the gift of new life. Help us to grow in virtue, to forgive one another from our hearts, and to live in peace all our days. Keep us strong in faith, persevering in prayer, diligent in our work, and generous toward those in need. May our home, O Holy Family, truly become a domestic church where we reflect your example in our daily life. Amen. Jesus, Mary, and Joseph, pray for us![211]

---

210 Calloway, *Consecration to St. Joseph*, 245.

211 Archbishop William Lori, Supreme Chaplain of the Knights of Columbus, "Consecration to the Holy Family," Knights of Columbus, accessed July 27, 2020, https://www.kofc.org/en/resources/domestic-church/consecration-to-the-holy-family10371.pdf

Litany of the Holy Family

God, the Father of Heaven, have mercy on us.

God the Son, Redeemer of the world, have mercy on us.

God, the Holy Spirit, have mercy on us.

Holy Trinity, one God, have mercy on us.

("Pray for us" is repeated as indicated by "...")

Jesus, Mary, and Joseph, most worthy of our veneration,...

Jesus, Mary, and Joseph, called "the Holy Family" from all time,...

Jesus, Mary, and Joseph, son, mother, and head of the Holy Family,...

Jesus, Mary, and Joseph, divine child, pure spouse, and chaste spouse,...

Jesus, Mary, and Joseph, restorers of fallen families,...

Jesus, Mary, and Joseph, image of the Blessed Trinity here on earth,...

Holy Family, tested by the greatest of difficulties,...

Holy Family, with much suffering on the journey to Bethlehem,...

Holy Family, without a welcome in Bethlehem,...

Holy Family, visited by the poor shepherds,...

Holy Family, obliged to live in a stable,...

Holy Family, praised by the angels,...

Holy Family, venerated by the wise men from the East,...

Holy Family, greeted by the pious Simeon in the temple,...

Holy Family, persecuted and exiled to a foreign country,...

Holy Family, hidden and unknown in Nazareth,...

Holy Family, faithful in the observance of divine laws,...

Holy Family, perfect model of the Christian family,...

Holy Family, center of peace and concord,...

Holy Family, whose protector is a model of paternal care,...

Holy Family, whose mother is a model of maternal diligence,...

Holy Family, whose Divine Child is a model of filial obedience, . . .
Holy Family, poor in material goods, but rich in divine blessings, . . .
Holy Family, as nothing in the eyes of men, but so great in heaven, . . .
Holy Family, our support in life and our hope in death, . . .
Holy Family, patron and protector of our Congregation, . . .
Jesus, Mary, and Joseph, pray for us.
Lamb of God, who takes away the sins of the world, spare us, O Lord.
Lamb of God, who takes away the sins of the world, hear us, O Lord.
Lamb of God, who takes away the sins of the world, have mercy on us.
Christ, *hear us.* Christ, *graciously hear us.*
Let us pray. O God of infinite goodness and kindness, who has deigned to call us to this Family, give us the grace to venerate Jesus, Mary, and Joseph, so that, imitating them in this life, we may enjoy with them the life to come. We ask this through Christ Our Lord. Amen.[212]

[212] "Litany of the Holy Family," Missionaries of the Holy Family, accessed July 27, 2020, https://msf-america.org/holy-family-prayers/prayers-devoted-to-the-holy-family/litany-of-the-holy-family.

APPENDIX B

FAMILY DELIVERANCE CASE HISTORIES

In this section are minor family exorcism histories personally known to me through my work with various priests and teams in the United States and sometimes in other places to which I was invited, such as Rome, the Caribbean, Canada, Ireland, and Poland. I have disguised personal details to provide utmost privacy while maintaining the integrity of the real family situation. This is a small sampling of deliverance cases—absent demonic possession cases, since they are relatively rare and horrific to share.

Personal testimony is very valuable for learning how to prevent or treat demonic attacks. The Lord said, "Behold, I send you out as sheep in the midst of wolves; so be wise as serpents and innocent as doves" (Matt. 10:16).

The Church prudently and charitably responds to those seeking help. I hear complaints from people about how difficult it is to find a priest who believes their story of possible demonic affliction. This is unfortunate, but please persevere. Priests may not have received training or instruction from a diocesan protocol. Some dioceses have not instituted one. God will not abandon you or your loved one, if, for good order and in obedience to your pastor or bishop, you must go through several steps to arrive at a date for ministry. You always have recourse to sacramental Confession and can make an appointment with your parish priest. Pray and practice the Faith to the best of your ability—exercise your baptismal authority in offering personal deliverance prayers daily. If you read these stories and recognize yourself or your family in them, stop, pray, and be grateful that divine providence led you to these insights.

CASE: A son
ENTRYWAY: Murder of a family member; obsession

This young man described as follows the suffering that he and his younger siblings experienced at the hands of his father:

> I feel the devil is near me ever since I saw my father murder my infant brother. My dad is in prison now. My mother left us; she was a drug addict, abused by my father. We (my brother and sister and I) were placed in foster care. We moved around to different families. The three of us were just happy to stay together. Ever since I saw my dad kill the baby, I've hated him and wished I could kill him. I hate myself for not being able to save my baby brother. I feel out of control when extremely violent impulses come over me. Rage consumes me. It's all I know—anger, hatred, violence. My father doesn't deserve to live after what he did to the baby—and my mom.

Accompanying the young man was the Protestant minister who legally adopted all three children out of foster care. He shared how he tried very hard to heal prayerfully his adopted children from their past traumas and wounds. He prayed daily Christian deliverance prayers with this eldest of the three children. He felt he had done everything he could possibly do, and now he needed the assistance of a Catholic priest.

The young man was open to receiving deliverance prayers. Beforehand, he underwent a consultation with our team psychiatrist, who ruled out psychological pathology and reviewed pharmacology regimens. The young man tried to pray with his adoptive dad, but struggled intensely with obsessive thoughts of hatred, violence, and self-degradation. He hated himself for not saving his baby brother. He hoped that he could keep the family all together, that his mother and father would be healed of their respective addictions and abusive behavior, and that they would be a family again.

As the priest led the first and second sessions of minor exorcism prayers, the manifestation of evil spirits occurred: superhuman strength (it took a team of six strong people to prevent him from lunging at the priest), thrashing on the floor, blasphemous language in a guttural voice, and unnatural facial contortions. Rage overcame his body.

After a few sessions, he felt improvement, but didn't continue with ministry. The adoptive father reported that the son ran away for days at a time and was associating with friends in a gang. Despite his tragic history, we perceived God-given talents in this young person. We could do nothing but entrust him to the Father's hands. I pray for him still—that those eyes so full of rage may one day know the peace and forgiveness that only God can give.

The Protestant minister who adopted these children appeared to have a big, paternal heart. Hopefully, his Christian charity for the younger brother and sister will bring good fruit. I perceived how hard it was for him to watch the eldest son suffer at the hands of the evil spirits who tormented him.

The reason I shared this case is to highlight that sometimes the best efforts made for a family member end up in apparent failure. Yet the beloved souls for whom we pray do receive needed grace in God's perfect time.

Once, I complained to my spiritual director that I saw no indication of God's hearing or answering my ardent daily prayer for a family member. Father shared that perhaps that person's heart was hard as nails presently. Still, I should continue to deposit prayer into the reservoir of grace so that, when God saw a tiny opening in the person's heart, He could pour torrents of grace upon my loved one from the reservoir of my prayers. This is what intercessors do. We may never see the moment of change except from heaven. That it will come is worthy of hope. Pray for those you love; please don't give up on prayer or your family.

CASE: A wife, mother, daily communicant
ENTRYWAY: Hypnosis, curse; obsession

> I suffered from sudden-onset severe insomnia. My physician's various prescriptions did not help after several attempts to find the correct medicine. I was desperately sleep-deprived. Online, I researched natural healing methods and found a local hypnotist who claimed to cure insomnia with hypnosis, so I made an appointment. Her website was professional, so I felt comfortable approaching her for help. It seemed like a natural, harmless remedy. The therapist practiced in her home. Upon entering her large and

tidy home, we exchanged pleasantries; I filled out a patient form and made payment arrangements. Then, she invited me to recline upon the patient table situated in her living room. She assured me that her results for curing insomnia were excellent.

Next, she asked if I practiced any particular religion. I told her that I was a practicing Catholic. She casually advised that for the best possible outcome, it was necessary that I *renounce the Bible and Jesus Christ*. Otherwise, she said, they would limit my *open-mindedness*; therefore, I would not receive the fullness of *her healing* through hypnosis. I was hesitant at first. I thought to myself that I would never renounce Jesus as she asked. But I could say the words, not meaning them at all. God would know that I didn't really intend it. I proceeded to say out loud that I renounced the teachings of the Bible and Jesus Christ as Lord. I just wanted the treatment so that I could finally sleep. After the session, in which I was apparently successfully hypnotized, I returned home and was grateful to be able to sleep finally.

After twenty-four hours, however, strange, dark thoughts and images crossed my mind, and I heard noises around me. These were unrelenting while I was awake, but I could sleep at night again. At first, I made no connection between these strange things and the hypnotist. Then, strife broke out in my immediate family for no apparent reason. It was then that I began to suspect what was done to me during the time I was under hypnotic trance. This is why I am seeking the help of the deliverance priest. I have done something foolish and now I need help.

After a medical and psychiatric evaluation, she met with the deliverance priest and team to receive prayers. We discerned that a curse had been placed upon her while she was under the hypnotic state. Father led the woman through prayers to cancel her renunciation of the Bible and Jesus Christ. Even if she didn't mean her words of renunciation, they went out into the spiritual realm and had effect. She underwent a few sessions of deliverance prayers without strong manifestations of evil spirits, but there were signs of serious discomfort during the prayers. Father led her in prayer for the conversion of the hypnotherapist, whom she now believes was practicing a New Age version of hypnosis—because of the suspicious crystals inside of her home. The patient employed the use of sacramentals on her person, in the home, and with her family. Life returned to normal in her home and for her family. She discerned that she was liberated from a spirit of witchcraft that attached itself when she was under the hypnotic state.

You may ask whether Catholics can use hypnotherapy. The Church has issued only a warning—not a condemnation—of hypnosis. Susan Brinkmann explains:

> According to the *Catholic Encyclopedia*, citing the Response of the Holy Office of June 2, 1840, "She has condemned only abuses, leaving the way free for scientific research. 'The use of the magnetism, that is to say, the mere act of employing a physical means otherwise permissible, is not morally forbidden, provided that it does not tend to an illicit end or one which may be in any manner evil.'"...
>
> The use of hypnosis by legitimate medical professionals was approved by the American Medical Association in 1958.

> Hypnotherapy is typically used as part of a broader treatment plan, rather than as a stand-alone therapy and is best known for helping people to change negative behaviors such as smoking and over-eating, and to conquer fears and anxiety.[213]

Brinkmann also cautions against a dangerous practice known as past life regression therapy, "which uses hypnosis to allegedly help patients remember past lives." One use is to "uncover suppressed memories of incest, satanic ritual abuse, space-alien abduction and regression into infancy. Proponents of these practices are generally an eclectic mix of feminists, Christians, New Agers, and science fiction enthusiasts."[214]

Suzanne Baars, a well-known Catholic therapist, adds: "It's important that people know that no one can be hypnotized without their consent, nor can they be coerced under hypnosis to do something they would not do in any other setting. Naturally, it's important that no one allow someone they do not trust to use hypnosis with them, as I do believe that the evil one can use that to his advantage—as he can many other things."[215]

Caution and prayerful discernment are necessary when seeking alternative methods of healing. I believe that this lady's outcome was quite good for several reasons: she was a practicing Catholic, a daily communicant; she was protected by God's armor. She brought everything to light as soon as strange things manifested. She humbly turned to the Church for deliverance ministry, and

---

[213] Susan Brinkmann, "Can Catholics Use Hypnotherapy and EMDR?," *Women of Grace* (blog), January 26, 2010, https://www.womenofgrace.com/blog/?p=11443.

[214] Ibid.

[215] Ibid.

she had remorse for renouncing the Lord—even if she didn't really intend to do so. She made an unwise choice in a desperate search for relief, suffered consequences, and was delivered by God's grace and the Church's ministry.

CASE: A single Catholic person in medical residency
ENTRYWAY: Pharmakeia; obsession

> I was exhausted from working long medical shifts and suffering lack of sleep. Insomnia was wearing on me, so it became difficult to keep up with patients at the hospital. When I had an opportunity to finally take a break at the hospital, I needed to fall asleep, but couldn't. It was easy to go to the nearby pharmacy cabinet to help myself to an injection of propofol, a drug used to slow the activity of your brain and nervous system—which is what I needed now before another long shift. Propofol helps patients to relax before and during general anesthesia for surgery. As I injected propofol into my arm, I clearly heard a mocking, guttural, otherworldly voice: "You're mine now! This drug will own you, and so will I. Yes, inject it into your veins and sleep, sleep well. I will help you."

Despite initially pushing that voice aside, the person quickly became addicted to propofol, repeatedly stealing it from the hospital's inventory and injecting it. Soon the person had to resign from medical residency to enter a rehabilitation center to be liberated from propofol. During rehab, the person reported recurring nightmares of a demon over the bed, laughing, mocking, and taunting: "You will never be free! Never! You're mine now!"

This person was almost done with rehab when I was contacted for an appointment for deliverance ministry. I arranged a prayer session for after the person completed rehab. The priest and team began to intercede. The person had a solid Catholic foundation from childhood. The person repented of sin, made restitution for the stolen drugs, and had a prayer session with a priest for minor exorcism prayers. In our last conversation, the person was doing well and had resumed the hospital residency program.

There is a Greek word, *pharmakeia* (*pharmacia* in Latin), that refers to the use of medicine or drugs, spells, sorcery, witchcraft, and the occult (see Gal. 5:20, Rev. 18:23, Rev. 9:21). Revelation 9:21, for example, reads, "Nor did they repent of their murders, of their sorceries, or their immorality or their thefts." Demons can gain rights over a person who does some illicit thing, such as stealing a drug from a hospital for personal use. There is a price to pay for such things. In this case, the person was likely going to be a very effective Catholic medical doctor. Perhaps this is why, after giving in to the temptation to steal and inject the propofol, the person was targeted immediately by an evil spirit.

We know many families who suffer because their relatives are addicted to drugs. A good portion of exorcism cases have a component of drug addiction. I want to encourage families to keep interceding for loved ones who suffer from drug addiction. Don't give up, please. Do what you must to maintain boundaries. Sometimes, tough love is the best medicine. There are many resources available. Enlist all the help you can get—from medical doctors, rehab centers, twelve-step groups, and so on. Many, many drug addicts and alcoholics have been beautifully restored in Christ.

CASE: A grandmother
ENTRYWAY: Curse, Santa Muerte; obsession

I was searching for a Catholic Rosary prayer group in my neighborhood. Hearing of a home in my neighborhood where people gathered to pray the Rosary, I approached one of the members to see if I could join their prayer group. When I entered the living room, I saw statues of Jesus and Mary and saints, so I felt comfortable. After praying the Rosary together, the host asked me to go to the kitchen with her. She said that she wanted to prick my finger—just a tiny bit to get a little blood. By this, I'd have a bond with the group; it was sort of my initiation. I asked what she would do with my blood. In a very casual way, she said my blood would be mixed with the blood of a chicken—just like everyone's blood was mixed with that of a chicken to create a close spiritual bond. Before I knew it, she had my hand, pricked it with a tiny needle, and squeezed drops of blood onto a glass bowl. Then she told me to return to the living room and continue praying the Rosary, which I did. That night I felt strange, like something had followed me home. Though I was uncomfortable, I decided that I should keep praying the Rosary with the group, so I returned. Over time, I realized that something had attached to me, causing emotional sadness and physical weakness. Everything in my life suddenly felt very heavy, like I was walking through mud. I decided to see a Catholic priest in my parish, and Father prayed with me. He discerned that I had been cursed and told me to

> stop attending that prayer group. When the priest prayed with me, I began to change into another person. My parish priest contacted the deliverance team for deliverance prayer ministry.

Father told us that when he prayed with her, she began manifesting evil spirits: superhuman strength, vulgar language, physical contortions of the body, and a strong aversion to blessed objects. When the deliverance priest and team prayed with her, it took five people to restrain this small lady in a chair while Father completed the minor exorcism prayers. Over quite a few hours, we had a tough physical battle to cast out the demon who had entered through that illicit blood covenant. It was discerned that the so-called Catholic Rosary prayer group was a front for Santa Muerte. They placed a curse on this unsuspecting grandmother. An authentic Catholic Rosary cenacle would never in a million years require that the blood of its members be mixed with the blood of a chicken. This timid, pious grandmother was too shy and went along with the ritual because she didn't know what else to do. In one long session, this lady was liberated. She continued under the care of a priest spiritual director without any further diabolical incidents.

CASE: An adult son
ENTRYWAY: Curandera, occult, drugs; oppression

A Catholic couple called for advice regarding their adult son, who was raised in the Faith. He had moved to Mexico and was living with a woman he met there. She practiced witchcraft that she claimed was benign (so-called white witchcraft). The son was intrigued and went along with the girlfriend, who claimed that her spirituality was to help them become prosperous—it would bring them good luck.

He began taking drugs that were readily available in their neighborhood and became depressed for the first time in his life. He had stopped practicing Catholicism. He was home in the United States to visit his parents when they saw how oppressed he was. With his parents, he was quite frank about his life in Mexico. They cautioned that he was playing with fire. His lifestyle was taking a serious toll on him, physically and spiritually. He wasn't argumentative; rather, he was open to their suggestions. That's when they called me. They had heard my talk at a national spiritual warfare conference. I advised them to seek a priest to counsel their son and suggest they give their son the book *The Devil in the City of Angels*.[216] I recommended that book because it addresses the occult practices in Los Angeles and Mexico.

The priest visited the family home and had a private meeting with the adult son. The son agreed to the priest's offer for Confession. The parents gave the book to their son. One month later, they called again to share that the book scared their son and opened his eyes to the dangers of engaging in the occult, witchcraft, and drugs. He broke up with his girlfriend when he returned to Mexico and began practicing the Faith again. Apparently, his ex-girlfriend was a curandera: a folk healer or shaman who uses herbs, hallucinogenic plants, magic, and spiritualism to treat illnesses. Curanderismo (from the Spanish word *curar*, meaning "to

[216] Jesse Romero, *The Devil in the City of Angels* (Charlotte, NC: TAN Books, 2019).

heal") is a centuries-old synthesis of Native Mexican culture and beliefs. More information is available in a research article published by the American Medical Association.[217] In California, where the Latino culture is growing rapidly, the proliferation of curanderos continues. We've seen many cases of spiritual harm done through the practices of the curanderos.

CASE: A mother, nurse
ENTRYWAY: Yoga; obsession

A successful yoga master and registered nurse approached us with the following story:

> My profession and my life are being destroyed. I took a long look at my life to discover what may be the cause of its destruction. I traced the timeline back to the start of supplemental income from a yoga practice. I studied to become a yoga master. I practiced and taught Kundalini yoga.[218] Presently my life, relationships, finances, and profession are terribly attacked. I am severely harassed and oppressed. I must have opened the door to something evil. Can you help me to renounce yoga and cast out any evil spirits?

---

[217] Daniel Alegria et al., "El Hospital Invisible: A Study of Curanderismo," *JAMA Psychiatry* 34, no. 11 (November 1977): 1354–1357, https://doi.org/10.1001/archpsyc.1977.01770230096009.

[218] Kundalini yoga includes breathing exercises and meditation to activate the life force that resides at the base of the spine. It is symbolized by a coiled serpent. The CDF's *Letter to the Bishops of the Catholic Church on Some Aspects of Christian Meditation* includes warnings about physical practices that are mixed with non-Christian spiritual teachings. Some forms of yoga include practices that involve rituals directed to the Hindu gods.

She was more than ready for repentance, renunciation, and conversion. In the presence of the priest and team, she spoke aloud the renunciation of each chakra that was opened intentionally through Kundalini yoga: *Muladhara* (root), *Svadhishthana* (sacral), *Manipura* (solar plexus), *Anahata* (heart), *Vishuddha* (throat), *Ajna* (third eye), and *Sahasrara* (crown of head).[219] This nurse was *not possessed*, but she was *obsessed* by spirits of destruction. She was liberated after two minor exorcisms and reported a sustained healing through reparation and daily prayer.

Notice the above list of chakras. Do they even remotely resemble anything in Catholic teaching or Scripture? This nurse, an expert in yoga, now warns about its potential for serious harm. See the chapter on diabolical disguises for more information about yoga.

CASE: My experience
ENTRYWAY: Curse—the evil eye

Years ago, I was in New Orleans to speak at a conference. Afterward, a group of us, accompanied by a priest friend, visited the St. Louis Cathedral. Upon arrival by taxi, I noted that in front of the beautiful cathedral was a long line of tables set up with voodoo, New Age, and occult items sold by peddlers. I was taking a prolonged look at this novel, jarring scene that contrasted with the beautiful facade of the cathedral.

One woman, dressed like a gypsy and selling trinkets, noticed me. I looked away, walked past her, and climbed the stairs to enter

[219] "7 Chakras of Kundalini Yoga," The Yoga Institute, accessed March 20, 2020, www.theyogainstitute.org/7-chakras-of-kundalini-yoga/.

the cathedral. Kneeling before the Blessed Sacrament, I began to pray. The priest and our friends joined me also. After twenty minutes, the priest and ladies arose from prayer and went to the back of the cathedral to wait for me. I couldn't move. I was seemingly frozen to the pew. I couldn't speak, and my arms and legs were paralyzed. Interiorly, I prayed *Jesus, Jesus, Jesus* and was mystified but not afraid.

After a few moments, Father approached me, saying, "Come on, Kathleen, we have to go!" I couldn't respond. Father knew something was wrong when he stood in front of me and realized I couldn't move or speak. He immediately, silently prayed deliverance prayers to break the spell. I was fine as soon as Father finished praying. Though I had the spiritual armor of thirty years of daily Mass and Adoration, sometimes God allows His servants to learn lessons such as this.

Fr. Gabriele Amorth writes about this type of spell:

> The evil eye is a spell cast by looking at someone. It does not come about by believing that some individuals caused bad luck by just looking at you; this is nonsense. The evil eye is a true spell; in other words, it presupposes the will to harm a predetermined person with the intervention of demons. In this instance the nefarious deed is achieved through the sense of sight. While I could never be certain that a particular spell was the result of the evil eye and whether a look had been sufficient, the effects were clear. Many times the perpetrator of the spell is not known, nor how it began. What is important is that the victim should not suspect everyone he meets, but

> forgive wholeheartedly whoever caused him evil, no matter who.[220]

When I traveled to Mexico City to the Shrine of Our Lady of Guadalupe, a similar parade of vendors surrounded the beautiful shrine. Fr. Daniel Leary warned our pilgrimage group not to linger or stare into their eyes. It's not that we're afraid, but prudence is always necessary to avoid evil spirits.

Case: A high school student
Entryway: Pact with the devil; obsession

The teenager's parents called Father for help when their child began to manifest evil spirits—thrashing on the floor like a snake, hissing, cussing, contorting the body. When the parents and siblings tried to calm the teenager down, they could not. At times, they had to keep the teenager in a room to prevent him from destroying the rest of the house.

In the teenager's bedroom, the furniture moved across the floor; the bed in particular moved from one wall to the next. The chest of drawers opened and closed on their own, the lights turned off and on, and the room was frigid.

When Father arrived, the teenager was calm enough to have a conversation with the priest. He told Father that he had made a pact with the devil. The teenager agreed to sell his soul to the devil if the devil made him the smartest student in his class. The teenager also desired to be the most popular person with the opposite

---

[220] Fr. Gabriele Amorth, *An Exorcist Tells His Story* (San Francisco: Ignatius Press, 1999), 132.

sex. The devil delivered his part of the pact; for a time, the student thought he had made a good deal.

Then the torment began—the physical whips of the devil, dark disturbing thoughts, intense temptations to hurt himself. Then, the noises and movement of furniture in the bedroom kept the teenager awake and exhausted from lack of rest.

Father asked, "Do you want to be set free?"

The teenager replied, "I like being popular and not having to study to get good grades."

Father explained that he could help only if the teenager wanted to break the pact with the devil. The teenager had to choose God. Once he decided that he couldn't stand the physical and mental torment anymore, the teenager chose to break the pact.

Some family members were ready to help Father restrain the teenager if necessary. While Father prepared for the exorcism, he asked the teenager if he knew any prayers by heart. The priest was surprised that the teenager had memorized the Magnificat (Luke 1:46–55). Father asked the teenager to pray the Magnificat aloud. At the end of the prayer, a series of loud screams came forth; the teenager shook physically, coughed repeatedly, and then became perfectly quiet. Father discerned that the demon had been cast out by the powerful anointing of the Magnificat. Father said more prayers for the teenager, and there were no diabolical manifestations. The Rite was not prayed. Our Lady had taken care of things. No more sessions were required, and the teenager was liberated.

It came to light that the teenager's mother had a strong Marian devotion and was praying the Rosary in another room during this episode. There have been other cases where the Rosary has accelerated liberation, especially when prayed by a parent for a child. If you haven't already taken up praying the Rosary for your children's protection, please start. I recall when a demon spoke through a person receiving the Rite: "Stop those wicked beads! Stop that chain! Stop the blasted beads!"

CASE: Infestation of a devout Catholic family's house
ENTRYWAY: Cursed objects, occult curses; infestation and obsession

---

A family experienced various strange phenomena in their home. Some of these phenomena coincided with thoughts and dreams that the mother and son experienced simultaneously. For example, they would mystically perceive three-inch-long nails being pushed into their skulls, causing excruciating pain. In the morning, they would find such nails scattered randomly on the floor. They collected them and gave them to the exorcist when he and I visited their home. This phenomenon occurred on a regular basis. The mother and son suffered a great deal of oppression, while the father did not.

The family also heard sounds within the walls of the master bedroom. A contractor had recently remodeled the home, so we encouraged them to search for cursed items. They discovered small figurines that looked like voodoo dolls inside the walls of the master bedroom and bathroom. These were given to the exorcist to dispose of per the protocol for cursed objects.

After parish priests as well as the exorcist performed a series of several house blessings, the family experienced relief. The son was liberated first. His pious mother continued to suffer, offering her prayers and sacrifices for her son, for priests, and for souls.

They placed a recording of Gregorian Chant in their attic to play continuously and to bless the atmosphere.

The mother and son were liberated by a series of deliverance prayer sessions. But the infestation of the home continued. Eventually, they learned that their next-door neighbor practiced witchcraft. They decided to move away and haven't experienced a problem in the new home.

CASE: Married, non-Catholic medical professional in RCIA
ENTRYWAY: Shamanic healing;[221] obsession

This man reported the following:

> I was having heath challenges that were not treatable by medical science. I resorted to shamanic healing that was recommended by a friend of mine. This led me deeper into alternative healing spirit work that caused a lot of problems in my life. Strange things happened with my health that were really unusual. I was attacked spiritually. My health kept getting worse even when I sought help from highly recommended *shamanic healing providers*. Medical doctors could not figure out a proper diagnosis and treatment for me. After the shamanic healing process, things got out of hand. My medical condition was worse than before I began. My physical condition became far more complicated and

[221] "Shamanism is based on animism, a belief that all created things have a soul and consciousness. Mountains, woods, forests, rivers, and lakes are perceived to possess spirits and to be living, thinking impassioned beings like man." Susan Brinkmann, "Ritual Sacrifice of Children on the Rise in Uganda," *Women of Grace* (blog), April 5, 2010, https://www.womenofgrace.com/blog/?p=83.

> unexplainable. I was unable to continue my full-time work. The income from the few hours that I could work had to be spent on out-of-pocket medical expenses. Dark spiritual attacks affected the other areas of my life also. My relationship with my children changed for the worse. Overall, it was as if my whole life was falling apart. Shamanic healing deals with the "spirit world" that is not of God (it is occult and antithetical to Catholicism) and it is quite dangerous. It may feel good temporarily but never does it bring you true healing. I urge you not to experiment with it. If you need physical healing that traditional medicine cannot provide, first pray to God, Jesus Christ, who is our true divine healer, then seek authenticated medicine and healing approved by the Catholic Church.

This person has received minor exorcisms, which included renunciation of shamanic healing. He has the assistance of a priest spiritual director for continuing prayer, and although he is improving, he is not yet completely free of physical symptoms. As this person is going through RCIA, it might be that evil spirits are retaliating against his eventual Baptism into the Catholic Church.

CASE: A priest
ENTRYWAY: Crisis of faith; oppression

An eighty-five-year-old priest who had served for years as the diocesan deliverance priest was hospitalized in cardiac intensive care for three months following open heart surgery. When I visited Father in his weakened post-operative state, he implored that I pray very much for him because, all night long, swarms of evil spirits were tormenting him. He said demons were bombarding him with dark thoughts that pierced like fiery darts:

> Your God abandoned you. You gave your life to the Church for nothing, old man. You thought you were doing what your God asked of you, but now your God rejects you completely! All those prayers—ha, ha, ha—they don't matter now. Your God is a tormentor: suffer, suffer, the Cross, the Cross—that's all he wants. You're being punished for wasting your life. There's no heaven. You will suffer forever—with me—into the pit we will go. Go ahead, now, call on your God. He won't listen, doesn't care. A mean one—that God of yours! No heaven for you—no heaven at all!

It seemed to him that the devil was trying to destroy his faith.

I asked Father how he fought against such attacks. For a priest in a vulnerable physical state to endure such demonic oppression is a mystery. Father calmly admitted that it was difficult to fight against the diabolical onslaught. He had the strength to pray only *one prayer* that he repeated all night, and it eventually cast the demons away:

> I slowly prayed and concentrated very hard on every word of the Apostles' Creed: *I believe in God, the Father Almighty, Creator of heaven and earth; and in Jesus Christ, His only Son, Our Lord, who was conceived by the Holy Spirit, born of the Virgin Mary, suffered under Pontius Pilate, was crucified, died,*

> *and was buried. He descended into hell; the third day He arose again from the dead. He ascended into heaven and sits at the right hand of God, the Father Almighty; from thence He shall come to judge the living and the dead. I believe in the Holy Spirit, the holy Catholic Church, the communion of saints, the forgiveness of sins, the resurrection of the body and life everything. Amen.*

The demonic attacks persisted for nine nights and then suddenly stopped.

As this story shows, the Apostles' Creed is a weapon in spiritual combat. Our Catholic prayers are anointed, packed with power to resonate in the spiritual realm. Quoting St. Ambrose, the *Catechism* says, "This Creed is the spiritual seal, our heart's meditation and an ever-present guardian; it is, unquestionably, the treasure of our soul" (CCC 197).

For years, Father had ardently prayed, "God willing, I'll do purgatory time on earth." Perhaps God is answering the desire of this priest's heart. Now, Father is ninety-one. He is frail and living in a monastery, praying most of the day. He says many Rosaries and the Liturgy of the Hours between dialysis treatments. This priest was my spiritual director for sixteen years, and our family owes a debt of gratitude to him. He always told us, "Pray that priests pray!"

Priests are on the frontlines of the spiritual battle over souls. They experience personal spiritual attacks and are in need of continuous prayers. I urge readers of this work to join an army of spiritual mothers and fathers in intercession for the holiness and protection of clergy: the Foundation of Prayer for Priests (www.foundationforpriests.org). On the foundation's website, you'll discover family resources on the subject of prayer, vocations, spiritual motherhood and fatherhood, and spiritual warfare.

Lord Jesus, graciously protect your priests from the spirit of the world, the flesh, and the devil. Guard and equip priests on the frontlines of spiritual warfare. Thank you for calling and forming priests to radiate the love of the Most Sacred Heart for your family, the Church. We commend all priests and families to the united and victorious Sacred and Immaculate Hearts.

ABOUT THE AUTHOR

Kathleen Beckman is the president of the Foundation of Prayer for Priests (www.foundationforpriests.org). She has served the Church for twenty-five years as an international Catholic evangelist, author, Ignatian retreat director, and radio host, and is often featured on EWTN TV and radio. For over a decade, Kathleen has served on the diocesan exorcist's team and is the administrator of her diocese's exorcism and deliverance ministry. She completed the Association of International Exorcists Rome course "Exorcism and Prayers of Liberation," and for six years was an exorcism case-study facilitator at the Pope Leo XIII Institute, the school that trains clergy for exorcism ministry. In 2001, Kathleen was invested into the Equestrian Order of the Holy Sepulchre of Jerusalem. She sits on the advisory boards of the Pope Leo XIII Institute, and Magnificat, A Ministry to Catholic Women. Sophia Institute Press published her last three books: *Praying for Priests*, *God's Healing Mercy*, and *When Women Pray*. A wife, mother, and grandmother, Kathleen lives with her family in Orange, California.

Sophia Institute

Sophia Institute is a nonprofit institution that seeks to nurture the spiritual, moral, and cultural life of souls and to spread the Gospel of Christ in conformity with the authentic teachings of the Roman Catholic Church.

Sophia Institute Press fulfills this mission by offering translations, reprints, and new publications that afford readers a rich source of the enduring wisdom of mankind.

Sophia Institute also operates the popular online resource CatholicExchange.com. *Catholic Exchange* provides world news from a Catholic perspective as well as daily devotionals and articles that will help readers to grow in holiness and live a life consistent with the teachings of the Church.

In 2013, Sophia Institute launched Sophia Institute for Teachers to renew and rebuild Catholic culture through service to Catholic education. With the goal of nurturing the spiritual, moral, and cultural life of souls, and an abiding respect for the role and work of teachers, we strive to provide materials and programs that are at once enlightening to the mind and ennobling to the heart; faithful and complete, as well as useful and practical.

Sophia Institute gratefully recognizes the Solidarity Association for preserving and encouraging the growth of our apostolate over the course of many years. Without their generous and timely support, this book would not be in your hands.

www.SophiaInstitute.com
www.CatholicExchange.com
www.SophiaInstituteforTeachers.org